Trauma and Recovery
in the Twenty-First-Century Irish Novel

Irish Studies
James MacKillop, *Series Editor*

Select titles in Irish Studies

Carmilla: A Critical Edition
Joseph Sheridan Le Fanu; Kathleen Costello-Sullivan, ed.

J. M. Synge and Travel Writing of the Irish Revival
Giulia Bruna

Kate O'Brien and Spanish Literary Culture
Jane Davison

Laying Out the Bones: Death and Dying in the Modern Irish Novel
Bridget English

Political Acts: Women in Northern Irish Theatre, 1921–2012
Fiona Coleman Coffey

Relocated Memories: The Great Famine in Irish and Diaspora Fiction, 1846–1870
Marguérite Corporaal

Revolutionary Damnation: Badiou and Irish Fiction from Joyce to Enright
Sheldon Brivic

Seamus Heaney as Aesthetic Thinker: A Study of the Prose
Eugene O'Brien

Trauma and Recovery

in the Twenty-First-Century Irish Novel

Kathleen Costello-Sullivan

Syracuse University Press

Syracuse, New York 13244-5290

First Edition 2018

18 19 20 21 22 23 6 5 4 3 2 1

∞ The paper used in this publication meets the minimum requirements of the American National Standard for Information Sciences—Permanence of Paper for Printed Library Materials, ANSI Z39.48-1992.

For a listing of books published and distributed by Syracuse University Press, visit www.SyracuseUniversityPress.syr.edu.

ISBN: 978-0-8156-3567-3 (hardcover)
978-0-8156-3585-7 (paperback)
978-0-8156-5433-9 (e-book)

Library of Congress Cataloging-in-Publication Data

Names: Costello-Sullivan, Kathleen, author.
Title: Trauma and recovery in the twenty-first-century Irish novel / Kathleen Costello-Sullivan.
Description: First edition. | Syracuse, New York : Syracuse University Press, 2018. | Series: Irish studies | Includes bibliographical references and index.
Identifiers: LCCN 2018004164 (print) | LCCN 2018004347 (ebook) | ISBN 9780815654339 (e-book) | ISBN 9780815635673 (hardcover : alk. paper) | ISBN 9780815635857 (pbk. : alk. paper)
Subjects: LCSH: English fiction—Irish authors—History and criticism. | English fiction—21st century—History and criticism. | Psychic trauma in literature. | Collective memory in literature.
Classification: LCC PR8803.2 (ebook) | LCC PR8803.2 .C67 2018 (print) | DDC 823/.92099415—dc23
LC record available at https://lccn.loc.gov/2018004164

Manufactured in the United States of America

For

Thomas and Matthew Sullivan,
Katie, Maeve, Ciaran, and Sabrina Costello,
Dana, Danny, Erin, and Krystal Basulto,
and Joey, Kaitlyn, and Jimmy Murphy—

Because what goes down in life
eventually, inevitably,

will come back up.

Contents

Acknowledgments

Like any work of long gestation, this study reflects the support provided by many individuals. Although any errors or shortcomings remain my own, whatever contributions this analysis might make are the product of the deeply appreciated efforts and aid from colleagues and friends across my home institution, my field, and my life.

I thank the Moore Institute at the National University of Ireland, Galway, for a Visiting Fellowship in the summer of 2014, which gave me precious writing and research time as well as access to the John McGahern Archive in both 2014 and 2016. Barry Houlihan in particular was enormously helpful, and I appreciated the conversation and insights of the scholars whom I met that productive first summer.

I thank James MacKillop for his initial openness to this project as series editor at Syracuse University Press and Deborah M. Manion for her wise and professional counsel and collegiality. The anonymous reviewers for Syracuse University Press provided crucial and focused advice to help me advance this argument through its final phase. It was a delight to work with copy editor Annie Barva again: I appreciate her skill and professionalism.

I thank the authors included in this study for their brilliant novels as well as for the permissions to quote from their work. John Banville's *The Sea* was the first novel I worked on for this project, and in many ways it set the research contexts I pursued. Colm Tóibín's canon set me on the path to pursue this project; his novels are the cornerstone of my intellectual life, and I am profoundly grateful for his generosity and accessibility as I worked on this study (as well as on my prior one). Anne Enright's powerful novel *The Gathering* challenged me personally more than any text I have ever read. Colum McCann's prose has moved and inspired me, and he has been incredibly kind and gracious to me as just one among many scholars who no doubt seek his time. Sebastian Barry's brilliant novel *The Secret Scripture* helped to consolidate my thinking on metanarrative in this study overall, and Emma Donoghue's novel *Room* expanded my thinking about literature's ability to represent what W. B. Yeats referred to, in a different context, as "beauty in a broken place" (which, of course, is also the title of Colm Tóibín's play from 2004).

Matthew Fee offered priceless advice and support over the past three years, and I am particularly indebted to him for his generosity, his insights, and his indefatigable support, friendship, and enthusiasm. Julie Grossman has offered much-appreciated readings and help and has been an intellectual mainstay and role model for me in my time at Le Moyne College. Claire Bracken offered immeasurably helpful comments on the final draft of the manuscript. Ellen Scheible was a needed resource to compare notes on the McGahern Archive, which both of us plumbed, and I value her thoughts and feedback. Patrick Keane and Lisabeth Buchelt offered thoughtful feedback in the later stages of this project. I also thank my Syracuse Irish literature reading group—Sandra Clarke, Colleen Wolf, Sally Huntington, Linda Conklin, and Alice Shafer—for allowing me to test out my ideas and thoughts with them, lo these many years.

I sincerely thank Inga Barnello, Kelly Delevan, and Wayne Stevens at the Le Moyne College Noreen Reale Falcone Library for their knowledge and assistance. Melissa Short, Alysson Malbouf, Allison Baldwin, Melanie Rose, Briana Tonzi, Ashley Atkins, and Megan Daigle helped by procuring articles for me and proofreading the manuscript. Dixie Blackely and Jeanne Darby provided professional support that helped me make time for this project. William Day and Steven Affeldt offered their expertise in research that strayed slightly far afield for me. My department chair, James Hannan, has been a reliable and appreciated support and sounding board. The president of Le Moyne College, Linda LeMura, granted me valued research funds to continue my scholarly work while in my position as dean and has my sincere thanks.

I am particular grateful to the provost and vice president of academic affairs at Le Moyne College, Father Joseph Marina, SJ, PhD, for his unflagging support of me as both a scholar and an administrator. Few academics could be as fortunate in the freedom to pursue such a dual path through scholarship and administration as I have been in working with him.

Jim Rogers of *New Hibernia Review* and John Brannigan of *Irish University Review* have my thanks for their careful editing and publishing of earlier versions of the last and first chapters of this study, respectively. Tim McMahon has been a friend, colleague, and mentor in our work together with the American Conference for Irish Studies, which has played a pivotal role in my evolution as an academic through the supportive and collegial network and productive conferences it provides. Margaret Kelleher offered help—as she has throughout my career—in shaping my thoughts about trends in Irish literature for this study when I visited Dublin in 2014.

Father David McCallum, SJ, has been a personal and professional resource for me, and I am deeply grateful. I could not have completed this project without the advice and support of Roger Di Pietro: I am forever in debt for his wisdom, kindness, advice, and professionalism. Ali Merola, Heidi Kinnally, Angie Sayles, Eileen Sweeney, Mary Buck, Michelle Hunt, and Kim Taffner have expanded my options and abilities as a working parent: I am so grateful to our "village" for the mutual cover, communal memory, support, and friendship they provide. I could not have completed this work without them.

Finally, I acknowledge with love and gratitude my husband and partner, Timothy Patrick Sullivan, and our incredible sons, Thomas Patrick and Matthew Peter. I thank them for never allowing me to lose sight of our family priorities and for the profound joy they give me amid the slings and arrows of our beautiful (and admittedly occasionally chaotic) life together.

Credits

The End of The Beginning of Love by John McGahern, copyright © the Estate of John McGahern, is reprinted by permission of A. M. Heath & Co Ltd.

Excerpts from *Texts for Nothing and Other Shorter Prose, 1950–1976* by © Samuel Beckett, published by Grove Press, are reproduced by permission of Faber and Faber, Ltd. (World excluding United States print and ebook.)

Excerpts from The Complete Short Prose: 1929–1989, copyright © 1995 by the Estate of Samuel Beckett. Used by permission of Grove Atlantic, Inc. Any third party use of this material, outside of this publication, is prohibited. (United States and Canada.)

Excerpts from *The Sea* by John Banville, copyright © 2005 by John Banville, are used by permission of Alfred A. Knopf, an imprint of the Knopf Doubleday Publishing Group, a division of Penguin Random House LLC. All rights reserved. (World excluding United Kingdom and European Union.)

Excerpts from *The Sea* by John Banville, copyright © 2005 by John Banville, are used by permission of Pan MacMillan. (World including United Kingdom, excluding United States and Canada.)

Excerpts from *The Gathering* by Anne Enright, published by Cape 2007, copyright © Anne Enright, are reproduced by permission of the author c/o Rogers, Coleridge & White Ltd., 20 Powis Mews, London W11 1JN.

Excerpts from *The Secret Scripture* by © Sebastian Barry, published by Viking Penguin 2008, are reproduced by permission of the author c/o Faber and Faber Ltd. (World excluding the United States and Canada.)

Excerpts from *The Secret Scripture* by Sebastian Barry, copyright © 2008 by Sebastian Barry, are used by permission of Viking Books, an imprint of Penguin Publishing Group, a division of Penguin Random House LLC. All rights reserved. (United States and its territories, Philippines, Canada, and open market.)

Excerpts from *Room* by Emma Donoghue, copyright © 2010, are reprinted by permission of Little, Brown and Company, an imprint of Hachette Book Group, Inc. (World excluding Canada.)

Excerpts from *Room* © 2010 by Emma Donoghue. Published by HarperCollins Publishers Ltd. All rights reserved. (Canada.)

Excerpts from © Colum McCann, 2009, *Let the Great World Spin* are reprinted by permission of Bloomsbury Publishing Plc. (World excluding United States, Canada, and Philippines.)

Excerpts from *Let the Great World Spin: A Novel* © 2009 by Colum McCann. Published by HarperCollins Publishers Ltd. All rights reserved. (Canada.)

Excerpts from *Let the Great World Spin: A Novel* by Colum McCann, copyright © 2009 by Colum McCann, are used by permission of Random House, an imprint and division of Penguin Random House LLC. All rights reserved. (United States, Philippines, and open market including the European Union.)

Excerpts from *Nora Webster* by Colm Tóibín, copyright © 2014, are reprinted by permission of the author. For US rights, permission was granted by Simon and Schuster.

I gratefully acknowledge permission to use material in chapter 1 that was originally published as "'My Memory Gropes in Search of Details': Memory, Narrative, and 'Founding Traumas' in John Banville's *The Sea*," *Irish University Review* 46, no. 2 (Autumn–Winter 2016): 340–58.

I also gratefully acknowledge permission to use material in chapter 6 that was originally published as "Colm Tóibín's *Nora Webster*: Peacemaking and Intertextual Redemption," *New Hibernia Review* 20, no. 3 (Fall 2016): 39–54.

Trauma and Recovery
in the Twenty-First-Century Irish Novel

Introduction

Trauma and Narratives of Recovery in the Twenty-First-Century Irish Novel

> I'll close my ears, close my mouth and be grave. And when they open again it may be to hear a story, tell a story. . . . I have high hopes.
>
> —Samuel Beckett, "Texts for Nothing"

In February 2014, the *Connaght Tribune* broke the story of local historian Catherine Corless's revelation that as many as 796 children were buried in an unmarked grave—what may have been a septic tank—on the property of a former mother-and-baby home run by the Sisters of Bons Secours in Tuam, County Galway.[1] Under the shadow of the film *Philomena* (Stephen Frears, 2013), presenting the story of Philomena Lee, a former mother-and-baby home inmate, and following the many revelations in recent years about scandalous conditions in industrial schools, Magdalene laundries, orphanages, and mental institutions, Irish society responded to the Tuam discovery with fury and horror.[2] The Irish nation was again asked to confront a painful history of silence, suffering, and abuse—a legacy of its colonial past.

The report provoked immediate reaction and ignited a firestorm of outrage. Minister for Children and Youth Affairs Charlie Flanagan actively engaged the Tuam situation, promising government involvement and response (if in general fashion).[3] On June 16, 2014, activists demanded that the "inquiry into mother and baby homes should be widened to include mental hospitals following further controversy over high death rates, unmarked graves and allegations of patient mistreatment."[4] Ireland's leading public intellectuals also spoke out. Recognizing that "Catholic Ireland locked up in mental hospitals, industrial schools, Magdalene laundries and mother-and-baby homes an astonishing 1 per cent of its entire population," for example, prolific writer and *Irish Times* commentator Fintan O'Toole argued that the factors that caused these travesties—"superiority, shame, cruelty and exclusion"—persist in Ireland and that, accordingly, "the past has yet to pass."[5] Although resistance remains, such responses do reflect a willingness to confront the traumas and crimes of the past so that contemporary Ireland might chart a trajectory away from its histories of silence and repression toward a more open and self-reflective society.

Revelations such as those at Tuam have thus catalyzed broad societal soul searching over the past two decades, whereby the impact of large-scale cultural forces and events on Irish individuals and society alike is revisited.[6] Such cultural discernment follows the long arc of reassessing Irish history and culture over the past several decades, arguably beginning with the Revisionist debates. Oona Frawley notes that these "'Revisionist' debates in Ireland from the 1960s onwards presented reinterpretations of Irish history from a variety of ideological positions that sought to use the past in order to explain the present, to create histories that provided a sense of release from traumatic or difficult pasts."[7]

With the advent of postcolonial theory in the 1980s, these discussions widened. As Joe Cleary has observed, postcolonial studies "destabilize[d] the cultural dominant [*sic*] represented by modernization discourse" as it sought to "articulate the systemic connections between the various crises that affect Irish society, North and South, . . . in a manner that controverts crucial tenets of the reigning orthodoxy."[8] The movement toward multiple and contested understandings of history and away from a privileged, dominant narrative catalyzed a broad reassessment of Ireland's history. It also led to explicit consideration of the consequences of large-scale social and cultural forces for Irish society as a whole.[9]

In her work on the groundbreaking series *Memory Ireland*, Frawley observes that this "consideration of 'history' from new and multiple perspectives" triggered an assessment of the role of memory as a social and individual force.[10] I return later to the issue of collective memory as it relates to trauma, but here it is worth noting Frawley's observation that "multiple subspecies of memories . . . can be said to function not just at the level of the individual mind, but at a social level." Although she carefully notes the hazards of a normative use of cultural memory, Frawley acknowledges that events can have a profound impact at both the cultural and the individual levels of memory and experience.[11] The broadening of historiography and consequent recognition of the complex role of memory dovetailed with the growing field of trauma studies, which had concrete implications for Irish literature.

The desire to confront traumatic subjects was a facet of Irish literature for much of the twentieth century. Yet just as the societal response to Tuam outlined earlier reflects a more direct and open approach to these issues than was common in the recent past, Irish authors have also evolved in their response to, and literary uses of, trauma. These most recent responses both capture and engage their cultural and historical, post–Celtic Tiger moment. This study considers not only the ways in which the Irish canon represents an ongoing awareness of trauma as a literary and cultural force but also how this representation has shifted since the turn of the twenty-first century. Previous Irish trauma narratives—for example, John McGahern's *The Dark* (1965), Patrick McCabe's *The Butcher Boy* (1992), Edna O'Brien's *Down by the River* (1996), and Seamus Deane's *Reading in the Dark* (1996), to name only a few—center predominantly on the role of silence and the individual, communal, or societal suffering that traumas induce. In contrast, twenty-first-century Irish narratives increasingly turn from just recognizing traumatic experiences toward also exploring and representing the process of healing and recovery, interrogating this possibility from the vantage of the authors' time and place. This shift is often manifest structurally—for example, through a metanarrative engagement with traumatic representation. The novels under consideration in this study infuse trauma into the narrative either by integrating it structurally or by writing it into characters' embodied selves as the physical markers of trauma.

According to Robert F. Garratt, self-consciousness about narrative is a hallmark of "trauma novels":

> A trauma novel . . . employs a narrative strategy in which a reconstruction of events through memories, flashbacks, dreams, and hauntings is as important as the events themselves. In a trauma novel, both subject and method become central: in addition to developing trauma as an element of the story and part of its dramatic action, it depicts the process by which a person encounters and comes to know a traumatic event or moment that has previously proved inaccessible. In so doing the trauma novel stakes its claim as a literary hybrid, a work that balances narration and narrative, a story that both describes an external violent action and portrays the mind's attempts to remember it.[12]

The more hopeful engagements with trauma evident in the novels I include here take this consideration a step further by emulating the process worked through by the traumatized. Their unreliable narratives mirror the nature of traumatic memory and thus model the process of recovery both structurally and narratively. In this way, I argue, such narratives go beyond just representing trauma; they also engage with the material nature of trauma for a victim by weaving it into the narrative, and they show how trauma victims can heal through narrative processing.[13]

This dual narrative and structural engagement are evident in various ways in all the texts I include in this study. John Banville's narrator in *The Sea* (2005) wrestles with the omissions and uncertainty of memory, even as the novel attests to both throughout its narrative arc; the process of recording past events becomes recuperative. Sebastian Barry's *The Secret Scripture* (2008) transcribes the memory and testimony of Roseanne Clear McNulty so she can find some degree of liberation from a torturous past. Anne Enright's *The Gathering* (2007) foregrounds Veronica Hegarty's processing of trauma and loss through narrative (re)construction to attain a degree of closure. Emma Donoghue's *Room* (2010) exposes the narrative structuration employed by the traumatized as a flawed coping mechanism, which is itself subject to revision; in *Let the Great World Spin* (2009), Colum McCann creates structural parallels throughout the novel to ground a recuperative narrative of suffering and recovery. Finally, Colm Tóibín's novel *Nora Webster* (2014) employs pointed intertextual references to highlight the constructed and subjective nature of both trauma and recovery. All of these texts thus engage to varying degrees with a metanarrative exploration of trauma and recovery, enacting a recuperative narrative simultaneously for the reader and by the character.

This shift from trauma toward recovery can also often be seen thematically, as in the novels' consideration of the traumatized body (in particular the gendered body). *The Sea* asks how "knowing" and speaking one's story relates to "being"; *The Gathering* consistently explores the physical imprint of trauma on and for Veronica as victim, subject, and woman. *The Gathering*, *Room*, *Nora Webster*, and *The Secret Scripture* all center in varying ways around motherhood, maternal embodiment, and their relation to trauma. McCann, too, explores the concrete physical repercussions of trauma for Father Corrigan in *Let the Great World Spin*. Paralleling the embedding of trauma in narrative, these works collapse boundaries between structure and content, making trauma a material object as well as the subject with which, and through which, they work. While capturing the physical consequences of traumatic experience, they thus correspondingly invite a conversation about healing. The authors in this study recognize that the act of representation is potentially curative: for individuals, these novels suggest, exploring and representing trauma can not only capture painful experiences but also catalyze a move toward recovery and away from the stifling silences of the past.

In this respect, many twenty-first-century trauma novels enact narratively the very process of recovery that they depict. The most recent of Irish novels assert possibilities for redemption, resolution, and some degree of recovery from traumatic experience by moving beyond expressing and representing trauma to a simultaneous exploration *in narrative practice* of the possibility for recovery. As I detail later, in the period in which these novels were written, the first two decades of the twenty-first century, Irish society had to negotiate the legacy of hubris, greed, and neoliberalism from the Celtic Tiger era, balancing cynicism over the errors of the past with a determination to move ahead differently and moderately. The language of reconciliation introduced by the peace process likely also influenced this shift. A product of their time, these novels thus reflect their historical moment and respond to what Irish society seeks: to recognize past failings and the very long shadow of societal abuses; to acknowledge the past without either occluding or overprivileging it; and to seek ways to move ahead productively as a society.

In this introduction, I briefly trace the evolution of trauma studies in relation to Irish history and literature. I selectively review some authors of important twentieth-century Irish novels that can be classified as trauma narratives in order to suggest how the representation of trauma in Ireland has developed and evolved over the past century. Finally, I suggest why this shift has occurred—that is, what changed to set the stage for the more redemptive, more hopeful responses to trauma, in addition to the limitations of this model, that characterize many twenty-first-century Irish novels.

Memory and Trauma Studies

Since the 1990s, trauma as not only a personal but also a cultural phenomenon has come increasingly to the fore in academic study. Late twentieth-century landmark psychology texts such as Judith Lewis Herman's foundational work *Trauma and Recovery* (1992) sparked a reassessment of the workings and social implications of trauma throughout the decade.[14] Herman's critical contribution to the fields of psychology and, indirectly, literary study is in her tracing of the characteristics of trauma as well as the process by which individual recovery is possible.

In addition to noting now familiar characteristics of post-traumatic stress response such as hyperarousal, dissociation, constriction (limiting one's emotional and social life), and intrusive thoughts, Herman observes the fundamental sense of alienation that trauma causes, its existential disruption of social and familial networks: "Traumatic events call into question basic human relationships. They breach the attachments of family, friendship, love, and community. They shatter the construction of the self that is formed and sustained in relation to others. They undermine the belief systems that give meaning to human experience."[15] In addition, because "traumatic events ultimately refuse to be put away," victims of trauma can never really evade those painful memories and are instead haunted by them throughout their lives.[16] Trauma's resistance to being "put away" is central to understanding the pressing need to confront and address traumatic experiences.

Given the destructive force and obdurate duration of trauma, the field of trauma studies also explores the means by which a survivor can move on. The joint work of Holocaust studies, psychoanalytic theory, and literary criticism has contributed crucially to this effort. Shoshana Felman's influential work on testimony—most notably *Testimony: Crisis of Witnessing in Literature, Psychoanalysis, and History* (1992), coauthored with Dori Laub—and Cathy Caruth's collection of essays *Trauma: Explorations in Memory* (1995) emphasize the damaging role of silence in trauma and the ways in which testifying to one's experience can alleviate suffering.[17] As Laub notes, "Survivors often claim that they experience the feeling of belonging to a 'secret order' that is sworn to silence. . . . [B]y never divulging their stories, they feel that the rest of the world will never come to know the *real* truth."[18] This impulse toward silence effectively reinforces the sense of isolation and vulnerability with which trauma victims already struggle.

Caruth argues that, equally important, the survivor's memory and understanding of trauma are experienced as unspeakable: "The traumatized . . . carry an impossible history within them, or they become themselves the symptom of a history that they cannot entirely possess."[19] Because traumatic memory is "inflexible and invariable" and "a solitary activity," its very processing in the brain is, according to trauma theorists, isolating and elusive.[20] These important contributions highlight both the difficulty of assimilating traumatic memory, which presents as a disrupted and often psychologically evasive history, and the simultaneously contradictory impulse between repression and revisitation that trauma inflicts. The obsessive return to traumatic memories and the seemingly contradictory parallel impulse toward silence profoundly mark the engagement with and representation of traumatic experience.

Literary critical interventions into trauma studies have thus proven to be rich and productive. Focusing on the means and modes of representation, such studies have deepened our understandings of the workings of traumatic memory. In *Writing History, Writing Trauma*, Dominick LaCapra notes that "trauma and its symptomatic aftermath pose particularly acute problems for historical representation and understanding." His study thus seeks to "come to terms with trauma as well as [with] the crucial role post-traumatic testimonies . . . have assumed in recent thought and writing." LaCapra observes that although traumatic memory is inherently unreliable, such memories capture the spirit of the traumatic event and so cannot be dismissed. As he explains, traumatic memory "may involve distortion, disguise, and other permutations relating to . . . narrative shaping," but such failures in strict accuracy "[can]not invalidate [a narrative] in its entirety."[21] Felman and Laub make a similar claim, noting that to offer testimony sometimes is not "simply to [give] empirical historical facts" but to provide the wider context that traumatic memory seeks to capture.[22] Such understandings add an important dimension to the nature of traumatic memory and to the challenges it poses to efforts toward its verbal and literary representation.

As each of the examples given earlier illustrate, the nature of trauma cannot be extricated from discussions of memory, and scholars have increasingly come to understand memory not only as an individual event but also as communal. According to Guy Beiner, "The founding father of the concept of collective memory was the French sociologist Maurice Halbwachs, who . . . claim[ed] [in the 1930s] that memory is fundamentally a collective function."[23] Although the precise mechanisms of such communal memory have been debated in the years since Halbwachs developed this concept, Beiner's essential point is that communities and their self-understanding contribute to establishing common memory—what he terms "social memory." Thus, individual responses to societal-scale issues are shaped and influenced by their communal setting, which tempers and grounds those responses in a shared worldview: "Social memory is an organic and dynamic synthesis. . . . It does not merely reflect the total sum of individual memories in a community at any given time, but is grounded in a set of frames of reference by which individuals can locate and reinterpret their own recollections. As a metaconstruct, social memory assumes collective characteristics."[24] The field of literary studies, too, has responded to the role of memory. Garratt rightly notes that "the advantage the novelist may have is that in the trauma novel the story is as much about *the act of memory* as it is about the event remembered."[25]

Ireland and Trauma Studies

As described earlier, trends in Irish historiography, combined with the advent of postcolonialism and conversations about collective memory, paralleled and deepened in an Irish context the developments discussed in the previous section. Indeed, as Frawley argues, "the conjunction of these two strands—historical movements away from more 'traditional' forms of historiography alongside the rising prominence of postcolonialism, and the impact of trauma studies in forcing a consideration of historical group trauma—is the point at which memory studies might be said to have met Irish studies."[26] Frawley's work on memory studies complicates the role of memory in Irish history and historiography in meaningful and thoughtful ways, recognizing both this field's potential pitfalls and its opportunities.[27] Particularly given the revelations in the 1980s and 1990s regarding the Kerry Babies case and the X case as well as the proliferation of studies on the Magdalene laundries, industrial schools, and other forms of institutional incarceration and abuse, Irish society became increasingly attuned to the notions of collective memory and, correspondingly, collective trauma. Indeed, the impact and reach of the documentary *States of Fear* (World Health Organization, 1999) reflect this attunement. Ireland thus fits within the wider trend in cultural and literary studies over the past two decades to assess the impact of traumatic experience at both the individual and the societal levels.

Among the best analyses of collective trauma in Ireland is Graham Dawson's excellent study *Making Peace with the Past? Memory, Trauma, and the Irish Troubles* (2007). Recognizing that "*personal* memory . . . is bound up in a reciprocal relation with . . . social and collective representations of the past," Dawson complicates our understanding of both individual and collective memory as mutually entwined and constitutive. He also explores the curative power of remembering and testifying to communal suffering and employs the idea of a "traumatized community" to acknowledge that "profound suffering has been inflicted on and endured by a community, a people or a nation, and that both the suffering and the response to it are integral to the historical record." Communal remembering can remediate such losses, he suggests, helping the individual and the community alike to process and integrate their experiences.[28]

Such efforts to explore the silences and suffering of the past were well under way in Ireland in the 1990s. Maria Luddy's book *Women and Philanthropy* (1995) was among the earliest inquiries into the Magdalene laundries and, according to James M. Smith, was also one of the earliest challenges to the religious orders to "make their archival records available" for public scrutiny, thereby breaking the long-standing cultural silences surrounding these institutions.[29] Smith's own later book on the subject, *Ireland's Magdalen Laundries and the Nation's Architecture of Containment* (2007), provides a comprehensive survey of institutions such as the laundries that, he contends, were used to police Ireland's national self-representation. Smith issues a direct challenge to the Irish state, society, and the Catholic Church alike to break the cultural silences surrounding the laundries, industrial schools, and orphanages, calling for "a collective movement forward—toward real action."[30] Such critical studies reflect awareness of the silences that have characterized Irish society from at least the nineteenth century on and recognize the possibility and the importance of breaking them.

In recent years, the application of trauma studies to an Irish context has correspondingly become increasingly common. In 2011, Anne

Goarzin edited a special issue of the journal *Études Irlandaises* dedicated solely to the topic of trauma in Irish literature. As she notes in the introduction, the volume "seeks to address some of the narratives that 'ghost' Irish history and culture (about the Travellers, the victims of child abuse or previously unquestioned interpretations of 1968 in Northern Ireland, for example). It also provides an insight into how literature perceives, deals with or memorizes [*sic*] inner or collective trauma."[31] In the same year, Garratt published his aforementioned study *Trauma and History in the Irish Novel: The Return of the Dead*, in which he considers how select novelists treat "common historical material within the frame of trauma" in order to present "a particular perspective on Ireland's past and on the ongoing discussions of historical interpretation." Focusing on novels written from 1970 to 2000, Garratt contends that "all of [these novels] place special emphasis on trauma and traumatic experience" as a means to process and represent the political violence and events of their times, and he concludes that such novels "present a view of Irish history that traumatizes those that are swept up by it."[32]

Although trauma studies as a field in general bourgeoned in the 1990s, the focus on trauma and its consequences has long been an aspect of literary and historical representation and criticism in Ireland. The very title of Margaret Kelleher's influential literary study *The Feminization of the Famine: Expressions of the Inexpressible?* (1997) highlights the long-standing tendency of Irish society to associate the Famine with the unspeakable. Kelleher recognizes this ineffable quality of suffering by asking, "Is it possible to depict the horror and scale of an event such as famine; are literature and language adequate to the task?" Her explanation of those silences anticipates conversations about cultural trauma more broadly: "Such a silence may denote depths of pain, of shame and of guilt on the part of those who survived, and a necessary repression of the past in order to move forward."[33] The Famine has long been held to mark what LaCapra would term a kind of "founding trauma,"[34] which contributed to the silences endemic in Irish society. The same is true of political discourse and Irish history more broadly. Dawson notes that "the Irish historical past is often described as 'traumatic,'" both in reference to specific events such as the 1641 Rebellion and the Famine and in broader strokes "from the nineteenth century down to the present . . . as a narrative of oppression and suffering inflicted on the Irish people."[35]

Trauma is a consistent undercurrent throughout the Irish literary canon. As referenced earlier, Kelleher's work on nineteenth-century Famine narratives explores literary attempts to express communal suffering. An argument could also be made that Anglo-Irish women's fiction as a whole, from the early nineteenth century with Maria Edgeworth on, reflects an awareness of societal trauma and the silences it invokes in a manner resonant with our understandings of Irish social silencing, particularly in the later work of Elizabeth Bowen and Molly Keane.[36] Yet one can look even earlier, for Irish folklore has long served this function as well: "The recital of folk history is a rudimentary form of commemoration. . . . Through mourning and memory, death—the most individual of human experiences—becomes a social event."[37] Writing out nightmarish scenarios in literature thus becomes a vehicle for interrogation, for bringing unspoken outrages and injustices to light. Although silence, commemoration, and anxiety are not synonymous with trauma, a desire to memorialize through representation has long been present in Irish society. Irish authors have taken up that challenge, increasingly exposing and engaging all kinds of societal oppressions and suffering through narrative.

Throughout the twentieth century, Irish authors increasingly confronted fictionally the hazards and crimes of a seemingly all-powerful Catholic Church, the systemic neglect and abuse of children, the suffocating nature of Irish domesticity, and the crippling familial and social silences that perpetuated and tacitly condoned such abuses. As Garratt argues, such works "tacitly assume a connection between political violence and partisan and distorted treatments of the past that invite vengeful responses."[38] Through their fictional representations of trauma, Irish authors made visible in the twentieth century what had been silent and initiated conversations that Irish society had avoided. As importantly, they provided a means and opportunity to engage with issues of history, memory, and loss.

Trauma and the Twentieth-Century Irish Canon

In the modern era, it is with James Joyce that—as in so many other things—the act of representing unspoken societal ills was arguably first enacted. In a talk at the celebratory launch of *Digital Dubliners* by Boston College in 2014, Fintan O'Toole argued that in many respects James Joyce's short story collection *Dubliners* (1914) set the stage for the interrogations of Irish societal ills that would follow throughout the twentieth century. As he rightly noted, *Dubliners* is the first modern text that sets out to portray both the vulnerability and the neglect and abuse of children as a central theme.[39] John McGahern noted the initial negative response garnered by *Dubliners*, a response that reflected Irish society's lack of preparation for such stark representation: "The first reactions to *Dubliners* were . . . that the work was depressing, with no uplifting message, too withdrawn and cold[,] and, *though all too accurate*, lacking in feeling and compassion."[40] Such literary representations would be commonplace by the late 1990s, however.

McGahern himself must be credited as a central figure in the twentieth-century shift toward representations of trauma in Irish literature. Born in Dublin in 1934, McGahern suffered the death of his mother when he was ten and, as is well known, went to live with his father in the Garda barracks in Roscommon. His father was professionally frustrated and abusive toward his children, and McGahern's canon plumbs both this painful personal history and its wider social context, revisiting and reshaping it throughout his career. Because of his personal and cultural history, it is worth considering him briefly as an exemplar of twentieth-century Irish interventions into trauma.

Perhaps of particular interest is the history of McGahern's first novel, "The End or the Beginning of Love." Written between 1957 and 1961, the novel was "accepted for publication by Faber and Faber, [but] McGahern decided to withdraw [it] . . . believing that it wasn't good enough."[41] A reading of this earliest, unpublished novel, however, reveals a fascinating parallelism between it and his later works, both in content and in many of the central themes—the pervasive power of the Catholic Church, silence, domestic abuse—that characterize these texts and would become staples of the twentieth-century Irish canon. Although it is thus tempting to read McGahern's entire professional writing life in part as a process of engaging and (in his case) perhaps working through the trauma of his early years, it is critical for our purposes here to recognize the shaping and craft that go into such appropriation.[42]

A few examples will serve. The earliest versions of "The End or the Beginning of Love" begin with a visit from the priest to speak to the "barefoot children" at school. In a conversation resonant with Joycean influence, McGahern traces the priest's encouragement to the boys to seek a vocation in passages that hint both to subtle pressure and a jarring sensuality: "'Come and be fishers of men[.]' He repeated the words with slow, dreamy emphasis, savouring them with his lips."[43] In another section, Jude looks scornfully at his collocutors, noting, "These people had no sense of sin; the levity with which they bandied the Holy Name and sex about terrified him; he almost expected the wrath of God would come like thunder and lightning to blacken this city off the face of the earth, this huge Sodom of the restless earth."[44] Like Steven Dedalus before him, Jude has a time in which he assumes subservience to the church and its expectations: "He believed completely with [his mother] that one day he would be a priest."[45]

Such references to the authority and power of the church, of course, came to be a hallmark of McGahern's work, and they illustrate the ways in which representations of trauma also served as a kind of social commentary. In an article titled "Whatever You Say, Say Nothing: Ireland 1950–1959," published in the *Irish Times* in 1999, McGahern reflected on the religious contexts that pervaded even his earliest writing: "In the South individual speech and thought were equally discouraged. . . . The demand for this subservience was driven most powerfully in the Republic by the Catholic Church. Against the whole spirit of the 1916 Proclamation, by 1950 the State had become a theocracy in all but name."[46] Similarly, his essay "The Church and Its Spire" reviews the internal pressures put on boys and young men to become priests that are so evident in "The End and the Beginning of Love"; in it, he avers, "After Independence, Church and State became inseparable, with unhealthy consequences for both."[47] Of course, this recycling has not gone unnoticed: as novelist Joseph O'Neill observed about McGahern in 1990, "The same themes and figures recur again and again in his writing: enraged fathers, dying mothers, shotgun marriages, priests, sisters, rosaries."[48]

Like Colm Tóibín after him, McGahern can be seen throughout his canon to rework repeated traumas clearly based on his own history—mothers dying, frustrated and abusive fathers, and alienated, oppressed children recur in texts such as *The Barracks* (1963), *The Leavetaking* (1975), and *Amongst Women* (1990).[49] It seems clear that, canonically, McGahern did not extricate his characters' personal sufferings from the wider context of Irish society. Yet perhaps as interesting as his revisitations of such traumas—and perhaps even more significant—is the way in which these revisitations evolve over time. This is particularly true in his narrative reworkings of troublingly sexualized passages in his work.

In the notoriously disturbing opening scene in McGahern's second published novel, *The Dark* (a novel that was, perhaps tellingly, originally named *The Pit*), for example, the father strips and threatens to beat his son.[50] This is a borrowing and reworking of a passage included originally about midway through a draft of "The End or the Beginning of Love." In the earlier novel, however, it is a daughter, not a son, who is terrorized: "Her stripped body shivered. A few adolescent pimples showed on the naked flesh. Hugh froze with horror. Even in the dim light he saw by his father's trousers that he was sexually aroused."[51]

A similar shift occurs when Hugh shares a bed with his father: in a later draft of "The End and the Beginning of Love" Hugh notes that his father's "heavy, rough hand was repulsive," but this novel does not feature the molestation scene included in *The Dark*.[52] Finally, although "The End or the Beginning of Love" includes many scenes of violence, as recur throughout McGahern's canon—such as when Hugh is beaten with a branch of heather and "the three children banded against their father. They wouldn't trust him"[53]—the degree of sexual undertone increases and of course explodes in his later work.

The representation of trauma evidenced here certainly became far more common over the course of the twentieth century. In this case, the author draws heavily on autobiographical suffering, but McGahern was self-conscious in his artistic appropriation of trauma and the craft that went along with it. A sense of compulsion and the ambivalent need to speak are tellingly juxtaposed with his view of art in a short nonfiction essay, "The Image": "For art is, out of the failure of love, an attempt to create a world in which we can live, if not for long or forever, still a world of the imagination over which we can reign . . . allowing us to celebrate even the totally intolerable."[54] Despite resorting to the same, clearly autobiographical themes, McGahern remained discomfited by their personal resonances. Asked whether he was "constantly mining that past and background," he averred, "No, I don't think that's true. I've never written about anything unless it is in my head for a long time. . . . One is trying to be true to the original experience, but seldom by the time it's finished has it anything to do with the way you imagined it in the first place."[55]

McGahern's oeuvre thus includes an element of working through that later authors would emulate, even as he clearly recognizes the parallels of personal and societal dysfunction. Through the narrative license McGahern takes and his resistance to the idea that his work is autobiographical, he offers an extended probing of the representation of trauma. For this reason, although he is hardly the only Irish author to tackle the representation of trauma in his work, his self-conscious engagement seems to me to be a central, if not the greatest, single influence on the creation and evolution of what some have called the Irish trauma novel.

No twentieth-century author may engage trauma canonically as graphically and relentlessly as John McGahern, of course, but many others do so to varying degrees. Equally influential—and perhaps equally as consistent as any other twentieth-century Irish novelist—is Edna O'Brien, whose brave and combative representations of social injustice have influenced Irish literature for the better part of almost six decades.

If McGahern's strength is capturing the impact of personal trauma against the backdrop of a claustrophobic and even damaging society, O'Brien's is in rendering the causal link between societal dysfunction and individual cost. O'Brien, too, directly confronts Irish regionalism and religious hypocrisy as well as the psychological consequences of an emotionally straitened life in Ireland, particularly for women, and she repeatedly addresses Irish prejudice and ethnocentrism, the Catholic Church's dominance, and the state's oppressive strictures on and for women. Novels as early as *The Country Girls* (1960) reflect her willingness to take on the stultifying strictures of church and society alike, and work as recent as *The Little Red Chairs* (2016) displays her recognition of the importance of acknowledging the suffering caused by societal norms as well as the suffocating nature of Irish rural town life.

O'Brien does not shy away from direct references to specific cultural taboos, aggressively tracing the pervasive and damaging impact of societal silences, sexual abuse, and family dysfunction on generations of Irish women and men alike. Her novel *Down by the River* (1997) caused a stir for its adaptation of a well-known contemporary crime in Ireland. As reviewer Ronan Bennett noted, "The novel was based on the real case of an underage[d] rape victim who sought an abortion in England and prompted one of Ireland's periodic bouts of soul-searching. [O'Brien's] style, though occasionally busy, was appropriately pared down. She was still writing intensely about love—more correctly, love's absence from damaged lives—but it was clear she was writing about Ireland."[56] In *Down by the River*, O'Brien captures the social tensions of sexual violence, shame, and a claustrophobically judgmental and intrusive society: "Only they will know. No one else will ever know. Except that they will." Importantly, she also stresses the centrality of "telling" to the process of healing: "She closes her eyes . . . thinking how it might be . . . that there would be a someone to whom she could tell it all, all of it, down to the last shred, but that there would be no need to tell it because it would be already known and that would be love."[57]

In the Forest (2002) was similarly direct, but such representations cost O'Brien a societal price. As Bennett notes,

> Though *In the Forest* garnered excellent reviews when it was published in America, in Ireland the response has been hostile. O'Brien has been accused of exploiting tragedy for profit, of intruding into private grief, of writing about an Ireland she no longer knows or understands. The intemperateness of the language and the contortion and inconsistency of the charges against her lead you to suspect there are other motives at work. . . . Literary Ireland can be a very petty place indeed; O'Brien can safely ignore it. But what we can be glad she has not ignored is the other Ireland, the Ireland that made Brendan O'Donnell/Mich O'Kane.[58]

I return later to her most recent novel, *The Little Red Chairs*, but here I would note that in a canon that spans monumental shifts in Irish society from the 1960s to the 2010s, O'Brien has been a consistent voice speaking out against the worst abuses that have plagued Irish society.[59] Her courage in tracing this horrifying tradition of silence and abuse has undoubtedly contributed to the more open climate we see in Ireland and in its literature today.

John McGahern and Edna O'Brien are thus emblematic of twentieth-century representations of trauma in the Irish canon. They are not alone; many twentieth-century Irish novelists pursued similar trajectories. Among the earliest progenitors is the oft-banned Kate O'Brien, whose work takes on not only the repressive structures of the Irish church and state but also the emotional consequences of such oppressions and repressions for her characters. Clearly, many late twentieth-century novelists followed these earlier writers' lead. It would be impossible to address all such novelists here, nor is that my task, but canonical writers as diverse as Colm Tóibín, Roddy Doyle, Julia O'Faolain, Jennifer Johnston, and Patrick McCabe, to name only a handful, trace the consequences of familial or societal dysfunction or both, often from within the wider Irish political context.[60] These authors, and many others, contribute to a body of work that consistently and directly takes up the representation of personal and societal trauma in Irish society.

Twentieth-century Irish novelists' engagement with societal and domestic trauma has thus opened the space for needed dialogue more broadly in Irish society. The representation of societally induced suffering grew organically from the repercussions of a postcolonizing society and the long history of the Irish literary tradition. The confluence of new directions in historiography, postcolonial theory, trauma studies, and cultural and literary theory contributed to that movement, as did the tendency (particularly of Nationalist historiography) to characterize Irish history as traumatic. This very act of opening up through representation has catalyzed the consequent shift that we are currently seeing in the twenty-first-century Irish novel. In the last sections of this introduction, I sketch the nature of that shift, its causes, and its implications.

Trauma and Representation

At their most recuperative, novels that engage trauma can (re)present a process that is in itself healing for trauma victims. As trauma studies have repeatedly shown, trauma survivors recuperate best when enabled to *narrativize* their suffering—to represent their own histories in ways that give them a sense of control and authorship over their own lives. According to Herman, in recovery the survivor "tells [his or her story] completely, in depth and in detail. This work of reconstruction actually transforms the traumatic memory, so that it can be integrated into the survivor's life story."[61] Trauma narratives thus can be seen to model the kind of process a survivor must pursue.

Holocaust studies, too, have long shown that "witnessing" is critical for recovery—acting not only as a witness to one's own experience but also as "a witness to the testimonies of others, and . . . *to the process of witnessing itself*."[62] Irish novels that engage trauma can emulate, through their characters and sometimes in their narrative structure, the kind of textual shaping that recovery from traumatic experience and memory requires. As Garratt observes, "To tell the story of a traumatic past, then, becomes both a task (in so far [*sic*] as it is difficult) and a 'cure' (in so far as it assimilates the unassimilated), since only with the ability to tell the event does it become true memory, relegated to the past, and therefore over."[63] Literary projects such as Damian Gorman's *An Crann*, which sought to promote healing after the peace process, and more recent efforts such as the Forgiveness Project reflect the widespread belief in Ireland, Northern Ireland, and the United Kingdom in the power of narrative to heal and to reconcile.[64]

Irish literature reflects cultural awareness of traumatic elements of Ireland's past and correspondingly of the ways that testimony and witnessing can be personally and socially curative. Although there is little doubt that literature has played a role in provoking needed social conversations, it is of course also important to differentiate such *representation* from an actual, psychological/therapeutic process. In one of the more skeptical treatments of trauma studies, Ulrike Tancke objects that trauma narratives artificially represent what is, in practice, largely inexpressible and thus betray a problematic and even "manipulative" ideological intention as a subgenre:

> The ubiquity of the concept which results is not, crucially, a mere reflection of themes and issues dealt with in literature, but rather a self-affirmative critical venture that confirms the relevance of criticism's key concerns. Importantly, trauma is used primarily as a critical category, allegory or theoretical construct; [*sic*] a shift which facilitates its ubiquitous usage and draws attention away from the material immediacy and violent impact of genuine traumatic experience.[65]

Such cautionary reminders are well noted: to imply a direct correlation between the *representation* of trauma and the *experience* of trauma or recovery would be irresponsible. This is not unlike the caution required in discussing concepts such as collective memory, as Frawley again helpfully notes: "Collective memory, understood as memory shared by a group[,] . . . is the *representation* of the past in the present."[66]

In *Making Peace with the Past?* Dawson speaks to the curative role of testimony for a "traumatized community" but rightly notes "the danger of ascribing to [a] group a collective psyche . . . as if it were *like* an individual."[67] More recently, in an article in the *Irish University Review* he wonders whether the "productivity" of trauma as a concept "may have become exhausted as the concept itself congeals into normativity." In particular, Dawson warns against trauma theory's potential to reinstitute a false binary between "the 'normal' and the 'pathological'"; to neglect the role of the "mediation [of trauma] in the internal world"; and to "inscrib[e] a privileged position and role to the trained cultural analyst" to the detriment of communal, interpersonal negotiations.[68] These cautions against a holistic application of trauma theory—of treating cultures as therapeutically akin to individuals and of leveling subtleties of individual and communal negotiation—are well founded.[69]

I am focused here not on the application of trauma studies to political and social reconciliation but rather on trauma's *representational use and value.* All of the authors in this study are engaged with the wider social, literary, and political forces that make trauma a relevant category of analysis, but here I am concerned with their use of trauma as a narrative device. I am interested in how literary representation can emulate cathartic testimony, just as it can capture the consequences and costs of personal and social trauma; it can identify and reflect real social patterns and emotional consequences as well as possibilities for healing while reflecting the interconnection of the personal and the political.

There are clear societal impacts when literature engages trauma, a causal correlation that requires acknowledgment of the representative function of literature. Indeed, some scholars argue that it is precisely *because of* the crafted nature of literature that it is empowered to engage such seemingly unspeakable traumas in cathartic and productive ways:

> Philosophical and artistic works are . . . capable of furnishing some extra, because indirect, insights into the enigma of horror. For both proffer an *unnatural* perspective on things—by virtue of

> style, genre and language. And this unnatural perspective is almost invariably absent from the all-too-naturalistic stance of most entertainment and mass media. . . . The advantage of art and philosophy is that they are critical discourses which underscore the character of such illusion.[70]

I hope that it will therefore be understood that throughout this study my use of trauma studies explores the ways in which authors self-consciously employ the concept of trauma as a narrative device rather than as an unself-conscious cultural process. Such representation can provide a commentary on suffering and trauma at both the individual and the national levels; at times, that representation seeks to model structurally the process it describes. Nonetheless, this act of what I call "*presencing* suffering"—making it tangible and thereby claiming a kind of narrative ownership—emulates the path pursued by the traumatized without claiming synonymy. In this respect, these novels can be seen to perform or model literarily the kinds of exploration sometimes required at the individual and national levels to confront suffering. Although subtle, the implication is clear: by modeling the sort of narrative engagement pursued by the traumatized, these texts gesture toward the kinds of recovery a therapeutic process would enable, but without claiming precisely to replicate that process.

Recovery in the Twenty-First-Century Novel

Although Irish novels throughout the twentieth century engaged questions of personal and societal trauma, a noticeable shift began to take place at the end of the twentieth century and into the beginning of the twenty-first. Rather than centrally focusing on capturing trauma, many novels from the late 1990s to the current day started to emphasize not only the representation of personal or cultural trauma but also the act of representation itself and the *curative* power of such representation. This metanarrative engagement with the process of narrativizing mimics the healing function of testimony as awareness of the process of telling empowers the trauma victim to author his or her own life story.

Needless to say, such a shift did not occur overnight, and the identification of its occurrence at the turn of the twenty-first century is of necessity somewhat imprecise. Colm Tóibín's novel *The Blackwater Lightship* (1999) is a twentieth-century novel, but it uses narrative recuperatively in its representation of Declan and his suffering body. Tóibín's focus on the *process* of engaging traumatic suffering narratively speaks to the idea of enabling recovery at the familial and national levels.[71] Similarly, James Ryan's novel *Seeds of Doubt* (2001) directly engages questions of silence and alludes to the power of storytelling. It is arguable that this shift can be seen as nascent in McGahern in that his canonical engagement with personal and literary trauma culminates in the autobiographical *Memoir* (2005), where he ponders the impact of such representation. Finally, Edna O'Brien's most recent novel, *The Little Red Chairs*, in many respects fits the kind of narrative engagement I examine in this study, with its emphasis on Fidelma's need to represent her painful past.[72]

Yet aside from the simple impossibility of including every novel that touches upon narratives of recovery, this study focuses on a distinction: although the texts cited earlier often end on the consequence of silence or seem to engage the curative power of telling, they do so without reflecting self-consciously on the empowering function of *narrative representation* as such. O'Brien's fine novel *The Little Red Chairs*, for example, is not given a chapter in this book despite being a twenty-first-century work because I read it as more consonant with a twentieth-century need to represent trauma, whereas the works in this study exhibit a metanarrative engagement with the representation of trauma itself as well as a focus on recovery.[73] Similarly, *Seeds of Doubt* is a powerful novel, but it focuses more on the cost of such silences than on modeling the process of telling itself: "It begins to dawn on him how ill served she and I were by all that secrecy, how ill served everyone was. . . . I cannot persuade him to let go of the belief that secrecy and silence are inherently worthy."[74] Tóibín's work from

1990 to 2014 trends increasingly toward narratives of recovery canonically, and, indeed, Tóibín is one of the earliest authors to engage this process self-consciously; however, that view is given fullest expression metanarratively not in *The Blackwater Lightship* but in his latest Irish novel, *Nora Webster*.

What may initially seem to be a most obvious omission on my part is excluded by the same logic—Eimear McBride's short, haunting novel *A Girl Is a Half-formed Thing*. Published in 2013,[75] the novel takes the reader into the mind of an abused, troubled young woman as she navigates a selfish and mercurial mother, a sexually predatory uncle, and the death of her older, disabled brother from a brain tumor. Tellingly, McBride uses a fractured narrative to emulate the broken thought processes of trauma. As Anne Enright has noted, "The style is . . . direct, simple and free of intertextual tricks and, after a while, the language becomes its own kind of object."[76]

This novel is often heralded for what some consider its re-creation of traumatic memory, given its use of fracture and disruption. It shares with the novels in my analysis an interest in form and structure, and it certainly models the ways in which language and experience can be bound as well as an interest in the physical manifestations of trauma. Nonetheless, *A Girl Is a Half-Formed Thing* falls beyond the bounds of this study because it does not utilize language as a vehicle to recovery or emulate the ways in which narrative can offer affective hope. Rather, it focuses its energies on re-creating the dislocations and reverberations of trauma.[77] In this sense, I would argue that it, like *The Little Red Chairs*, resonates more with earlier novels that exhibit a trauma-focused sensibility than with the novels centered on narratives of recovery that I examine here.

I have thus elected to mark this shift at the turn of the twenty-first century because the tendency toward a self-conscious engagement with the process of narrative and recovery becomes more common than occasional in novels written after 2000. As Garratt notes in *Trauma and History in the Irish Novel*, many of the novels that appear between 1996 and 2009, after the central bounds of his survey, "strike off in different innovative directions" from earlier Irish trauma novels.[78] I suggest that it is this self-conscious engagement with form as well as with the process of recovery that differentiates these texts.

☼

This differentiation leaves the practical question: Why did this shift occur? In the broadest sense, the sociopolitical valences of Irish literature that I identify here are consistent with the practice of much Irish literature throughout the preceding centuries. In 1834, Maria Edgeworth famously noted the social impact of Irish literature when she observed, "It is impossible to draw Ireland as she now is in the book of fiction—realities are too strong, party passion too violent, to bear to see, or care to look, at their faces in a looking-glass. The people would only break the glass and curse the fool who held the mirror up to nature—distorted nature, in a fever."[79] Just as W. B. Yeats claimed the necessity to read Irish literature "if you would know Ireland—body and soul" because Irish literature is "Ireland talking to herself,"[80] the novelists I focus on in this study recognize the contextual forces at play on their work and the dialectic of influence between sociopolitical contexts and the literature that would mirror them. If twentieth-century trauma narratives began or at least reinforced needed conversations about the past, the novels discussed here invite critical dialogue about the future.

More importantly, historically speaking, there are good reasons why the turn of the millennium was ripe for such a movement from the literary representation of despair to the representation of hope, from the expression of loss to the portrayal of a realistic willingness to look to the future. First, this time period, from the late 1990s to the early 2000s, saw such catalytic moments as the advent of the Peace Process—a culmination of hundreds of years of conflict at last productively engaged. The Peace Process set off a dramatic reassessment not only of the political violence that had affected the Irish Republic, Northern Ireland, and England but also of its cost. As Dawson notes, this reassessment required "the attempt to resolve the underlying causes of division" and "to address the damaging effects of violence."[81] Given the social and theoretical trends I have reviewed here, the language of trauma and reconciliation would naturally infuse the popular imagination as well as the literary milieu.

The exposure of multiple political scandals and a frank confrontation of the history and legacy of sexual abuse in the Irish (and global) Catholic Church also were at play. For example, the year 1997 saw the establishment of the Tribunal of Inquiry into Payments to Politicians and Related Matters (also known as the Moriarty Tribunal) to inquire into the financial affairs of politicians Charles Haughey and Michael Lowry. The year 2000 saw the establishment of the Commission to Inquire into Child Abuse, which marked a major governmental move toward acknowledging systemic child abuse by the government and the church. The inquiry into sexual abuse by priests in Ferns, County Wexford, followed soon thereafter in 2003. In short, this revolutionary time period marked the confrontation of troubling histories and painful truths in Ireland at both the cultural and societal levels.[82] Such direct engagement reflects a society not only looking to explain its past but also proactively seeking closure and a better future. It is clear that all of the novels in this study see their representations of trauma as in conversation with the wider social discussions going on in Ireland at the time.

The influence of the Celtic Tiger economy—and of its demise, to which I referred earlier—is also critically relevant here. Susan Cahill notes, "Celtic Tiger Ireland [was] a historical moment that reveals complex attitudes towards relationships between past, present and future."[83] The Celtic Tiger period forced a reassessment and break from readings of the past, and it consequently catalyzed changes in literary representation. As Cahill argues, "I would mark the last decades of the twentieth century and the initial years of the twenty-first century as offering . . . writers a milieu different in kind from that which had preceded it. . . . This period of economic prosperity facilitated major developments in Ireland's social, cultural, and ideological landscapes."[84]

In the post–Celtic Tiger period, social shifts in perspective are equally relevant. Mary McGlynn has compellingly argued that post–Celtic Tiger fiction—in particular the work produced by women—challenges the ideologies of that prior period and in so doing suggests a shift away from extremes toward a more moderate and practical worldview. If the Celtic Tiger period was marked by "excesses" and the "monetization of the domestic," post–Celtic Tiger literature moves "towards the apolitical and the realist" and away from "magical thinking about unending economic expansion."[85] McGlynn's sense of a post-Tiger awareness of the troubles of the past, paired with a willingness to acknowledge the country's own culpability, echoes unmistakably in the narratives of trauma and recovery I trace here:

> Ireland cannot absolve itself from the materialism of the Boom, nor treat the dismal aftermath as disconnected from what came before. At the same time, the variety of yesterdays here contests neoliberal notions of teleology, a cautionary warning for a nation eager to move past its recent recession—if there is no difference among the different kinds of yesterday, then no narrative of progress can downplay or obscure those moments that challenge fantasies of an upward trajectory.[86]

Although such literature remains marked by the neoliberal ideology of the Tiger era, it also reflects a rejection of extremism (as in its resistance to "triumphalist Tiger-era narratives of teleology and progress"[87]).

As a result, the texts I explore balk at the linear notion of history. They instead acknowledge the cost of traumatic experience and the possibility for recovery through recursive narrative engagement. At the same time, while recognizing the lingering costs of trauma, they also reject any magical belief that recovery can offer either erasure of the past or complete healing from traumatic experience. This understanding of trauma cannot be extricated from the larger social context in which these novels were born. In this regard, then, these novels' investigation of recovery is potentially as much an ethical as a literary intervention. If Cahill is correct that "the recession itself [was] experienced as traumatic for the culture at large,"[88] then it is worth considering whether these novels also function as a potential response to prior traumatic representation—a response that takes post-Tiger reality under advisement.

Interestingly, McGlynn also recognizes that post-Tiger texts engage with their subject matter structurally as well as narratively: as she artfully states, in her reading she can "move beyond detailing thematic similarities or generic preoccupations and connect literary form to a changing social landscape, one indelibly imprinted by its neoliberal era."[89] Although McGlynn's focus is on neoliberalism and the lingering effects of the Celtic Tiger worldview, it does strike me as telling that a similar confluence of content and form arises in relation to the representation of trauma against this background of profound social and historical change. Clearly, twenty-first-century Irish fiction is self-conscious about the relationship between structure and content, seeking to enact narratively the subjects with which it is engaged.

The turn of the millennium was thus a time of reassessment; of intellectual, cultural, economic, and social disruption; and of a pronounced turn away from previous histories and understandings. The post–Celtic Tiger period itself built upon the earlier patterns we have seen in historiography and literature, catalyzing the kind of sober yet realistic and hopeful novels we see in this study. In this regard, Irish authors' movement from the presencing of trauma to the representation of recovery is consonant with that cultural shift.

☼

The novels included in this study thus share an underlying hopefulness, a focus on representing the possibility that the word is powerful enough to effect and forge a new reality. Each text not only offers a direct representation of trauma but also goes beyond this representation to emulate a way *through* trauma by engaging with it structurally. The authors self-consciously reflect on the power of narrativizing trauma—of representing it and acknowledging it—as curative in itself, and they model such engagement structurally. Thus, the novels I have included here embody a kind of awareness not necessarily seen in earlier, twentieth-century novels; not only do they represent trauma both thematically and structurally, but they also recognize that the act of *telling* itself is a potential redress to the very traumas they represent.

They thus self-consciously reflect on the process of narrative representation as a vehicle toward recovery.

The novels I consider here span the period from 2005 to 2014. Each text engages with representing trauma metanarratively and through that engagement explores the process of recovery. Perhaps tellingly, this awareness of narrative structure increases over time, which is perhaps symptomatic of the objectivity gained with time and distance. In addition, all of these texts consider the physical, material nature of suffering, the sociopolitical context of Irish society, and the opportunity for recovery and for hope in the face of a traumatic past.

In the first chapter, "'My Memory Gropes in Search of Details': 'Founding Traumas' and Narrative Recovery in John Banville's *The Sea*," I argue that although critical scrutiny has focused on the structure of Banville's Booker Prize–winning novel of 2005, the text also merits reassessment for its commentary on suffering and its self-conscious engagement with narrative remediation. I consider main character Max Morden's past and his symptoms through the lenses of secondary traumatic stress and traumatic memory. The novel presents a classic example of a person who has experienced significant trauma, but it also models the potential alleviation of symptoms through narrative reclamation. Banville thus remains consistent in his engagement with narrative structure but in this case harnesses that awareness to emulate the process of testimony through content and form.

The second chapter, "'A Whole Fucking Country—Drowning in Shame': Gender, Trauma, and Recovery in Anne Enright's *The Gathering*," moves to a far more direct use of narrative structure to explore traumatic representation. Criticism of this novel often concentrates on its representation of memory and trauma, particularly with respect to how they influence an individual, against the backdrop of Ireland's troubling histories of silence and sexual abuse. My reading complicates such analyses by considering the novel's specifically gendered intervention into this narrative of past, memory, and trauma both structurally and narratively.

Through the acerbic yet funny, motherly yet "child-battered" figure of Veronica Hegarty, *The Gathering* engages the complex questions not only of the role of family secrets and cultural silences in one's contemporary construction of—and engagement with—the past through memory but also of how those complicated dynamics are influenced and in part determined by the vehicle of gender. By presencing the physical, gendered body as grotesque rather than romanticized, the novel subversively recuperates the traumatized body. This recuperation effects a double reclamation of gender and traumatized subject at once. In giving a sometimes scathing and often defiant engagement with the past to a female narrator, *The Gathering* thus contemplates the role of the past in the present and enacts a gendered intervention into, and reclamation of, that narrative and imaginary space.

The third chapter, "'Surmises Held Up against the Truth': Traumatic Memory and Metanarratives of Recovery in Sebastian Barry's *The Secret Scripture*," examines the relationship between historical trauma and traumatic truth. Barry's novel, too, re-creates the process of testimony that it explores narratively. This chapter suggests not only that Roseanne Clear McNulty's omissions, contradictions, and uncertainties reflect the fragmented nature of traumatic memory but also that her reconstruction of the past serves as a counterpoint to dominant narratives' authority and as an assertion of the relevance and legitimacy of personal truth, even when that truth is factually contested. As importantly, I reassess the novel's controversial ending: I argue that rather than giving a reductive or idealized conclusion, the text performs a metanarrative intervention that recognizes the mechanisms of traumatic memory and the hopeful but conditional nature of recovery from trauma.

The fourth chapter focuses on Emma Donoghue's painful and beautiful novel *Room* (2010). A text that is both moving and experientially suffocating, *Room* creates a fantasy space through its young narrator's observations—a space outside the trauma from which his mother bravely and creatively protects him. This reading focuses not only on the imaginative recourse available to victims of trauma but also on the metaphorical valences of "room" as both emotional and psychological space and the ways in which the narratives one employs to survive trauma can and must be revised in recovery. The novel also questions the dominant social narratives it inherits in the post-Tiger era. I suggest that Jack and his mother's challenge is thus one of reconciling the competing narratives of traumatic memory and healing space and experience.

The fifth chapter, "'Nothing Is Entirely by Itself': Recovery, the Individual, and the Solace of Community in Colum McCann's *Let the Great World Spin*," considers Colum McCann's acclaimed novel from 2009. I suggest the novel privileges the abstract nature of human suffering and healing and narratively enacts the very "balancing act" it promotes. Its Yeatsian inversion in claiming "things don't fall apart"[90] reflects McCann's ultimate reassertion of hope in the midst of suffering and a dogged declaration of the cyclical nature of good and evil, hope and despair. I consider how McCann stresses the very bodily reality of John Corrigan, an Irish priest, against the more commonly noted metaphorical valences of the tightrope walker Philippe Petit. Although using the microcosm that is New York City and the symbolically freighted site of the Twin Towers as its setting, the novel employs a specifically Irish literary tendency to narrativize trauma, thus reflecting not only McCann's well-recognized leanings toward empathy but also the Irish tradition considered here. *Let the Great World Spin* offers the promise of recovery transcending the individual or the nation without dismissing the relevance of either.

The last chapter considers Colm Tóibín's latest novel set in Ireland, *Nora Webster* (2014). By narratively giving voice to Nora's point of view, Tóibín creates a remarkably sympathetic portrait of a mother figure—a figure who in his other Irish texts is painfully limited or emotionally stunted. It is the novel's dense intertextuality that interests me here, for the novel effects a kind of canonical revisitation of a trauma that runs throughout Tóibín's oeuvre. As a result, *Nora Webster* thus serves as a kind of answer to Tóibín's earlier Irish texts and responds to familiar thematic issues such as the loss of a parent and painful familial silences. It provides an important meditation on the centrality of perspective in narratives of recovery, even as it explores that notion of recovery from trauma intertextually across a canon.

Throughout the twentieth century, Irish novelists showed tremendous courage and moral responsibility in attempting to portray some of the darkest aspects of Irish society and their consequences for individuals and society alike. The novels in this study do something equally brave and perhaps even more risky by representing trauma as they do. By detailing such traumatic experiences even while reflecting on the act of narration itself, these authors dare to look beyond trauma into the uncertainty that is recovery. In so doing, they model an acknowledgment of accountability for the past and a simultaneously hopeful yet realistic turn toward the future. Such a representation can benefit not only individuals who have survived trauma but also the wider Irish society seeking a path to a more liberated, hopeful future.

1

"My Memory Gropes in Search of Details"

"Founding Traumas" and Narrative Recovery in John Banville's The Sea

In his well-known op-ed for the *New York Times* in 2009, "A Century of Looking the Other Way," John Banville reflected on the findings of the Irish Commission to Inquire into Child Abuse. Addressing the "terrible revelations" coming to light, he observed that he had "heard no one address the question of what it means, in this context, to *know*"—and he chillingly concluded, "We knew, and did not know. That is our shame today."[1]

This observation interestingly dovetails with another that Banville made in an interview that same year by Belinda McKeon for the *Paris Review*, where he unexpectedly invoked notions of trauma when asked about growing up in Wexford. At first wryly quoting that "children should be loaded with as much trauma as they can bear," he went on to state, "My traumas were Wexford, Ireland, the fifties, and especially the Catholic Church. The first thing the Catholic Church does to a child is instill guilt in his little soul. . . . *The Sea* is a direct return to my childhood, to when I was ten or so."[2] In both of these commentaries, Banville suggested an historical awareness of the cultural conditions that some have identified as traumatic in Irish history and society, and

An earlier version of this chapter was published as "'My Memory Gropes in Search of Details': Memory, Narrative, and 'Founding Traumas' in John Banville's *The Sea*," *Irish University Review* 46, no. 2 (Fall 2016): 340–58.

he implied in the interview that his Booker Prize–winning novel *The Sea* (2005) is in conversation with those issues.

The role of trauma has played a relatively minor role in critical approaches to this text: *The Sea*'s narrative style and technique have driven most readings.[3] Yet in an interview with Joe Jackson in 1994, John Banville stated that "at some level, . . . all my art is about grief and loss and . . . the awareness of death."[4] Little surprise, then, that *The Sea* traces protagonist Max Morden's attempt to come to terms with the loss of his wife to cancer. Although many of Banville's novels reflect an engagement with issues of loss, memory, and identity, *The Sea* arguably provides the most comprehensive portrait of traumatic loss in Banville's canon. The narrative foregrounds the unprocessed nature of Morden's mourning; his memories and struggles with the past present a classic example of someone who has experienced significant trauma. Morden's fragmented, unreliable memories, his dissociated affect, his self-destructive behavior, and his obsessive recourse to the past reflect typical manifestations of emotional and psychological distress and traumatic memory.

In this chapter, I argue that *The Sea* re-creates for the reader what Judith Lewis Herman terms trauma's "twin imperatives of truth-telling and secrecy" as well as the disruptions to but inescapability of memory that trauma effects.[5] However, the novel does not end on this issue of traumatic representation—a theme that can be identified in earlier Banville texts. Rather, by painstakingly tracing the experience of trauma and its remediation through narrative, *The Sea* replicates the frustrating and often painful process of identity reconstruction pursued by the traumatized. As a result, although the novel serves as another Banvillean exploration of narrative or modernity, I suggest it does more than this.[6] *The Sea* also reflects on identity, loss, and, just as importantly, on the possibility of healing from a traumatic past through the vehicle of narrative engagement. In this respect, Banville harnesses his canonical sensitivity to form in order to engage metacritically with the nature of recovery from trauma in a manner that is unlike his prior novels.

The Sea follows the physical and psychological journeys of Max Morden.[7] A recent widower and art historian, Morden travels to the Cedars, an erstwhile summer rental home cum boardinghouse on the southern coast of Ireland. Morden's return to the town of Ballyless is shadowed by an earlier history of interactions there with the Grace family, who were of higher social status and who occupied Max's summer in his tenth or eleventh year. As Max's narrative alternates between memories of his life with his wife, Anna, and recollections of that fateful summer, we learn that the Grace children, twins Chloe and Myles, drowned in the sea in front of Max. Anna's recent death has thus triggered his return to the space and place of an earlier, formative trauma.[8]

Most frequently in reading this text, critics situate the novel within the author's oeuvre as a whole and thus debate whether it reflects his voice, authorial or otherwise.[9] Those who do engage the novel in terms of plot tend to identify a scarcity of actual content, with one reader even referring to it as "relatively plotless."[10] As Rüdiger Imhof has observed, "Hardly any reviewer has refrained from commenting on Banville's supreme prose-style [*sic*]."[11] The focus on Banville's style in *The Sea* seems to pose a distraction, sidetracking readers from considering how Morden's language reflects his character rather than reflecting Banville himself or his stylistic tendencies.[12]

Morden is certainly consistent with the author's wider oeuvre. He is overly concerned with language, and, like other Banville narrators, he provokes an analysis of the act of writing itself.[13] Morden is pedantic, engaging in wordplay with names such as the oncologist's, "Mr. Todd"—a slant reference to the German word *Tod*, "death"—and speaking in an unnaturally florid style: "The repetition there . . . is an uncharacteristic infelicity in Dr Thomson's usually euphonious if somewhat antiquated prose style."[14] Morden also focuses obsessively on his word choice: "This one took place—no, was exchanged—no, was consummated, that is the word" (106). Moreover, his narrative is overloaded with intertextual references, which suggests a certain degree of pedantic self-consciousness on the part of the speaker: "Once again in

Banville," states Imhof, "here is a narrative voice that intertextualizes, turning the account into an echo-chamber of literary quotations and allusions."[15]

Such literary self-consciousness is characteristic of Banville. In his novel *Shroud* (2002), for example, Axel Vander reflects a similar interest in language. His reflections on identity become pointedly orthographic as he considers the meaning of *I* as symbol and letter: "On the one side there was the *I* I had been before the letter arrived, and now there was this new *I*, a singular capital standing at a tilt to all the known things that had suddenly become unfamiliar."[16] Similarly, in Banville's earlier effort *The Untouchable* (1997) Victor Maskell demonstrates a comparable pedantic interest, noting "one has to be scrupulous with tenses" and self-consciously reflecting on the relationship between language and identity: "The personal pronoun is everywhere, of course, propping up the edifice I am erecting, but what is there to be seen behind this slender capital?"[17] As Monica Facchinello argues, "To the reader of Banville's earlier work, the writing of the novel's narrator Max Morden will . . . sound uncannily familiar."[18]

Morden's artistic references similarly invite intertextual associations that draw readers' attention to form. An art critic, Morden remembers his daughter, Claire, as "remarkably like" a "ghostly figure" in a painting by Bonnard (103).[19] This focus on the visual, too, redirects attention to Banville's metanarrative tendencies and to style over content.[20] That this focus on art is a familiar element in Banville's canon reinforces that perception: Victor Maskell is an "art critic," and Axel Vander is a celebrated literary scholar.[21]

Last, Morden is generally rather unsympathetic, which is in keeping with Banville's tendency to treat his characters critically for intellectual posturing.[22] This tendency again pushes readers to focus on *The Sea*'s structural similarities to other novels rather than on Morden as a character in his own right. Morden admits that he was never particularly able to relate to or know his wife, noting, "How little I knew her, I mean how shallowly I knew her, how ineptly" (159). He is coldly analytical of Claire, describing her as "not beautiful, . . . too tall . . . [with] rusty hair [that] is coarse and untameable and stands out . . . in an unbecoming manner" (32). He resents that she left her studies in art history to teach underprivileged children, averring, "I could not forgive her, cannot still" (46), and he accuses her of abandoning her dying mother, noting that "she had been conveniently abroad . . . while I was left to cope as best I could" (49). Finally, his resistance to her potential suitor has caused Claire emotional distress, leading her to accuse him of having "*driven Jerome away*" (49, emphasis in original).

Morden not only is aloof with his family but also displays misanthropic tendencies throughout, such as when he observes, "One is inclined to imagine that people who are fat must also be stupid" (153). He is an unapologetic alcoholic, and he is prone to violence and cruelty when intoxicated. Like Gabriel Godkin in *Birchwood* (1973), who flatly asserts that "people are easy to replace" and that love is "wasted,"[23] and Axel Vander, who describes life with his wife, Magda, as "the state of mutual incomprehension,"[24] Morden appears to be another "self-conscious intellectual" man in Banville's canon who "suffer[s] an extreme version of . . . excessive self-awareness" and endures "a sense of doubtful self-identity, suspect authenticity, and an agonized yearning for a sublimely idealized, preconscious, and therefore innocent, self."[25] Through his pedantry, his focus on language, and his generally unsympathetic nature and representation, Morden fits a broader pattern across Banville's works.

Despite these familiar character traits, however, attentive readers will find a distinctive and more sympathetic depiction of Morden evolve over the course of the novel. As Patricia Coughlan wisely reminds us, "However aware we are of Banville's multiple allusions to other texts and histories, ultimately his fictions cannot but posit their own sufficiency as free-standing objects, which do project worlds with complete moral systems."[26]

His references to art and literature reflect his insecurity as a writer and art historian. Assessing his own writing, for example, Morden notes that at times he is "immersed in words, paltry as they may be, for even the second-rater is sometimes inspired" (72). He states that he is a "person of scant talent and scanter ambition" (148) and claims that his daughter "will do what [he] could not, and be a great scholar" (130).[27]

Morden acknowledges that his book is "a modest project in which [he has] been mired for . . . years" (30), and he admits that he "had not the heart to tell [Claire] that [his] Big Book on Bonnard . . . has got no farther than half of a putative first chapter and a notebook filled with derivative and half-baked would-be aperçus" (191–92). Whereas characters such as Maskell and Vander successfully built careers despite their senses of inauthenticity, Morden is, in fact, a failure; he hides behind his academic facade, using bravado to obscure a vulnerable internal state.[28] His florid language thus goes beyond mere academic insecurity. His arrogant posture, unsympathetic nature, and linguistic play reflect emotional and psychological limitations as well as an effort to create a functional self from an otherwise fragmented identity.

☼

Morden's sense of alienation and attempts to reconstruct his past hail from a series of unprocessed traumatic events. In *Writing History, Writing Trauma*, Dominick LaCapra notes that experiences "may . . . give rise to what may be termed *founding traumas* . . . that paradoxically become the valorized or intensely cathected basis of identity."[29] Two major events in Morden's past—the nature and collapse of his parents' dysfunctional marriage and the deaths of twins Myles and Chloe—predispose him to an aggressively traumatized reaction to Anna's death.

Morden's treatment and abandonment by his father when he was a child are habitually underemphasized in readings of *The Sea*, but it is evident that his family dynamic had considerable impact. Morden notes that his parents' marriage was unhappy and that he was subjected nightly to the sounds of their verbal battles: "I lay in my narrow metal bed . . . hearing . . . my mother and father in the front room fighting, . . . going at each other in a grinding undertone, *every night, every night*, until at last one night my father left us, never to return" (53–54, my emphasis). The stress placed on "every night" through repetition emphasizes the painful impact of his parents' troubles, even though the adult narrator offers no emotional response—a repressive gesture consistent with unprocessed trauma.

Morden's relationships with his parents individually are also problematic. Morden calls his father "a violent man, a man of violent gestures, violent jokes," and he remembers when he "twisted out of his [father's] grasp in a panic" after what he recalls as aggressive, almost sadistic play (27). He implies that he took the brunt of his mother's bitterness after his father's abandonment: "And she gave me a level look, harsh and unblinking, the same look she would often turn on me after my father had gone, as if to say, *I suppose you will be the next to betray me*" (79, emphasis in original).[30] As an adult, Max accepts responsibility for his mother's unspoken accusation, ceding, "I suppose I was" (79), and as a boy he imagined himself into other realities, later admitting he was "ashamed of [his] origins" (153) and had wished he could "[cancel his] shaming parents on the spot" (28). Morden's simultaneous attempts to deflect blame from his parents and to distance himself from them emotionally reflect the stress of his familial situation.[31]

Morden's fascination with the Graces as alternatives to his nuclear family also suggests his escapist desires: "I had managed to scramble from the base of those steep social steps all the way up to the level of the Graces. . . . The gods had singled me out for their favour" (80). References to the Graces as "Gods" recur throughout the novel (e.g., 3, 45, 79, 87, 91).[32] Such escapist gestures can signal an attempt to alleviate the stress of a traumatic situation by dissociating from it: according to Herman, "perceptual changes combine with a feeling of indifference, emotional detachment, and profound passivity."[33] Morden's alienation from his parents as well as his willingness to accept responsibility and his escapist tendencies reflect the stressful, unhappy climate of his childhood and its damaging consequences.

Morden's sympathy for his mother also reflects his identification with her; his loss of Anna evokes memories of his father's betrayal. "Oh, Ma, how little I understood you, thinking how little you understood" (66). Not unlike his mother, to whom he listened "in helpless anger" and whom he would "hear as she wept, a knuckle pressed against her mouth" (146–47), Morden suffers from what he perceives as Anna's betrayal in "leaving him" and explodes with obscene suppressed rage at the thought of her: "You cunt, you fucking cunt, how could you go and leave me like this, floundering in my own foulness, with no one to save me from myself. *How could you*" (145, emphasis in original). Morden's rage echoes his mother's depressive behavior and suggests his own, earlier sense of abandonment.

Although Morden's renaming of himself is usually read as a metanarrative act of self-creation,[34] his gesture is, in this light, clearly escapist, reflecting a desire to flee from anything associated with his past. Max seeks to forge a new identity: when his mother protests that his "name is not Max," Max simply replies, "It is now" (156). His renaming signals the pain he associates with his family life and his desire to escape from it.

Needless to say, in practice the past proves harder to elude. The deaths of Chloe and Myles likely constitute the most foundational trauma of Morden's past, to which he is cast back associatively by his wife's death.[35] Already vulnerable owing to his conflicted family life, Morden was shocked by the suddenness of the twins' death: "What did I feel? Most strongly, I think, a sense of awe, awe of myself, that is, who had known two living creatures that now were suddenly, astoundingly, dead" (182). His description of himself immediately after their deaths as being "a thing of air, a drifting spirit," speaks to his sense of disconnect in the wake of that immediate, reality-altering horror (182).[36] This sense of alienation and unreality is typical of those experiencing trauma: "This altered state of consciousness might be regarded as one of nature's small mercies, a protection against unbearable pain."[37] In this regard, one might consider the aptness of protagonist Veronica Hegarty's statement in Anne Enright's *The Gathering*, when she notes of historical trauma and suffering, "We default to the oldest scar."[38] Morden notes the irresistible drive to return to a space so laden with trauma after the death of his wife: "[I] felt that I had been traveling for a long time, for years, and had at last arrived at the *destination to where, all along, without knowing it, I had been bound*, and where I must stay, it being, for now, the only possible place, the only possible refuge, for me" (117, my emphasis). His sense of the inescapability of the Cedars is directly associative: it reflects the seductive pull of his unprocessed trauma, which he confounds with the present and which complicates his ability to deal with Anna's death. Morden's sense of the Cedars' place in his life reinforces Cathy Caruth's argument that the "impact of [a] traumatic event lies precisely in its belatedness, in its refusal to be simply located, in its insistent appearance outside the boundaries of any single place or time."[39] Morden's reflexive return to the past signals the continuing influence and lingering effects of the twins' deaths.

Although critics often analyze the collapsing of Morden's life with Anna and his childhood experiences with the Graces through the lens of memory, the more specific context required here is that of traumatic memory. Hedda Friberg-Harnesk has argued that the novel reflects "a quest for selfhood and self-knowledge . . . linked to a sharp awareness of memory"[40] as well as concern with the "inescapable dependence of the present on the past" and the "distorting processes of memory."[41] The latter reading focuses on the fallibility of memory and how the present inflects, and perhaps distorts, our understanding of the past.[42]

It is true that Morden feels he cannot trust his recollections, so he consistently questions them: he notes that a sign featured "a lifebuoy, or a ring of rope—was it?—" (10), and he often questions what memory brings to mind: "Where was Chloe? Where was Myles? Why was I left alone with their mother?" (63). Max's recollection of Mrs. Grace is riddled with such doubts and hesitations, ending on the meaningless admission that a dog seems to have strayed in—and out—of his memory (64–68).[43]

Some of this uncertainty reflects the nature of memory itself, but Morden's inability to remember details is characteristic of traumatic memory. As Dori Laub notes, "The horror of the historical experience is maintained . . . only as an elusive memory that feels as if it no longer resembles any reality."[44] Indeed, the very gaps Morden observes are symptomatic of traumatic memory: "The historical power of the trauma is not just that the experience is repeated after its forgetting," states Caruth, "but that it is only in and through its inherent forgetting that it is first experienced at all."[45] Although all memory is subject to unreliability, such radical indeterminacy is inherent to traumatic memory.

The memories that Morden *does* recall are also prototypically traumatic. Traumatic memories are in their very nature imagistic: "Traumatic memories lack verbal narrative and context; rather, they are encoded in the form of vivid sensations and images," Herman explains.[46] Bessel A. van der Kolk and Onno van der Hart likewise characterize traumatic memory as "unassimilated scraps."[47] These descriptions evoke the frozen nature of such memories, which can remain "unmodified . . . ten, twenty, or thirty years" after the experience.[48] The largely imagistic memories Morden has of the Grace family, which he describes repeatedly as "tableaux," reflect the memory fracturing typical of traumatic experience (92).

Morden's reduction of Chloe to parts literalizes the process of fragmentation effected by traumatic memory:

> Her hands. Her eyes. Her bitten fingernails. All this I remember, intensely remember, yet it is all disparate, I cannot assemble it into a unity. Try as I may . . . I am unable to conjure her as I can her mother, say, or Myles. . . . I cannot, in short, see her. She wavers before my memory's eye at a fixed distance, always just beyond focus, moving backward at exactly the same rate as I am moving forward. (104)

This passage perfectly exhibits the force of trauma on Morden's memories in that he can envision Mrs. Grace but not Chloe. Although some images can be sharp and haunting, the images associated with a traumatic event often remain an incoherent jumble that is difficult to reassemble.[49] Beyond the usual unreliability and subjectivity of memory, Morden's recollections clearly carry the hallmarks of traumatic memory in their uncertainty and fragmentation.[50]

The inability to differentiate present from past is also typical of traumatic memory. Morden repeatedly conflates past and present: he recognizes his difficulty in keeping memories separate, noting, "everything for me is something else" (103). In addition, even as he compulsively returns to the past, it blurs and blends with the recent past or present. Morden cites the power of the past in the present and its destructive capacity: "There are moments when the past has a force so strong it seems one might be annihilated by it" (35).[51] Obviously, the sense that the past can "annihilate" one is a reference to the painful realities the past embodies.

Morden also collapses memories of Anna and Chloe. In thinking of Chloe, for example, Morden wonders, "How could she be with me one moment and the next not? How could she be elsewhere, absolutely?"—only to have that memory shift to something Anna said in her illness (104–5).[52] This recollection also parallels the language Morden uses in remembering his response to Chloe's and Myles's deaths, mentioned earlier. Such moments not only reflect the association he makes between two traumatic losses he has suffered but also suggest the collapsing of past and present typical of traumatic memory. As LaCapra has stated, in trauma "one is haunted or possessed by the past and performatively caught up in the compulsive repetition of traumatic scenes—scenes in which the past returns and the future is blocked or fatalistically caught up in a melancholic feedback loop." The memory work of healing trauma, then, involves learning to distinguish between past and present and to recognize something as "having happened to one . . . back then."[53]

Obviously, the most recent loss Morden suffers—that of Anna to cancer—heightens his distressed condition. He despaired upon her diagnosis, noting later that they endured "a new version of reality" and "a panic-stricken sense of not knowing what to say, where to look, [or] how to behave" (15, 17). He now recognizes the alienation this caused: "From this day forward all would be dissembling. There would be no other way to live with death" (17). Morden associates this alienation with a loss of verbal ability: "The notion seized me that I would never again be able to think of another word to say to her, that we would go on like this, in agonised inarticulacy, to the end" (16). His sense of isolation reflects the way in which "traumatized people feel utterly abandoned, utterly alone,"[54] and replicates his previous abandonments, both by his father and, in practical terms, by his first romantic attachment, Chloe.

I return to the issue of Morden's "inarticulacy" later, but I would note here that his alienation also signals the emotional distance in his marriage. He admits that "there were strains, there were stresses . . . the shouts, the screams, the flung plates, the odd slap," and he ruefully concedes, "Yet for all that, I cannot rid myself of the conviction that we missed something, that I missed something, only I do not know what it might have been" (161). Danielle C. Brousseau, Marvin J. McDonald, and Joanne E. Stephen note that partners of cancer patients are vulnerable to "secondary traumatic stress," which is defined as "emotions resulting from knowledge about a stressful event experienced by a significant other."[55] In their findings, the authors observe that "couples' higher relationship ratings [i.e., how close the couple is] may be indicative of less overt conflict and lower relational distress."[56] The emotional distance in Morden's marriage exacerbates his reaction to Anna's death and heightens his traumatic stress as a result.

Equally telling is Morden's sense of removal from Anna's suffering. Confronted with sympathetic funeral goers, Morden feels undeserving of sympathy: "I felt I should stop and hold up a hand and tell these people that really, I did not deserve their reverence, . . . that I had been merely a bystander, a bit-player, while Anna did the dying" (151). However, studies show that witnesses to traumatic events can experience trauma: "traumatic events . . . [can include] a close personal encounter with violence and death."[57] Morden's inability to recognize his own suffering is symptomatic of his emotional distancing from it—perhaps even of his dissociation—and speaks to his traumatized response.

Morden's response to Anna's death, his distance from Claire, and his self-isolating return to the Cedars all reinforce a long-standing tendency to retreat from intimate relationships. Herman observes that trauma victims often limit their emotional accessibility in a self-protective gesture: "The attempt to avoid reliving the trauma too often results in . . . a withdrawal from engagement with others, and an impoverished life."[58] Morden clearly leads an alienated life. He claims, "I know nothing, nothing" (158), and admits that he has "never had a personality, not in the way that others have" (160).

Morden's sense of alienation from Anna thus may be not simply the natural sense of confusion, despair, and unreality experienced by those confronting cancer: when taken in tandem with his rejection of Claire, his general misanthropy, and the associations he makes between Anna and Chloe, Anna's death evidently disrupts Morden's carefully constructed distance from Chloe's death, allowing the founding trauma of her loss to collapse into the hurt he suffers over Anna.[59] Morden does not, then, return to the Cedars only to cope with Anna's death: his return to the Cedars is also a return to the site of his founding trauma, reflecting an attempt to negotiate both.

Morden's alcoholism also marks his attempt to cope with trauma. John Kenny notes that many of Banville's characters are like Morden, "troubled soul[s], with a painful past . . . [they] assuage[] . . . through alcohol."[60] Although Morden initially only alludes to his drinking by referencing his "hip-flask" and Claire's insistence on driving (44, 49), it becomes clear that he is drinking excessively: he states that he is "in need of consolation and the brief respite of drink-induced oblivion" (148–49). Not surprisingly, "traumatized people . . . may attempt to produce . . . numbing effects by using alcohol."[61] Anna's death leads him to self-medicate in an effort to alleviate his suffering.

Even Morden's commitment to mourning is a marker of a traumatic experience: "One's bond with the dead . . . may invest trauma with value and make its reliving a painful but necessary commemoration."[62] This description resonates with Morden's desire to hold on to Anna even if only as a shadow: "Send back your ghost. Torment me, if you like. Rattle your chains, drag your cerements across the floor, keen like a banshee, anything. I would have a ghost" (183). Through his return to the Cedars, Morden similarly invites the past back into conscious memory, compulsively returning to the scene of his suffering. Ultimately, the fundamental unreliability of Morden's recollections; the fragmented nature of his memories; his dissociation, alienation, and alcoholism; and his tendency to collapse past and present all reflect not only the very recent trauma of Anna's illness and death but also his life-long struggle to deal with the unprocessed trauma of Chloe's death and, perhaps, with his parents' neglect and abandonment.

If "all [Banville's] art is about grief and loss," then it is worth considering how Morden compares to other Banville narrators who bear the scars of a painful past. In the early novel *Birchwood*, Gabriel

Godkin's home life is riddled with cruelty and madness, so much so that he runs away to join the circus; he, too, returns to his originary space, where he survived a childhood characterized by parental neglect and cruelty. This early novel also offers a meditation on the unreliability of memory, with Godkin observing, "We imagine that we remember things as they were, while in fact all we carry into the future are fragments which reconstruct a wholly illusory past."[63]

Yet Godkin does not display the same fragmented memory or paralysis as Morden; Godkin systematically traces his history and escapes his family home. One might argue that the original loss of his twin or even the Famine itself as a form of cultural trauma catalyzes a kind of return, but, as Kenny notes, the novel follows the form of a bildungsroman, and as such it speaks more to growth than to traumatic entrapment in the past.[64] Rather, Godkin acknowledges the losses of his past, stating, "I began to write, as a means of finding them [people from his past] again. . . . I was wrong. There is no form, no order, only echoes."[65] *Birchwood* suggests independence from one's past: "Godkin's position at the end of *Birchwood* is tantamount to [an] . . . assertion of creative freedom from history," Kenny argues.[66] And writing in this case offers no relief.

Banville's narrator in *The Untouchable* also shares some characteristics I have identified as symptomatic of trauma in *The Sea*. Victor Maskell, too, finds himself wandering the past in memory: "What am I doing here, straying amongst these importunate wraiths?" He, too, is emotionally disconnected from his children, saying of his daughter, Blanche, "She will never marry, now; I can see her at sixty, all brawn. . . . My poor girl." He, too, drinks—"Time for a gin, I think"—and wrestles with the nature of his own identity.[67] Maskell's interest in the past, emotional distance from his family, and tendency to drink parallel—or perhaps even foreshadow—Morden's character.

But here, too, there are significant differences. As noted earlier, Maskell has had a successful career: as director, he shapes an institute into "*the* greatest centre of art teaching in the West."[68] Similarly, although Maskell suffers from self-doubt, no single catalyzing traumatic event has precipitated his behaviors; rather, he embodies the political cynicism—and idealism—of his age.[69] He, too, rejects his family, but this rejection is grounded more in an attempt to construct a self than in a desire to break from a painful home life. And although Maskell's narrative is also an attempt at reconstruction, the focus is on identifying the act of betrayal that caused his downfall. Thus, whereas Morden's life is stultified and reflects a fear of "agonised inarticulacy," Maskell's is one of duplicity, so rather than seeking a true self, he constantly performs false ones: "Have I any authenticity at all? Or have I double dealt for so long that my true self has been forfeit?"[70] Readings of *The Untouchable* in terms of memory, identity, and authenticity are thus appropriate, but Maskell does not form the kind of totalizing picture of trauma we see in Max Morden.

Perhaps the character most similar to Morden is Axel Vander in Banville's immediately prior novel, *Shroud.* Like Morden, Vander has experienced profound trauma, his entire family having been killed in the Holocaust.[71] Antisocial and hostile, he, too, is a rampant alcoholic, in fact giving himself alcohol poisoning halfway through the novel.[72] Vander, too, claims that he is, "like everyone . . . thrown together from a legion of selves," suggesting that his sense of identity is artificial. He, too, has visions of his dead wife, wondering, "Why could she not leave me alone?" and he, too, seems unsure whether he is capable of "real" love, noting, "I must have loved [her] or else I would have left."[73] Finally, the possibility of exposure terrifies him because it shatters the protective identity that he has constructed painstakingly over a lifetime. It would be plausible to argue that Vander is a victim of trauma, as his alcoholism, alienation from self and others, and repression attest.

Yet even with all these similarities, there are again meaningful differences. Vander is less concerned with the uncertainty of memory than with evading the past: like Maskell, he focuses on intentional lies more than on repressive constructions. Whereas Morden compulsively seeks out his past, even describing his return to the Cedars as "the only possible place, the only possible refuge, for me" (117), Vander is forced to confront his history and his past life.

At the same time, Vander's relationship with Cass Cleave is clearly recuperative; he notes of his relationship with her, "For once . . . it was others I was thinking of. . . . Out of the . . . blastula I had set swelling in her belly there had already sprung the new beginnings of my people, my lost people. . . . My gentle mother, my melancholy father, my siblings put to summary death before they had lived, all would find their tiny share in this new life."[74] Here, Vander acknowledges the central trauma of his life and displays the ability to love and to hope. He also achieves peace with Cass, for he realizes that his wife, Magda, knew and kept his secret.[75] Thus, as much as Vander, too, bears the marks of traumatic history, he displays a degree of self-awareness and an ability to self-actualize that Morden has not achieved. Morden's attempt to overcome his past occurs not through interpersonal relationships but through recursively reviewing and ultimately expressing his suffering.

Most importantly, *Shroud* is profoundly engaged with questions of (self-)representation. As Kenny notes, "Banville's men . . . feel that they are potentially fakes, fraudulent in motivation as well as in being";[76] this assessment holds not only for *Shroud* but also for its effective sister novel *Eclipse* (2000). In contrast, *The Sea* concentrates on one character's historical *inability* to access self-representation successfully to this point: his identity is always already dwarfed by traumatic experience. This explains why *The Sea* seems arguably "plotless": it looks centrally at Morden's act of reconstructing, of telling, and of coming to know. Thus, as Kenny argues, in *The Sea* Banville "focuses . . . more clearly on what is deep down within the self and on what comes from these depths to the surface." Because Morden is "more *human*,"[77] the narrative concentrates primarily on the internal process he undertakes rather than on secrets kept, as in *Shroud*, or on mysteries solved, as in *The Untouchable*. As a result, Morden represents not the only but certainly the most complete portrait of a traumatized individual in Banville's canon. *The Sea* thus considers how one so positioned can best negotiate this state.

☼

It is precisely because *The Sea* focuses on what one "comes to know" that it does not end on trauma. Morden's attempts to construct a linear narrative as well as his self-conscious gestures of construction and authorship mark a "style and narrative technique . . . [that] . . . centres upon a process of self-reconstruction."[78] Morden, like many trauma victims, seeks to gain control over the fragmented narrative of his life; his self-conscious act of rewriting and his relentless return to the past model traumatized individuals' attempts to verbalize and thus to integrate their experiences.

Morden's unreliable narration reinforces the nature of traumatic memory precisely because it is fragmented and inherently unreliable.[79] People who have experienced trauma "often tell their stories in a highly emotional, contradictory, and fragmented manner which *undermines their credibility* and thereby serves the twin imperatives of truth-telling and secrecy."[80] Morden's unreliability mimics the process that victims undertake in trying to confront their traumatic pasts by engaging uncertain traumatic memory, surrendering the avoidant behavior that historically protected them, and embracing the desire to speak a truth that is often impossible to capture in its entirety. Trauma victims must eventually confront the need to subordinate a painful past to words: "There is, in each survivor, an imperative need to *tell* and thus to come to *know* one's story, unimpeded by ghosts from the past against which one has to protect oneself. One has to know one's buried truth in order to be able to live one's life."[81] As a character who repeatedly cites his own deadened state, claiming he was "tested for vital signs; for signs of feeling; for signs of life" (31; see also 3, 47), Morden clearly requires such an intervention.

His act of writing can therefore be understood as a self-conscious effort to engage a traumatic personal narrative. His obsessive revisitation of the past reflects an effort to control it, and in its inconsistency and unreliability his narrative mirrors those of the traumatized:

> [Testimony] may involve distortion, disguise, and other permutations relating to processes of imaginative transformation and narrative shaping, as well as perhaps repression, denial, dissociation, and foreclosure. But these issues have a bearing only on certain aspects of [an] account and could not invalidate it in its entirety. . . . [The victim] is not simply reliving or compulsively acting out the past but to some extent *working it over and possibly working it through*.[82]

Morden attempts to gain mastery over the past through a self-conscious process of narration. In referring to "the town," for example, he states, "I shall call [the town] Ballymore. . . . The town is Ballymore, this village is Ballyless, ridiculously, perhaps, but I do not care" (7). Morden acknowledges the unreliability of memory and the simultaneous need to *author* it through the self-conscious construction of his narrative.

Perhaps most telling is Morden's recognition of the centrality of narration to his very being, as reflected in his fear, upon Anna's illness, of "agonised inarticulacy." As he grasps for words to represent and express his suffering, he recognizes that such accuracy will capture his very essence: "What I am looking forward to is a moment of earthly expression. . . . I shall be expressed, totally. . . . I shall be, in a word, *said*" (137, emphasis in original). This interdependence of the ability to communicate and the ability *to be* as well as his inability to avoid the effort—"I cannot stop" (149)—reflect a common need of the traumatized: "The testimony is . . . the process by which the narrator (the survivor) reclaims his position as a witness: [he] reconstitutes the internal "thou."[83] Morden's attempt to narrate his past is also an attempt to control it.

At the same time, this stress also reflects his sense of the crucial place self-expression plays in his very essence. His emphasis on himself as a potential *be-ing* contrasts tellingly with his prior self-perception as "a thing of air," without materiality or substance. This linking of self-expression to material subjectivity gestures toward the physical nature of trauma and recovery; it is also an increasing focus in twenty-first-century novels of recovery, as we shall see throughout this study.

Only with his belated verbalizing of the twins' death does Morden seem poised to gain balance and perspective. His narration segues meaningfully from his review of Anna's final hour—a section introduced, tellingly, with the phrase "last words" (175)—to a long, linear narration of the twins' death, where he finally acknowledges the long-term consequences of that experience: "Often in my dreams I am back there again, wading through that sand that grows ever more resistant. . . . What did I feel? . . . But did I believe they were dead?"

(182). Morden's self-questioning, like his attempt to make sense of his experience now, marks a shift in his relation to this trauma precipitated by linear narration.

Morden continues to suffer, to drown his sorrows, and to employ some of the self-destructive tendencies that have buoyed him. However, his acknowledgment that the current landlady of the Cedars, Miss Vavasour, is also the twins' former governess, Rose, suggests a dawning willingness to engage the past on the terrain of the present rather than on the shifting and traumatic sands of the past. His recognition in the novel uncannily echoes the observation Banville would make four years after *The Sea* was published, when he speculated on the child abuse scandals wracking Ireland: "Human beings . . . have a remarkable ability to entertain simultaneously any number of contradictory propositions. Perfectly decent people can know a thing and at the same time not know it."[84]

Morden's acknowledgment brings his experiences into full consciousness, yet his act of narrative representation offers not magical remediation but a more manageable relationship to loss and psychological harm. As discussed in chapter 4, Emma Donoghue's novel *Room* makes a similar move, suggesting that people can know and not know at the same time and stressing the critically important role of the stories survivors tell. As I argued in the introduction, this sense of recovery as conditional or incomplete is consistent with the general climate of post–Celtic Tiger Ireland, when the excesses of Celtic Tiger bravado were abandoned in favor of more realistic expectations.[85] Morden's process of relaying and narrativizing his past becomes the vehicle for his negotiation of that past; it is not a magical remedy for the trauma induced by a painful or traumatic past.

The Sea thus portrays for the reader Banville's most comprehensive representation of the psychological consequences of traumatic experience to date: the fracturing of identity, the effect on memory, the self-destructive behaviors, and the temporal distortions. Although each discrete trauma in the novel has its own consequences—self-blame and alienation from his family, the fragmented memory from Chloe's loss, dissociation and constriction from the secondary trauma of Anna's illness and death—all traumas are combined through the workings of traumatic memory as Morden navigates his recent loss and painful past together. The novel's focus on this struggle privileges Morden's emotional and psychological journey above all else, reinforcing the parallels between his multiple losses and illustrating the collapsing effect of both traumatic memory and founding traumas. In doing so, the novel offers the most comprehensive portrait of negotiating such emotion and loss of any Banville text to date.

The self-consciousness of the novel's narration is consistent with Banville's wider canon, as is the intertextual and linguistic play so typical of the author's oeuvre. Yet in this instance Banville harnesses his self-conscious narration to re-create narratively the process of self-discovery and reconstruction that is critical to recovery from trauma—a scrutiny that has been both evident and evolving in his canon, as we have seen. Given Banville's somewhat playful retrospective reference in the *Paris Review* interview in 2009 to *The Sea* as embedded in his own early "traumas," one cannot help but wonder how much contemporary social issues in the Ireland of 2005 informed his thinking at the time he wrote this novel.

Fittingly, the understanding of the relation of traumatic past to narrativized present complements Morden's final description of the sea: "The whole sea surged, it was not a wave, but a smooth rolling swell that seemed to come up from the deeps, as if something vast down there had stirred itself, and I was lifted briefly and carried a little way toward the shore and then was set down on my feet as before, as if nothing had happened" (195). Just like the ocean, trauma can swell up when engaged, threatening to engulf one. *The Sea* captures the possibility of riding out such disorienting and overwhelming waves of memory and emotion through testimony, as Morden learns. The next chapter, on *The Gathering*, reflects on how that ability to engage can be the difference between drowning, like Liam Hegarty, and keeping one's head above water, like Veronica Hegarty.

2

"A Whole Fucking Country—Drowning in Shame"

Gender, Trauma, and Recovery in Anne Enright's The Gathering

Unlike in the case of *The Sea*, studies of Anne Enright's Booker Prize–winning novel *The Gathering* (2007) often focus on the text's narrative representation of trauma and traumatic memory. Analyses of the tortured and fragmented narrative of protagonist Veronica Hegarty recognize how this story of personal suffering and abuse mirrors the troubling backdrop of Ireland's cultural tendencies toward silence and the Catholic Church's Irish sex abuse scandal. Focused on its caustic yet sympathetic and struggling narrator Veronica Hegarty, the novel provokes concomitant questions about the role of gender in the text. *The Gathering* challenges the conscriptive role to which women were relegated, whether by the church or by the state, in Irish history: Veronica's self-protective act of traumatized forgetting can thus be read allegorically as signaling the consequences of national neglect and abandonment for Irish society's most vulnerable.

Although critics recognize Enright's self-conscious engagement with form in the text, what is often understated in readings of *The Gathering* is the mechanism by which the novel intervenes in the narrative of trauma and gender through its use of *bodily language* and the harnessing of the *domestic space*. Veronica traces the historical suffering of her family through a specifically matrilineal line, narrated and reimagined through aggressive bodily imagery and pointedly located in domestic spaces and spheres. Enright's novel thus effects a kind of gendered intervention into the experience of trauma. Employing the narrative and imaginary spaces of motherhood and the domestic, *The Gathering* appropriates and undermines gendered norms, even as its problematic response to the female body reflects Veronica's traumatized worldview. By so doing, the novel traces Veronica's processing of trauma through narrative even as it converts both the domestic and the gendered body from sites of oppression and containment to vehicles of potential liberation and reclamation. Veronica's self-conscious narration highlights the act of telling while representing the ways in which narrativizing trauma can be both empowering and subversive at once.

The Gathering follows the thoughts and actions of narrator Veronica Hegarty, whose closest sibling, Liam, has recently committed suicide in England. As she struggles with rage and sorrow over Liam's death, ambivalence over her large family, burgeoning alcohol abuse, and seeming disaffection in her marriage, Veronica slowly and painfully constructs a fragmented narrative of past and imagination, memory and fiction. This process of narrativizing ultimately reveals the abuse of her brother and possibly herself by her grandmother's friend and landlord, Lamb Nugent, when they were children. By novel's end, however, Veronica seems to be moving toward a more stable and accepting place in relation to her marriage, her family, and her brother's death.

As Liam Harte has skillfully argued in his fine article "Mourning Remains Unresolved: Trauma and Survival in Anne Enright's *The Gathering*," Enright's text reflects many of the hallmark signs of trauma in Veronica's attempts to reconcile herself to the death of her brother and her role as witness of Nugent's sexual abuse, not the least of which is forgetting in the first place: "Hers is the story of a self formed under the burden of a trauma that has remained cognitively unprocessed."[1] Like much major trauma, Veronica's has been inadequately assimilated or remembered only as an absence in a manner that Cathy Caruth also has described: "it is only in and through its inherent forgetting that [the trauma] is first experienced at all."[2] As a result, Veronica's desire to "write down what happened," even though she is "not sure if it really did happen,"[3] reflects how traumatic memory is almost always already foundationally compromised.

Unable to engage the enormity of her traumatic experience, Veronica instead repressed her memories and resorted to behaviors typical of traumatic coping. Thus, like Max Morden, she drinks heavily, noting, "It is the only way I know to make the day end" (38); she sews her fingers together and stabs herself with needles in classic signs of cutting and self-harm (127, 129);[4] and she suffers from a considerable amount of guilt—for example, reading a "dark look, full of blame," in her sister's gaze (25). As psychiatrist Judith Lewis Herman observes, a tendency toward self-harm is a typical, if unfortunate, coping mechanism for child abuse victims: "feeling can be most effectively terminated by a major jolt to the body . . . through the deliberate infliction of injury." Similarly, as we saw in the previous chapter, victims of trauma often self-medicate in an attempt to cope: "Traumatized people . . . may attempt to produce . . . numbing effects by using alcohol."[5] As a result of the trauma she suffered, Veronica thus lives her life as what Harte calls "a defensive performance, a simulation of . . . control. . . . [S]he has been surviving rather than experiencing life."[6]

Veronica's performance of normalcy thus cloaks a profound pain: "Liam's death stirs up a virulent pack of demons that had been only temporarily kept at bay."[7] Although Veronica fulfills the role of successful Celtic Tiger wife and mother, she also displays unexplained emotions that, in retrospect, are telling: her sometimes inexplicable rage at her family (10–11), her sudden flashes of violent imagery pertaining to sexuality (35), and her hostility toward her husband (36–38), for example, strike the reader as unexplained as they occur because we, along with Veronica herself, are determining and unearthing the reasons for these emotions. It is thus natural that many view this text primarily as what Robert F. Garratt has called a "trauma novel."[8]

In the attempt to manage and deal with the fragmented memories of her past and the emotionally fractured state of her present, Veronica, like Morden, turns to narrative. Veronica, too, wrestles with questions of truth and accuracy, but she also focuses heavily on her own act of authorship. Her insistent imaginings of the life of her grandmother

Ada with Lamb Nugent thus reflect her compulsive but inventive engagement with the past, for, as Herman notes, "traumatized people find themselves reenacting some aspect of the trauma scene *in disguised form*," a psychic return that has "a driven, tenacious quality," like a compulsion.[9] Veronica notes, "But mostly, I write about Ada and Nugent in the Belvedere, endlessly, over and again" (38). Veronica's attempts at narrative mastery over her past carry this obsessive quality; her insistent but redirected return to the past reflects the pressures of "an event that has not yet come into existence" for her, "in spite of the overwhelming and compelling nature of the reality of its occurrence."[10] Her reference to her narrative constructions of her grandmother's life as "all my romance" (21) not only speaks to her attempt at authorial control but also hints at her resistance to lived history through a less-painful, avoidant, even romantic reconstruction of the past.[11]

Of course, as I suggested earlier, the very evolution of the novel slowly reveals, both to Veronica and to the reader, the hard truths that she has sought both to engage and to deny. Harte has ably traced Veronica's narrative as "a form of traumatic memory" in that it re-creates the alienating and fragmentary nature of that form of memory.[12] Carole Dell'Amico, too, recognizes that "testimonies involving traumatic events are often fraught with distortions and riddled with gaps,"[13] which Veronica's own narrative includes. As we have seen, such gaps are inherent to this form of mental processing.[14]

The novel's ability to re-create for the reader the gaps, confusions, and inconsistencies of traumatic memory are in fact one of its profoundest strengths. Just as Veronica "reassemble[s]" Nugent, "click clack" (14), from his bones and the skeleton of a narrative, trauma survivors' stories *bring their trauma into being* through the process of narrativizing: "Knowledge in the testimony is . . . not simply a factual given that is reproduced and replicated by the testifier, but *a genuine advent, an event in its own right*."[15] Thus, there are moments when Veronica's unconscious knowledge of her brother's plight draws nearer to the surface, as when she states, "It is possible that Nugent is imagining it all—or that I am" (17). Similarly, imagining Nugent's interaction with his sister, she observes, "In those days, people used to be mixed up together in the most disgusting ways" (35). Enright's text traces, even as it enacts, Veronica's process of reconstructing her traumatic memory through narrative. As in the case of *The Sea*, *The Gathering* reflects the fractured and distorted nature of traumatic memory and how narrative can be a means to try to reconstruct and process such experience.

Even with nontraumatic recollections, of course, Veronica faces the natural slipperiness of memory. Enright has noted that engagement with the inherent unreliability of memory is a facet of her work as she tries to wrestle with issues of memory and the instability of identity construction:

> The past changes because of events in the present; the past becomes more apparent. And the characters learn about their own pasts by the good functioning of their memory. So you could also say, that they don't remember things properly, even though they have really good solid memories, even though this is the scaffolding of the work. . . . *The Gathering* is interested in the edges between, certainly fantasy or imagination and memory, between memory and history and where we let go of memory, where it ossifies and turns into history.[16]

Thus, when Veronica tries to remember the clothing worn at her grandfather's funeral, she recognizes the improbability of her own recollections: "My memory has them all bundled in shawls. . . . But this was 1968: there would have been patterned headscarves and big-buttoned coats that smelt of the rain" (60). Similarly, when remembering a childhood scene, she recognizes that her memories are probably not accurate or perhaps not even hers at all: "Here's me eating Ada's rubber bathing hat. . . . Though, of course, it must have been Kitty's nappy—hardly mine, at the age of three. . . . Did this happen? . . . More probably, it was Liam put the hat over my face and nearly killed me. Or it was Kitty who got smothered by the two of us" (99). *The Gathering* does not shy away from the fundamental unreliability of memory.

This recognition of memory's treachery heightens the sense of urgency we detect in Veronica's efforts to "bear witness to an uncertain event" (1); it deepens our understanding of the critical need for her to come to terms with what she does not, perhaps cannot, know. As a result, Veronica cannot even be sure whether her recollections of the trauma itself are correct, and her remembrances often take on an almost hallucinatory quality. Thus, when she does remember Nugent's assault on Liam, she recognizes the unreliability of that image: "And even though I know it is *true* that this happened, I do not know if I have the true picture in my mind's eye . . . the bridge of flesh between the man and boy. The image has too much yellow light in it, there are too many long shadows thrown" (144, emphasis in original). Similarly, Veronica is not sure where or how the assault happened or even if she, too, were a victim: "Whatever happened to Liam did not take place in Ada's good room—no matter what picture I have in my head. . . . I wonder, . . . did it happen to me too. What can I say? I don't think so" (223–24). Veronica's memory is distorted by time and trauma. *The Gathering*, like *The Sea*, thus reflects the fractured and unreliable nature of traumatic memory as well as the narrative attempt to gain some control over that memory and therefore to gain some level of mastery over one's life.

Because the re/membering of her own personal trauma is triggered not only by her brother's suicide but also by the associations evoked through the contemporary scandals in Ireland, Veronica and Liam's tragedy invariably assumes a national as well as a personal significance in the novel.[17] Veronica admits, "I never would have made that shift [to remember Mr. Nugent] on my own—if I hadn't been listening to the radio, and reading the paper, and hearing about what went on in schools and churches and in people's homes. It went on slap-bang in front of me and still I did not realise it. And for this, I am very sorry too" (172–73).[18] As Dell'Amico concludes, "The book's abuse is shrouded in ambiguity in order to call attention to this particular failure [to recognize child sexual abuse] while still allowing for inquiries into other related histories of neglect," such as the histories of the asylums, industrial schools, and Magdalene laundries.[19]

Veronica's and Ireland's related traumas thus become entangled, and "it [is] increasingly impossible to separate the individual's dissociation from the agony of unspeakable trauma from the pervasive denial of memory and responsibility by state and society."[20] As we will see in the following chapter on *The Secret Scripture*, such an entangling of narratives can be symptomatic of the interdependence of personal traumas and national traumas caused by Ireland's many scandals and its dysfunctional societal "architecture of containment."[21] In such readings, Veronica's experience is effectively a kind of allegory for the many victims of the Irish state.

Because gender has been so entangled and problematically dealt with in the construction of the Irish state, scholars understandably recognize it as specifically related to national allegory in this novel. Harte sees Veronica's traumatized alienation from the body as inherently gendered, arguing that she is "blinded . . . by the male body's latent capacity to inflict sexual suffering."[22] Dell'Amico, too, suggests that the novel invokes "Irish cultural misogyny and institutionalized abuse in Roman Catholic institutions."[23] Finally, Laura Sydora has recently read the novel as reflecting "a desire to investigate contemporary societal change . . . to recover what has been silenced in Ireland's public historiography, particularly female identity."[24]

There is, of course, no debate about the historical devaluing of both women and children in traditional postrepublic Irish society or about the systematic suffering this devaluation caused. Yet the novel's subversive use of gender remains in one way underexplored: the allegorical comparison of Veronica to nation is often held separate from her narrative construction as embodied subject, save as victim. For example, Harte observes Veronica's parallel to victims of the state, noting that "the coercive power of the social and psychological forces that render the traumatic memories of *both daughter and nation* untellable will not yield easily to articulation or communication." He rightly recognizes that "personal, familial, and cultural amnesia must . . . be systematically undone" and that the novel refuses any easy personal (or national) resolution to trauma;[25] however, he reads Veronica's body through trauma and through allegory, but not through her physical embodiment as an agent or through her descriptive appropriation of the body. Thus, he can observe that Veronica's trauma is "displayed and replayed through the body,"[26] but he does not address the ways in which her engagement with bodily function and the novel's narrative representation of it undermine and disrupt that use of body as object.

Dell'Amico offers a more subversive reading of gender in the novel. She broadens the comparison to nation that the text effects, noting that *The Gathering* is concerned with "feminism's unfinished work" and the "lingering gender inequalities that threaten feminist gains," but she also recognizes that the novel's concern encapsulates "all of the book's marginalized individuals and groups." Dell'Amico's reading ultimately grounds women's resistant power in the domain of "feeling": "*The Gathering* enacts a feminist agenda in its focus on the feminine-coded realm of feeling. . . . Enright asserts the force of a *womanly realm of experience* against the patriarchal notion that mainstream historiography offers greater understanding and meaning through a rational, objective, masculine frame."[27] Seeking to reclaim feminine power, she reads the sense/sensibility dichotomy subversively. In the process, however, the body itself drops out.

Although most readings of *The Gathering* accurately capture the representation of trauma, the resonances of nationalist critique, and the novel's allegorical engagement with gender, I want to argue for its subversive, disruptive, and appropriative use of gender and the domestic. Veronica's narrative employs the language of motherhood and the domestic as metonyms to indict the mores of the state while *reclaiming* the physical reality of woman as subject. Veronica certainly does refer to the timeworn tropes of Mother Ireland and the domestic space, but her construction and use of those spaces create a subversive counter-narrative without denying the inherent challenges of those spaces.

This use of the body and the domestic is clear in Veronica's references to her grandmother. Lamb Nugent enacts the violence of the text by molesting Liam, but Veronica's obsession with her grandmother and her family history as the site to which she must return to understand Liam's death (13) repeatedly uses domestic space and an overemphasis on the raw female body as its loci. As a result, *The Gathering* harnesses these long-standing tropes disruptively—not as empowering in and of themselves but as subversive sites from which gendered imbalances and systemic sexual abuse can be confronted and disrupted as bodily, inherited aspects of a family or a society.

Thus, in imagining her grandparents' wedding night, Veronica sketches Ada's "overused pubis" (57), later comparing it to the "breast of an underfed chicken" (67). She imagines this encounter in the space of that most loaded of signifiers for the centrality of the Irish domestic ideal, the marriage bed, and the reference to chicken perversely invokes and recasts the domestic roles of cooking and sustenance.[28] By rendering her grandmother's body in a graphically and evocatively physical way, her narrative hyperbolically emphasizes the objectification of the woman's body.[29] She also undermines what Anne Mulhall has called the "cultural and social prohibitions around the gendered body,"[30] stressing the grandmother's bodily reality even while reconfiguring the maternal as a physical subject burdened by the domestic space. Thus, although it is true, as one critic argues, that the novel captures "a distinct sense of alienation from [women's] own bodies,"[31] which it recuperates physically, it simultaneously represences and rewrites raw physicality as not celebratory but grotesque and conditioned by the domestic space.

A similarly condemnatory reclamation occurs when Veronica imagines her grandmother having an extramarital liaison with Nugent. The imaginary encounter occurs in the kitchen, another locus of the domestic, where, we learn, Ada would stand at the sink and cry—just as Veronica herself will later do by the dishwasher (89). During her narration of that encounter, Veronica describes their unsanctioned sex with the metaphor that "they pulled the house down around their ears" (139)—a telling image and space for an act destructive of the idealized marital state. Locating scenes of women's misery and imagined adultery in the kitchen suggests both a disruptive appropriation and an undermining of the domestic space. Of course, this image of deconstruction also contrasts ironically with the seemingly endless growth of Veronica's family home, with its cancerlike, monstrous expansion and images of perverse maternity: "I was inside [this house], as it grew: as the dining room was knocked into the kitchen, as the kitchen swallowed the back garden. . . . The place is all extension and no house" (4).[32]

Significantly, Veronica employs her narrative reshapings self-consciously. When she acknowledges her narrative control as "bend[ing] . . . [Nugent and Ada] in the rudest possible ways," she imagines herself as masculinized, her narrative as a kind of ejaculation in both senses of the word: "I would love to leave my body. Maybe this is what they are about, these questions of which or whose hole. . . . [T]hey are a way of fighting our way out of all this meat (I would like to just swim out, you know?—shoot like a word out of my own mouth and disappear with a flick of my tail . . .)" (139–40). Word-as-sperm becomes an act of both rejection and reclamation: Veronica hopes to discard her female corporeality, thereby attaining freedom from her gendered physicality. At the same time, however, she acknowledges that the act of narratively presencing the body is a generative and therefore a recuperative gendered act, even as she claims the traditionally male role of sexual actor for herself.[33]

Veronica also locates the blame for her and her brother's fate in her grandmother through their bodily connection. Having recognized that she has Ada's feet, Veronica immediately reverts to a meditation on her own value as a sexualized object, noting, "Lawyers want to breed out of me" (21). Dell'Amico reads this scene as a mark of Veronica's Celtic Tiger–era commodified sexuality[34]—rightly, I think—but that her sexuality is directly connected back to her matrilineal inheritance seems significant as well.

Ada's body becomes, through its very fertility, the generative site of suffering. Veronica observes, "She *must* know what lies ahead of them now. . . . She knows because of all the things that have happened since. She knows because she is my Granny" (17, emphasis in original). By establishing a bodily connection to her grandmother, Veronica not only traces the generational subjection of women to a sexualized role but also suggests the centrality of past constructions of reproduction in the present day and the damaging consequences of that role.[35] Her grandmother's and her own shared tears in the domestic space, to which I referred earlier, work similarly; the sink and the dishwasher stand in metonymically for the pain-inflicting domestic space. Thus, the issue is not only that Veronica indicts "Ada's failure to protect [Liam]" and sees in her a "more . . . thoroughgoing failure," as Dell'Amico rightly suggests,[36] but also that she sees Ada as coextensive with her own subordination and potential failure, thus establishing a matrilineal inheritance of both sexualized objectification and complicity.

Veronica's condemnation of her mother and her sense of abandonment are also directly correlated to the understood prohibitions against contraception and the expectations of Irish marriage that undergird the text. And, as in her treatment of Ada, Veronica turns to the body and the domestic space to make her critique of her mother. She describes her mother, like her grandmother, as oversexed in the most graphic of ways: she indicts her parents for the "stupidity of so much humping" and complains that her parents "bred as naturally as they might shit" (8, 25). The bodily imagery again rejects the sanctity of the celebrated marriage bed, with Veronica complaining that her father's "bed was all the reality that this woman [was] asked to bear" (9).

Veronica's mother, like her grandmother, is presenced in her raw physicality when she is described as "this piece of benign human meat" (47). Enright's bodily language, combined with her use of the domestic space as a metonym for the familial ideal, once again undermines the abstracted and idealized Irish mother, marking the sites of domesticity as destructive or even grotesque while presencing the oft-elided maternal body. This combination reflects Enright's tendency, as Mulhall notes, to work against the absenting of women in the Irish canon: "In place of the real mother, Enright has observed that Irish writing has traditionally either appointed 'the iconised mother figure,' or posited an absence. . . . The mother is the unspeakable phantom, the gap enclaved within the novel's genealogy. Enright works to make this absence present, to answer to its uncanny insistence."[37] Notably, this absenting is treated as a constant threat in the novel and implicitly linked to motherhood. Veronica frets that if she does not speak to her children, she "will just fade away," just as Mammy is "always vague, . . .

now completely faded" (38, 197). As Susan Cahill argues, "The blankness of the mother in the symbolic economy is shown to negatively affect female subjectivity."[38] Representing both Ada and her mother in this way, even as she links her own vulnerability to theirs, Veronica highlights the objectification of women even as she subverts it by resorting to graphic, bodily, often grotesque descriptions.

Just as Veronica holds Ada accountable for her role in Liam's molestation—which, tellingly, Veronica relates as occurring in the drawing room, the site of middle-class respectability—so too does she consider her parents' generative prowess to have led directly to Liam's assault. She notes bitterly that she and Liam were "farmed out" to their grandmother owing to the sheer unmanageable number of children in their household (49). She attributes Liam's inability to settle down to this abandonment, observing that "one of the effects of our stay at Ada's [was] that if [Liam] made a home, it was only ever to leave it" (121). She also correlates the ironic undervaluing of children—that prized goal of domesticity and marriage—as causally related to Liam's abuse: "[Nugent] did what he liked with the children passing through . . . [b]ecause children in those days were of little account. We three Hegartys were manifestly *of little account*" (235–36, emphasis in original). As Harte notes, "Veronica is struck by how fundamentally inhospitable to children's welfare and well-being the public and private spaces of patriarchal, postcolonial Irish society were."[39] More importantly, that abandonment directly correlates to the enforcement of a form of motherhood that undermines children's happiness, here even ejecting them from their "proper" domestic space into a threatening, damaging one. In Veronica's musing whether "it would be possible to unbuild [her childhood home] and start again" (24), we see once more how the domestic space generates not only history and children but also suffering.

Not surprisingly, Veronica feels she is the inheritor of this problematic model of motherhood, and her representations of the domestic space and the maternal body reflect this indictment. Her repeated references to her home as "oatmeal, cream, sandstone, slate" speak metonymically to the blandness of the performative domestic space, where her "girls are just a residue," already an absence, as she was in her childhood home (36).[40] As Mulhall has noted, this representation fits a pattern within Enright's wider work, where "domestic spaces . . . are themselves crypts of the transgenerational trauma of abuse."[41] Recognizing that the domestic space and children's and women's bodily vulnerability in particular are entwined, the novel engages both: "Veronica seems to realize that the edifice [of her family home] has rotten foundations."[42]

Thus, Veronica's observation of herself as happy and her corresponding response—"So, I am happy. That's nice to know" (68)—also speak to this performative element of the domestic. In the absurd, sad, and quite funny scene where she drunkenly drives around her neighborhood, she muses on the ridiculousness of the entire domestic model: "There is something so bare about our little estate at night; the neighbours, each in their madness, asleep in a row. Nothing matters. . . . The urge to drive is very strong. . . . Still—and I am officially mad now, I am a mad housewife—I ease the car away from the kerb and, drinking all the while, move around the estate in first gear" (149). Even as she sees her "life in inverted commas" (181), she cannot help but run through a performance of this domestic role—for example, crying on the escalator in the Brown Thomas department store while buying tellingly empty containers to fill with dry goods (189); considering buying a new carpet when confronted with her dead brother's body (193); and imagining buying and redecorating her grandmother's house (238), an imaginative, metonymic attempt literally to paper over the crimes that took place there. Veronica sees her own home, like her grandmother's and mother's homes, as an unnatural, deadening space, where the domestic causes not bliss but perversion and harm.

Not surprisingly, Veronica is as aggressive in her descriptors of her own sexualized, maternal body as she has been of her mother's and grandmother's corporeality.[43] In imagining sex, she notes, "My image of these nights is of a woman (myself) lying on a bed, with her back arched, and her mouth open, and her hand scrabbling for the wall" (88). She also famously describes her own corporeality as both damaged by motherhood and capable of inflicting harm: "I look at my hands on the railings, and they are old, and my child-battered body, that I was proud of . . . just feeding the grave, *just feeding the grave!* . . . I want to call for an end to procreation" (79, emphasis in original).

This passage not only stresses the real, bodily consequences of motherhood versus the ideal but also suggests that the maternal body, as societally constructed, can be a site of violence and hereditary harm. By stressing both concrete womanhood over idealized abstraction and the capacity for harm and damage versus the usual celebration of motherly sacrifice, Enright doubly undermines the maternal ideal—a gesture consistent with her wider work. As Enright has observed, "The imperative I feel to turn my women into subjects is part of a broader set of problems about gender and the objectification of women. We're always breaking out of those stereotypes or images, or we're always insisting on our subjectivity. And we're relentlessly turned into objects."[44] Veronica reasserts her own physical reality, as unpalatable as it at times may be, and undermines at once the traditional celebration of life-giving maternity.[45]

Veronica also describes her own genitalia, like her mother's and grandmother's, and the sex act itself as grotesque and yet somehow domestic. Thinking of nights spent with Michael Weiss, she remembers "the sex still warm and hurting between [her] thighs" (88). When reflecting on sex with her husband, she observes, "I felt like a chicken when it is quartered" (40)—both a domestic reference to a kitchen activity and emblematic of the unexpectedly destructive force of marital sex. Of course, this description also harkens to the same metaphor she used in reference to her grandmother, linking the marriage bed and the domestic with violence and raw physicality. She later repeats this domestic/grotesque imagery by saying, "I felt like meat that had been recently butchered" (219), and she pronounces her "private parts" to be a "spreading bruise" (220). The repeated imagery of butchery takes a traditional domestic chore to its most violent extreme. It also captures the potential harm of the domestic even as it subverts the traditional celebration of women's sexuality and supposed marital bliss, while narratively presencing the embodied maternal all at once.

Veronica thus treats her own body the same way she treats her grandmother's and mother's. Reflecting on sex with Michael Weiss, she describes her genitalia as "a meaty flower" (93), a grotesque image that stresses the bodily reality of her sexuality and perverts stereotypical associations of women with flowers. By refusing to treat women's bodies as either abstract or sacrosanct—she also describes her grief as "almost genital" (7) and vodka as "crotch-like" (165)—Veronica undermines traditional reverence for the abstracted maternal body and reconfigures the maternal and marital as both corporeal and somehow abject.[46]

This reconfiguration is not entirely unproblematic: the association of the feminine with abjection is hardly an immediately recuperative gesture and, it could be argued, seems to reinforce the negative associations with women's bodies and female sexuality against which feminism has long labored.[47] Yet this is where the element of trauma is significant. Veronica's foregrounding of her bodily trauma as well as her metonymic evocation of the domestic as a site of trauma simultaneously engage her suffering through narrative and write that trauma on the suffering body *while gendering it*. If, as Ulrike Tancke (paraphrasing Whitehead) has argued, "traumatic events . . . are essentially corporeal in nature,"[48] Veronica's representation of suffering bodies serves the multiple purposes of acknowledging that suffering, presencing the body, and yet contesting the body's social construction as an object. Through this act of reclamation, Veronica thus stakes the right to *reauthor* what her own body and bodily reality—as well as, of course, her trauma—mean. In disavowing traditional configurations of motherhood and body-as-object, her narrative empowers her to speak her trauma and to author herself as at once a suffering but recoverable subject.

Veronica's narrative throughout thus implicitly blames the domestic ideal for a personal and societal history of harm, even as it aggressively reclaims female bodies through graphic, even grotesque emphasis on their corporeality. Inevitably, this reclamation also has implications allegorically for the status of women in Irish society as a whole.

Although these descriptions can be shocking, they reflect Veronica's attempts to work through and narrativize her trauma as well as her rejection of the traditional domestic roles and gender constructions that have facilitated such objectification in the first place. Trauma written on the body as object/abject is thus resisted by Veronica's reclamation of authorship—not only of her own physicality but also of her matrilineal line. This act of narrative subversion/perversion hollows out the maternal ideal and presences women as lived, physical subjects even as it works through Veronica's traumatic pain and grief.

☼

Despite Veronica's ambivalence over her matrilineal forebears, the novel does not end with a condemnatory representation of motherhood. It instead seeks to reclaim motherhood as a lived, bodily experience, grounded not in its idealized abstractions but rather in the bodily reality and bond between mother and child. In this way, the novel makes another reclamation—one that is generative rather than abstract or idealizing and that counters the memory of physical abuse and exploitation with investment in nurturing and love. In other words, without romanticizing motherhood, Enright reclaims the maternal body as physical subject, not object, and provides an alternative, reclamatory narrative to the reductive inscription of trauma.

Claire Bracken and Susan Cahill have observed that "motherhood is a central theme throughout Enright's fictions" and that the author often engages "the cultural silence surrounding the embodied experience of pregnancy and motherhood."[49] *The Gathering* is consistent with this pattern as it posits the concrete, bodily relation between mother and child in defiance of a domesticated, objectifying, and often harmful ideal.[50] This is not to say that Veronica does not fear re-creating the matrilineal inheritance she condemns, and the sense of women's vulnerability, the falsity of the maternal ideal, and her bodily trauma are linked. As noted earlier, Veronica imagines her daughters to be a kind of "residue"—a figurative parallel to her concern that she herself will "fade away." Her worry that the cause of her own "fading" will be a failure to communicate with her daughters reflects her lifelong experience of neglect by her own mother. That Veronica also refers to the lunatics who were housed and abandoned in the asylum as a "residue of skin" (159) reinforces her fears for her daughters.

At the same time, Veronica's fear of what is written on the body is clear in her own role as mother. Just as she traced the destructive elements at play in her own matrilineal inheritance, she links her daughters to herself physically. Seeing that her daughter Emily has the "Hegarty-blue eyes" (38), she anticipates as her daughters' potential fate the same institutionalized neglect and inherited familial and cultural vulnerability to which she was subject.

Veronica thus recognizes the potentially generational impact of such a social construction of motherhood. Referring to her mother as a "kind of collective guilt" (3), she lashes out at the maternal, rejecting the celebration of mother love as a type of hoax or myth: "I just didn't buy it, and neither did Liam. We just didn't buy the whole Hegarty *poor Mammy* thing" (184, emphasis in original). At times, her resistance to this ideal leads her even to project such disconnect ahead to her daughters: her suspicion that her children, like her husband, will prove "too lazy even to love" her (27) betrays a sense that the mother–child bond is potentially transitory or contingent—a love, like a grief, that can be "biological, idiot, timeless" (11).

This sense of the potential implication of the matrilineal in her traumatic experience culminates when Veronica implies that her mother's neglect—in violation of the maternal ideal—directly caused Liam's death: "I am saying that, the year you sent us away, your dead son was interfered with, when you were not there to comfort or protect him, and that interference was enough to send him on a path that ends in the box downstairs. . . . Because a mother's love is God's greatest joke" (213). Noting her mother's failure to "comfort or protect," Veronica directly gives the lie to the idealized role of mother.

Yet Veronica's ability to reclaim motherhood ultimately catalyzes her ability to heal. Although Liam's body is a locus of violation and betrayal, and Veronica's sense of history reflects her troubled inheritance of the tortured history of Irish domesticity, trauma, and the objectifying cult of motherhood, she also insists on and revels in the physicality of her daughters and her bodily connection to them, and she celebrates this connection narratively. Veronica details her examination of her newborn daughter, studying the "eyes, fingers, toes, the tiny pores on her nose plugged with yellow stuff that made [her] panic" (53). Similarly, as a counter against the grotesqueness of her own and her foremothers' pregnancy-abused bodies or, for that matter, against the domestically inflected representations of the sexed female body in pain, she holds up the concrete, biological connection of mother and child. In her role as mother, she sees that connection as a site of generation, symbiosis, and care, a passage I believe is worth quoting at length:

> I do not know what she smells like, she is like a perfume you have been wearing too long, she is still too close to the inside of me. So I can not [*sic*] smell her, quite, but I know that her smell is there as I lie down with the thought of her beside me. I want to run my hand down her exquisite back, and over her lovely little bum. I want to check that it is all still there, and nicely packed, and happy, that my daughter's muscles agree with her bones. I want to find the person that I built from my body's own stuff, and grew on ten thousand plates of organic sausages and sugar-free beans, and I want to squeeze every part of her tight, until she is moulded and compact. I want to finish the job of making her, because when she is fully made she will be strong. (152)

Unlike the narrative construction of Nugent, "who must be reassembled; click clack; his muscles hooked to bone" (14), this passage offers us the image of creation, nurturance, and care, where she will "check" to see that her "daughter's muscles agree with her bones." The earlier, grotesque, imaginative narrative engagement is replaced by the concrete physical reality of creation, but, importantly, without absenting either her own or her daughter's body. At the same time, this process is close and interpersonal, not generational: Veronica says her daughter is "built from my body's own stuff," not that her daughter "has" her eyes, feet, and so on. In this respect, she suggests symbiosis rather than inheritance, commonality rather than descent.

Veronica also rejects the interpretation of children merely as a legacy, an inheritance, or a product of the maternal or the marital—in other words, as objects—"fiercely" insisting, "It's not what children are for" (199). She instead privileges the physical bond of mother and child and the concreteness of those beings as subjects. In the physical reality of motherhood, Veronica can evade the type of objectifying, poisonous fate that taints both her personal and national history. It is thus perhaps telling that when she phones her daughter and is offered in return only one word, "love" (257), this conversation occurs in an airport—the universal symbol of transience and movement—rather than in the symbolically overloaded and overly cathected domestic space.[51] In the same way, when the Hegartys learn of the existence of Liam's only son, Rowan, endowed with the biological mark of the "Hegarty-blue eyes," the stress shifts to fatherhood instead of motherhood—a kind of symbolic rebalancing that destabilizes the overprivileging of the mother.[52]

The Gathering clearly reflects on trauma, on the nature of memory, and on the problematics of cultural silences and omissions in the Irish state, but it is also an aggressive intervention into the narrative construction of women and motherhood and the ways in which that history has been transmitted from generation to generation. If, as Veronica argues, "this is the anatomy and mechanism of a family—a whole fucking country—drowning in shame" (168), then her bodily language emphasizes the lived realities that her family, like Irish society as a whole, has so often sought to deny and the traumatic consequences of that denial. That shame is as organic as it is historical: the bodily oath speaks to the generative as well as the damaging aspects of traditional Irish society, even as "drowning in shame" evokes the pervasiveness of that societal culpability and the consequence of such shame in the drowning suicide of her brother.

At the same time, through an aggressive narrative foregrounding of the physical female body, often metonymically bound to the domestic space that has been site and ideological origin of so much damage, *The Gathering* rejects the abstracting or appropriation of women's bodies as either site of trauma or as object. The novel highlights the consequences of objectifying and dehumanizing models of domesticity for women and society. Veronica offers a recuperative narrative that counters this domestic ideal with the real, physical, and productively generative forces of motherhood, even as she subverts the idealized human body through the vehicle of her traumatic experience. If trauma is written on the body, *The Gathering* suggests that such a narrative can be malleable. By reworking that narrative through counteractive representations of femininity and motherhood, the novel is doubly reclamatory. The next novel we consider, *The Secret Scripture*, asks similar questions and invites us to ponder the implications of authorizing competing narratives—for trauma victims and Irish society alike.

3

"Surmises Held Up against the Truth"

Traumatic Memory and Metanarratives of Recovery in Sebastian Barry's The Secret Scripture

> I know, there is no one here, neither me nor anyone else, but some things are better left unsaid, so I say nothing.
>
> —Samuel Beckett, "Texts for Nothing"

As we have seen, in his critical work *Writing History, Writing Trauma* Dominick LaCapra observes that traumatic memory "may involve distortion, disguise, and other permutations relating to . . . narrative shaping," but such failures in strict accuracy "[can]not invalidate [a narrative] in its entirety."[1] This disclaimer clearly applies to Sebastian Barry's novel *The Secret Scripture* (2008), in which main character Roseanne Clear McNulty's attempt to unravel her traumatic life history is riddled with doubt, contradiction, and ambiguity. Like Max Morden in *The Sea* and Veronica Hegarty in *The Gathering*, Roseanne finds her recollections to be contested and uncertain, a clear reflection of the fragmented nature of traumatic memory.

Traumatic memory is not the only "story" in *The Secret Scripture*, however. As occurs implicitly in *The Sea* and explicitly in *The Gathering*, Barry's novel is in conversation with the larger Irish social contexts that frame the character's experience. Roseanne's omissions, inconsistencies, and uncertainties as well as her reconstruction of the past engage that context. They also serve as a counterpoint to dominant narratives' authority and as an assertion of the relevance and legitimacy of personal truth.

Ultimately, however, the novel suggests that questions of which account is "true" are largely ancillary to the main point, which is instead fundamentally the process of *telling*. Roseanne's narrative in *The Secret Scripture* not only echoes the workings and omissions characteristic of traumatic memory but through its metanarrative consideration of what constitutes a "story" also highlights the cathartic and healing properties of narrativizing trauma. Although such healing comes regardless of claims to authenticity or validated "truth," the novel's provocative awareness of its own, highly crafted conclusion simultaneously challenges the reader to consider what "recovery" means in light of traumatic personal and cultural experience.

The Secret Scripture focuses on Roseanne McNulty, a one-hundred-year-old mental asylum in-patient who has suffered under the pressures of Catholic Ireland and the concomitant institutionalized policing of women's bodies. Essentially orphaned as a teenager by her father's death and her mother's mental breakdown, Roseanne is thrown on the dubious mercy of the local Catholic priest, Father Gaunt, who urges her to convert from Presbyterianism and to marry posthaste. When Roseanne marries a Catholic but remains unconverted and is seen walking out with an Irish Republican, Father Gaunt assumes she has had an affair and arranges for her effectively to be imprisoned in her house in Strandhill and for her marriage to be annulled. Years later, when Roseanne becomes pregnant from a one-night liaison with her erstwhile brother-in-law, Eneas, Father Gaunt arranges for her to be institutionalized on the grounds that she is a nymphomaniac. In other words, for much of her life Roseanne is not in control of her own life or life story.

Like *The Gathering*, this novel clearly engages with the social contexts at work on Roseanne and in twentieth-century Irish society at large. Father Gaunt's all-controlling power over her reflects his own (potentially repressed and lascivious) attraction to her.[2] More importantly, it also mirrors the almost boundless authority of Catholic priests in the fledgling Irish state.[3] Roseanne recognizes this power: "The word of a man like that was like a death sentence."[4] Roseanne's physician, Dr. William Grene, describes Father Gaunt as an "all-knowing, stern-minded, and entirely unforgiving" priest, who feared not only Roseanne's Presbyterianism but also her basic femininity:

> He betrays at every stroke an intense hatred if not of women, then of the sexuality of women, or sexuality in general. For him it is the devil's cloak and hood. . . . It is also crystal clear that he regards her Protestantism as a simple, primal evil in itself. His anger that she would not let herself be made a Catholic . . . is absolute, long before she married her Catholic husband, and likewise remained what she was. This in itself for Fr Gaunt is a real perversion. (227, 230)

This response to Roseanne echoes what Linda Hogan has identified within the Catholic Church as a "theology of sexuality['s] . . . particular disgust of the female body."[5] It also reinforces the obstacles Roseanne faced as a Dissenter in a rabidly Catholic new Ireland[6] and as a female unprotected from the moral strictures imposed on women by the new state.[7]

As a female non-Catholic, Roseanne is thus doubly disempowered. Father Gaunt's reference to Roseanne's beauty as "a mournful temptation" (94) to the men of Sligo clearly gestures toward the history of vulnerable women remanded to institutions on the basis of their physical attractiveness alone.[8] Dr. Grene, too, acknowledges that patients were often "sectioned for social rather than medical reasons" (16, 27), and he signals the truth of such facilities when he says, "I was going to say incarceration, but I mean of course her sectioning" (135).

As in the outside world, so within the asylum Roseanne is thoroughly unprotected—which was, sadly, so often the history of such institutions in Ireland and elsewhere throughout the nineteenth and early twentieth centuries.[9] The physical conditions within the asylum are deplorable. Roseanne's room is so cold that it is covered with a "rheum of frost," against which she must wear all four of her dresses to stay warm (24). Dr. Grene acknowledges that many parts of the facility are virtually uninhabitable: "The rooms have gone beyond the beyonds, with the ceilings endangered, horrible swathes of dampness up the walls. Anything iron, such as bedsteads, rusts away" (44). Such descriptions bespeak the dehumanizing conditions so often encountered in these facilities as well as Roseanne's vulnerability within the institution.

Perhaps worst of all, it is clear that Grene himself has been at best a disengaged doctor and at worst a fundamentally irresponsible or complicit one. As he considers relocating his longtime patients because the asylum is slated for demolition, Grene recognizes that he is "interviewing them for . . . their expulsion, *their ruin*," but he concludes, rather counterintuitively, that he must "resist compassion at every turn" (45, my emphasis). He recognizes that there are "bats in the roof and . . . rats in the cellars," but he accepts this state of affairs just as he accepts that the old women in the "central block" are covered in bedsores (15). Roseanne notes that Grene has been generally inattentive to her over the years, only recently actually engaging with her as one would hope a doctor should: "It is only so recently he has been coming up here to me regularly. I do remember when I only saw him twice yearly, at Easter and Christmas, when he would come in quite briskly, ask how I was, not really listen to the answer, and go off again" (126). Dr. Grene has clearly allowed the status quo, which even he recognizes as not only unhealthy but also damaging, to be maintained.

Perhaps most damning is Grene's and the other staff members' willingness to look away from the violence and violations perpetrated in their facilities. Grene recognizes that "somewhere in the distant past, in just such an institution as this, [Roseanne] suffered in some way at the hands of her 'nurses'" (117). Roseanne, too, acknowledges the perception that hospital employee John Kane is a potential sexual threat, observing "with a small degree of dread that his flies were open" and that "in the gossip of this place he has a very poor reputation" (30), about which nothing is done. Finally, when a patient is apparently sexually abused, Dr. Grene and the staff worry about word getting out, not about the patient:

> And of course the worst was suspected, as it always is. . . . All thoughts turned to John Kane because of course he has been implicated in such matters before, and let off. . . . But there is no proof, nothing, and we must simply all be vigilant. . . . The staff seems to gather

> together and roll itself into a ball, needles outward. I must confess I feel the same myself. Perhaps it would shock an outsider the level of things going wrong we feel we can tolerate. . . . Things are best handled in-hospital. (163–64)

Both in the outside world and in the world of the asylum, then, Roseanne has been subject to appalling conditions and left entirely unprotected, even by those whose professional or pastoral responsibilities would dictate they act otherwise, and her fate has been determined by others.

As Tara Harney-Mahajan observes, by portraying a woman whom society has silenced, rejected, and contained, Barry invariably raises the specter of the Magdalene laundries and current debates in contemporary Irish society: "*The Secret Scripture*, thus, enters into a timely and highly charged debate ongoing in Ireland about social justice, the complicity of society, and questions of reconciliation and forgiveness."[10] Dr. Grene has certainly been complicit in society's erasure of the asylum's inmates, and Father Gaunt is a symptom of the containment of what was perceived to be socially "aberrant."[11] By consigning Roseanne to the asylum, society renders her and her sufferings unseen—an attribution of invisibility that she subsequently internalizes.

In recognition of her ostracism and social exclusion, Roseanne perceives herself as a "thing left over, a remnant woman" (4), and, having been forcibly separated from her husband, Tom, she thinks of herself as "more and more like a ghost" (205).[12] Once in hospital, she situates herself as one among others whom history has relegated to oblivion. Thinking of the other elderly women marooned in the hospital, for example, she reflects, "Who were they? Why, they were your own people. Silent, silent, sleeping towards death. . . . The human town not so far off, sleeping and waking . . . forgetting its lost women there" (31, 32). Roseanne embodies one such "lost woman": she both represents and recognizes her own cultural invisibility.[13] Like Veronica Hegarty, who fears her own and other women's potential role as a "residue" or an absence, Roseanne recognizes her social erasure, particularly in gendered terms.[14]

The inaccessibility of Roseanne's story is in part a function of the very conditions that consigned her to a mental hospital from the outset and is symptomatic of her trauma. Her act of voicing her own account serves as a kind of counternarrative to the authorized version of her history that landed her in the asylum. Her "testimony" is thus "a fundamental undermining of the prevailing official story of Roseanne" and therefore can be read as an attempt to suggest that "the path forward [for Ireland] must be predicated on an engagement with official history . . . and . . . the opportunity to voice one's own story."[15] In this respect, *The Secret Scripture* uses Roseanne's story to represent all those women silenced and forgotten by Irish history; the overwriting of her narrative by Father Gaunt's "authoritative" version reflects the experience of many women in Irish history.

☼

As we have seen, trauma carries direct implications for memory and narrative. Given the loss of her child, her incarceration, and her years of physical abuse in the institution, Roseanne has many reasons for traumatic response. As the epigraph that begins this chapter suggests, Roseanne (perhaps wisely) believes that silence may be the safest recourse for her, noting that her "secrets are [her] fortune and [her] sanity" (23)—all that she has to protect her from a world that is willing to hide whatever it sees as aberrant or nonconformist, such as babies "that were embarrassments" best consigned to the river, "a great friend to secrecy" (3). Her self-protective silence is one indicator of her traumatic past: she notes, "All speaking is difficult, whether peril attends it or not[,] . . . [w]hen *to speak at all* is a betrayal of something, perhaps a something not even identified" (76). Roseanne implies that the speech-act itself—in addition to its content, which signals the impact of trauma—is problematic.

Roseanne's difficulties with trust are also symptomatic of her traumatic past. Even as she considers the sincerity of Dr. Grene's kindness, she hesitates: "At least Mrs. McNulty was always openly hostile, whereas Jack and Fr. Gaunt always presented themselves as friends. . . . Now I am having a bad thought, for doesn't Dr. Grene also present himself as a friend?" (127). Her difficulty with trust matches a tendency among those held long in captivity: "Prolonged captivity disrupts all human relationships and amplifies the dialectic of trauma. The survivor oscillates between intense attachment and terrified withdrawal."[16] Roseanne's silences, fears, and distrust of her own memory are consistent with her history of trauma and abuse.

Her persistent willingness to accept responsibility for her past, despite her clear powerlessness and vulnerability, also reflects her trauma as well as the insidious power and reach of dominant narratives. In talking with Dr. Grene, Roseanne is overcome by shame, even though she clearly has been a victim: "Violently ashamed. It was as if some wood and leaves were suddenly cleared from a spring, and the head of water blossomed up. Painful, painful shame" (80).

Similarly, even as she records her history, she repeatedly feels driven to defend the very individuals who have caused her so much suffering. She notes, "I don't mean to describe all this in a bad way. God forgive me" (159), and insists, "I must be careful to write of her fairly" in discussing her heartless mother-in-law (160). When narrating details about Father Gaunt, who ruined her life, she observes, "I do not mean this critically," and she insists, "I know . . . that he was trying to do his duty. . . . I know this" (92–93). This observation clearly suggests Roseanne's sense of vulnerability and worthlessness—common reactions in a victim of trauma—and exemplifies how dominant narratives have contaminated her own.

Although Roseanne fears speaking, she does see the value in penning her tale, if only for her own peace of mind. She acknowledges, "For dearly I would love now to leave an account, some kind of brittle and honest-minded history of myself, and if God gives me the strength, I will tell this story" (5). Recognizing that "no one even knows [she has] a story" and that she writes on "unwanted paper" (4), she emphasizes the significance of the act of telling and the importance to her that she get it right: "Oh, I must remind myself to be clear, and be sure I know what I am saying to you. There must be accuracy and rightness now" (31).[17]

Yet Roseanne is clearly not a reliable witness. Some of her memories seem to signal their own unreliability without her awareness. For example, she relays—in great detail—a memory of her father's purported experiment in dropping hammers and feathers from the cemetery tower to test the speed with which they would fall. Father Gaunt directly contradicts this memory in the official record he compiled for the mental hospital, indicating that it actually was a traumatic episode in which Roseanne's father was beaten with hammers in front of her by members of the Irish Republican Army (IRA). According to Dr. Grene's summation of Father Gaunt's account,

> [Her father's] mouth was stuffed with white feathers. . . . [H]e was beaten with hammers, and an effort made to push him out the little window at the top of the tower. Roseanne herself was below looking up. Awful noises no doubt of horror from the small room at the top. . . . The hammers had not really killed him either, and as he roared, the feathers burst from his mouth. . . . [O]ne of the men flung the bloody hammers out the window. (180)

At various moments in the narrative, Roseanne unconsciously echoes these contested memories when she is under duress, suggesting that perhaps Father Gaunt was (at least this time) potentially correct. The first instance of corroboration is provoked by her thinking about IRA soldiers' experiences with violence, when she offers a telling aside: "They had charged into an unknown place with God knew what danger, and now it seemed the thought of lugging John's brother Willie was a *feather too far. Or a hammer*" (53, my emphasis). In a second instance, as she tries to explain the bitter, excluded past of her paternal Dissenter ancestors, she observes that her grandfather "thought of the Protestant religion as an instrument *as soft as a feather transformed into a hammer* by the old dispensation, and used to *batter the heads* of those that laboured to live in Ireland" (62, my emphasis). Such instances suggest the functions of the subconscious at work in revealing repressed traumatic narratives that Roseanne has worked to deny. This repression is in keeping with the understanding of traumatic memory as "a history that [the traumatized] cannot entirely possess."[18]

At other times, Roseanne is fully cognizant of the unreliability of her memories, whether conscious or unconscious. She notes that people, as authors of their own stories, can "hold up a wall made of imaginary bricks and mortar against the horrors and cruel, dark tricks of time that assail us, and be the author therefore of themselves" (3–4). Similarly, she claims that at times a "foul and utter lie [is] the best answer" (26). Such observations suggest the willful resistance to certain stories, a potentially self-protective gesture against a narrative that may be too painful to tell. Although Roseanne is unwilling to speak her history, she is willing to write her account. Her statement stresses the *craftedness* of such written personal histories and stories, a point to which I return later.

Roseanne's uncertainty over the details of her own narrative suggests the power and elusiveness of traumatic memory. As Dori Laub notes, "The horror of the historical experience is maintained in the testimony only as an elusive memory that feels as if it no longer resembles any reality."[19] Roseanne strives for accuracy, but both her recognition of memory's failures and her inability to work through some details reflect her trauma and her emphasis on the attempt to produce something emotionally true, "honest-minded," if not therefore necessarily wholly accurate.

Dr. Grene identifies these powerful symptoms of traumatic memory at work when Roseanne notes the fragmented and unreliable nature of her recall. After she explains, "I do remember terrible dark things, and loss, and noise, but it is like one of those terrible dark pictures that hang in churches, God knows why, because you cannot see a thing in them," he replies, "That is a beautiful description of traumatic memory" (101). As noted in the discussion of *The Sea*, "Traumatic memories lack verbal narrative and context; rather, they are encoded in the form of vivid sensations and images."[20] Roseanne is thus unreliable not only because of the constraints imposed on her from without but also because of the emotional constraints imposed on her from within by trauma. The nature and uncertainty of her memories and their entanglement in the dominant narratives complicate her ability to provide a reliable or stable counternarrative and therefore reflect the impact of wider social conditions on the individual.

As in *The Sea* and *The Gathering*, this novel thus acknowledges the inherent fallibility of memory. Roseanne recognizes that even when one tries to tell the truth, that truth may not hold up under scrutiny: "Friend or enemy, no one has the monopoly on truth. Not even myself, and that is also a vexing and worrying thought" (127–28). She also acknowledges that the ability to generate such stories is a potentially losing battle in the face of dominant societal narratives that seek to undermine them. Roseanne recognizes that truth is always subjective and contested: "The fact that I never saw the soldiers, never spoke to them, never even thought of doing so . . . is in the informal history of Sligo neither here nor there. For history as far as I can see is not the arrangement of what happens, in sequence and in truth, but a fabulous arrangement of surmises and guesses held up as a banner against the assault of withering truth" (54–55). In her uncertainty, her avoidance, and her recognition of the limits of—and challenges to—her own assertions, Roseanne reflects the challenges of traumatic memory; she also acknowledges that her memories are to a certain degree always societally influenced, if not determined. As importantly, she implies that history itself is radically indeterminate, an "arrangement of surmises" rather than the careful ordering and recording of certainty or fact. The best one can do, she suggests, is to offer something that contains a kind of sincere intent, is "honest-minded" if not necessarily true.

Roseanne's hesitation thus reflects more than only the symptoms of societal forces. As her inconsistent recollection of the feather-and-hammer incident and her distrust of her own memories show, her recollections bear the hallmarks of trauma. In her uncertainty, Roseanne reflects a common difficulty of traumatic memory, which "can be grasped only in the very inaccessibility of its occurrence" and which is in fact defined by its fundamental opposition *to* memory.[21] Roseanne protests, "I have to be very careful with these 'memories' because I realise there are a few vivid remembrances from this troubled time that I know in my heart cannot have happened" (234). As Garratt observes, in her memories "we see the difficulty for the trauma victim in attempting any reconstruction of the past."[22] Roseanne finds that her memory is compromised not only by the pressures of societal revision and selectivity but also, as in the cases of Veronica Hegarty and Max Morden, by the fractured nature of traumatic memory itself.

☼

Like the texts considered in the preceding chapters, *The Secret Scripture* considers how the act of writing becomes a vehicle both to reflect and to negotiate Roseanne's trauma. The novel traces parallel journal entries compiled sometime around 2007 not only by Roseanne but also by Dr. Grene: he is the approximately sixty-five-year-old head of the sanatorium to which Roseanne has been consigned for decades. Roseanne is secretly and self-consciously compiling her life story, which she does not share with anyone. Dr. Grene, for his part, simultaneously records his personal thoughts and his professional attempt to ferret out Roseanne's history in order to determine her mental state in advance of the impending destruction of the asylum and the patients' relocation to another, newer facility.

As the parallel stories evolve, the reader sees that both characters bear an uncanny resemblance in terms of the way they tell their stories, in their distrust of the reliability of their memories, and in a shared compulsion to seek some kind of emotional closure from past traumas through self-expression. By the text's end, when it is clear that Roseanne and, by extension, Dr. Grene have been victims of gross—and shared—injustice, the reader has attained not only a sense of the social mechanisms that brought them to this common fate but also an awareness that this story, so laboriously crafted, will never be entirely certain or complete.

Roseanne's emphasis on silence and her ambivalence over her own accuracy rather than on the *content* of her narration stresses the *act of narration* itself, which suggests that accuracy per se is not central here. Her narrative and its relation to the dominant narrative are also complicated by Dr. Grene's own storytelling: because Dr. Grene's process of narrative discovery happens in parallel to Roseanne's, the novel clearly privileges not one counternarrative but *two* occurring in tandem.[23] In addition, because Dr. Grene is a literal and figurative part of the architecture that contains Roseanne—the institution and the building itself—his narrative can hardly be considered straightforwardly recuperative. Grene's narrative seeks to retell Roseanne's even as he attempts to assemble his own. Rather than another attempt at appropriation or a "critical analysis" juxtaposed with her "traumatic narrative," however, Grene's tale represents an intermediary step in Roseanne's narrative as he seeks to piece together "her true story" from fragments and insinuations and from his own deductions based on the dominant narrative.[24] As he notes, "[Perhaps] she was being cagey because she feared me, or was even perhaps in dread of speaking. . . . Of course either way I know she has suffered enormously. . . . So perhaps there is a certain usefulness in *writing in this book*. And anyway, I would like in some way to find the heart and the thread of her story, as one might put it. Her *true history* or as much of it as can be salvaged" (121, my emphasis). This passage captures the complicated imbrication of narratives within the text: recognizing her avoidance, he still hopes to access her truth, and as he seeks her story, he is simultaneously penning hers and his own.

Grene's story is not just a retelling of Roseanne's; he also parallels her *in practice* by writing out his sorrow over his lost wife and his infidelities as well as over his lost brother. Grene's narrative about betraying his wife, Bet, for example, parallels Roseanne's self-reproach for having gone to meet John Lavelle: just as Roseanne asks, "Why did I go up to Maeve's cairn that very Sunday following [to meet Lavelle]?" Grene asks, "Why did I have to betray [Bet] in Bundoran of all places?" (176, 177). His narrative re-creation of the painful memory of his brother's death also reflects a similar narrative of repression, loss, and self-reproach:

> I am astounded to read back over what I just wrote. I have made an anecdote out of the tragic death of my brother, for which, as is clear to me from the cooled syntax, I obviously blame myself. . . . I never discussed this. . . . It is a scandal in the halls of myself. I see that,

> clearly, staring at the bare facts. But how on earth would I . . . ever heal myself? . . . I am clearly content to be beyond help. It is disgusting. I am not only crying now, . . . but trembling also. (182–83)

Finally, Grene's narrative, like Roseanne's, is marked by uncertainty and confusion. As illustrated earlier, Grene apparently was unaware of his own sense of guilt until he wrote it, and he questions both his memory and his contemporary motives, noting, "I must interrogate my own motives now in everything" (184). Grene's process of narrativizing his own life thus weaves into and overlaps with Roseanne's process, complicating our ability to isolate or prioritize her account of herself.

This sense of parallel is heightened structurally throughout the novel. Although Dr. Grene does not know for most of the narrative that he is Roseanne's son, there are clear ironic indicators present throughout that this convergence is coming. Tellingly, that convergence is grounded in the language of history and narrative. Roseanne notes that "a person without anecdotes . . . [is] more likely to be utterly lost not only to history but the family following them" (11); Dr. Grene, in his turn, observes unwittingly that Mrs. McNulty "is rather a touchstone for me. She has been a fixture, and not only represents the institution, but also, in a curious way, my own history, my own life" (16). Dr. Grene's sense of Roseanne's centrality thus retroactively reinforces her claim, as her act of writing provides her a place in history and family at once. Similarly, Roseanne supposes "it is odd that I am trying to write out my useless life here, and resisting most of his questions," while admitting, "Maybe the truth is, I am writing it for him, as he is really the only person I know, in any full sense of the word" (126), even when she is not aware that indeed she writes for and to her own progeny. Of course, this sense of parallel also echoes the sense of generational impact of trauma that we saw in *The Gathering*.

Most importantly, Dr. Grene's narrative revelations parallel Roseanne's by improbably using the same language. Just as Roseanne refers to her story as written on "unwanted paper," Dr. Grene suggests he lacks an audience: "Whose sleeve do I have to grip, to tell my story to?"

(47). Roseanne protests that she has "not looked in a mirror for about fifteen years" (138)—an aversion Dr. Grene also expresses when he notes that he had not looked in the mirror "in many years," observing, "I had glanced every morning in the mirror, . . . but had not *looked* in it at myself" (116, emphasis in original). His sense that he has a "slightness as a person, as a soul, [but that] keeping this book has somehow helped me" (89) parallels Roseanne's desire to leave what she calls "a history" of herself, however "brittle and honest-minded" (5). Roseanne describes herself as an "old, old woman now, . . . a scraggy stretch of skin," who nonetheless has "a story" (4); Grene refers to her as "Old lady. The cailleach of the stories. So ancient, and yet, one of those faces that is so thin" (118). The reference to Roseanne as the "cailleach" not only evokes the idea of Roseanne as older woman but also highlights metanarratively her role as a character in a story and the supernatural imagery that subsequent religious language invokes.[25] I return to these points later, but the parallels between the two narratives in both style and content are unmistakable.

The improbable parallelism of Roseanne's and Dr. Grene's stories thus functions not only at the level of the characters' stories, as both seek catharsis and self-discovery through telling, but also at the level of narrative, language use, and uncertainty with memory. One might note as an example of this self-conscious engagement with authorship a moment late in the text when an unlikely convergence of unreliable memories occurs, again pertaining, perhaps not surprisingly, to the hammer and feathers. As we have seen, Dr. Grene records that before Roseanne's father was beaten with hammers, his mouth was "stuffed with white feathers no doubt to characterise his former work" (180) as a police informant. Later, however, Dr. Grene realizes that he himself added this detail about the feathers: "I find to my absolute astonishment and even shame that in his [Father Gaunt's] account of the events in the tower, he doesn't actually say Roseanne's father's mouth was stuffed with feathers, just that he was beaten by hammers. . . . [M]y own brain must have supplied this detail, stealing it from Roseanne I would like to think, except at that point of course *I hadn't read her account* [yet]" (279–80, emphasis in original).

In the meditation that follows, Dr. Grene acknowledges the uncertainty of memory in the versions of Roseanne's history that he reads and hears: "I believe [both Roseanne and Father Gaunt] have written not so much wrongful histories, or even competing histories, but both in their human way quite truthful, and that from both of them can be implied *useful truths above and beyond the actual veracity of the 'facts.'* I am beginning to think there is no factual truth" (280, my emphasis). Like Roseanne, Dr. Grene here admits not only his own fallibility but also the historical devaluation—and perhaps even irrelevance—of actual truth in storytelling. Thus, the parallels between Dr. Grene's narrative and Roseanne's narrative occur on multiple levels—word choice, self-revelation, process of writing, recording of trauma, and uncertainty of memories—culminating in this moment when their stories literally blur into one another and reject the need for strict accuracy in narrative.

This very parallelism and convergence are often considered the greatest weakness of *The Secret Scripture.* Harney-Mahajan notes that the ending of *The Secret Scripture* was generally found to be both "melodramatic and implausible" and that "almost no one liked the ending."[26] Not only do Roseanne's and Dr. Grene's two stories merge into one, but Dr. Grene also learns that Roseanne is the mother who gave him up for adoption (or, more properly, from whom he was stolen by Roseanne's in-laws and Father Gaunt). In general, the improbability of this narrative and of its parallel presentation strikes some readers as contrived or too neat.

I would suggest, however, that this conclusion should be read against the overarching role of trauma and narrative remediation that the novel champions. As the examples of parallel narrative given earlier suggest, both Roseanne and Dr. Grene are engaged in a symbiotic and therefore highly improbable process of narrative reconstruction and remediation. Yet both characters are very aware of the act of telling in which they engage, and they are equally aware that this act involves a degree of craft and authoring. Both address a "reader"—but neither specifies to whom she or he speaks. Roseanne says, "Dear reader! Dear reader, if you are gentle and good, I wish I could clasp your hand. . . . Although I do not have you, I have other things" (23). Similarly, Grene ironically says, "Oh, and I forgot to say (but to whom am I saying it?)" (254). Such reference to a "reader" stresses not only the character's awareness of the act of storytelling but also a metanarrative engagement with the act of narration itself.

Indeed, the use of the word *story* itself also recurs throughout the novel. Roseanne repeatedly refers to her "story," the story "no one even knows" she has (4), and she literalizes this occlusion by hiding the manuscript in the very fabric of the building that contains her, under a floorboard.[27] The word *story* occurs with relentless consistency not only in reference to Roseanne's process of narration but also in relation to the others involved in her past. Roseanne speaks of Eneas's "dark *story*," (134); the "*story*" of Joe Brady and "the huge *plot he had plotted* with Fr. Gaunt" (105); "the *epic story* of Jack" (134); "the presence of . . . unwashed *characters*" in Sligo" (128); and the "strange *chapters* of this country's bewildering *story*" (181, my emphases). For his part, Grene notes, "We are missing so many threads in *our story* that the tapestry of Irish life cannot but fall apart" (183, my emphasis). Again, the text is riddled not only with recognition of the nature of traumatic memory and its unreliability but also with a self-conscious reflection on the fictional nature of the text itself.[28]

Reading the conclusion of the novel in terms of this self-conscious engagement with narrative and narrativizing changes our understanding of the novel's ending. In many respects, its very improbability weaves together that "tapestry of life" that has been broken by Roseanne's fragmented and oppressed history. With both characters' histories merging, the denouement feels almost like magical realism: it is a fantasy fulfillment of the restoration of wholeness—a reunion of mother and son as well as a moment when the *craftedness* of the text in its entirety is thrust before the reader as evidence of the very process that the characters (and by extension, of course, Sebastian Barry) have pursued throughout the novel.

By intertwining Grene's and Roseanne's narratives, *The Secret Scripture* undercuts the claim that "the tapestry of Irish life cannot but fall apart" (183). What arises is not a unified, authoritative, and comprehensive narrative but rather a patchwork of meanings that, when presenced equally, is both legitimate and curative without necessarily even being assured truth. In addition, it is the process of storytelling itself that forges this communal, healing narrative. Like *Let the Great World Spin*, discussed in chapter 5, the novel thus generates a sense of hope and coherence from its disparate threads and by the very means of narration.

Roseanne testifies to the importance of such smaller, personal stories in speaking of her father: whereas he saw "a little gift of narrative," "little scraps of stories," as constituting "a ragged gospel," her mother was "singularly without stories" and thus unable to be saved (11). Similarly, Dr. Grene refers to Roseanne's records as a "little apocryphal gospel as may be" (120). Each of these descriptions focuses not on a grand counternarrative but rather on the ways that the act of telling even small personal truths or dubious apocryphal ones carries the authority of scripture, a kind of functional alternative that is both inclusive and healing to those who work toward its composition.[29]

Such personal narratives, the novel suggests, can also provide a necessary reminder of the need to question and interrogate dominant narratives in their exclusive claims to truth, but the question of truth itself is largely ancillary. The almost oxymoronic juxtaposition of "apocryphal" and "ragged" with "gospel" suggests that such narratives, whether tattered or even somewhat untrue, nonetheless carry an authority that is in its way nearly divine and that is clearly a route to at least some degree of emotional, post-traumatic salvation. As Dr. Grene notes of his mother's narrative, once he has at last found it, "What is wrong about her account if she sincerely believes it? Is not most history written in a sort of wayward sincerity? I suspect so" (278).

I thus suggest we read the ending of *The Secret Scripture* as an acknowledgment of a wished-for but in some respects unattainable happy ending, which nonetheless holds out hope for the future. On this note, it is perhaps telling that the novel ends without Dr. Grene's revelation to Roseanne that he is her son. This leaves the conclusion literally inconclusive. Grene recognizes his own role in the system that could have potentially destroyed his mother, a recognition that the reader might hope will lead to a cathartic apology and restoration: "Professional man though I am, I confess to feeling very sorry for her. And retrospectively, rather guilty" (275). However, when he learns she is his mother, he defers the revelation, despite his guilt: "I tried to tell her, there and then. But I hadn't the words. I will have to wait for the words" (291).[30]

Through its refusal to provide neat closure, the novel's ending exposes an awareness of the improbability of such completely cathartic and redemptive endings in practice—a reflection, perhaps, of the more moderate expectations typical of post–Celtic Tiger literature noted in the introduction. It also suggests that the generational story of Dr. Grene and his mother—and by extension of all those whom society had consigned to secrecy or invisibility—is not yet wholly written, just as Grene "hadn't the words." *The Secret Scripture* imagines a restoration of a familial and, on another level, societal wholeness to Irish society through the process of telling, but the deferral of that happy ending suggests such a resolution is yet to be attained through the compilation and combination of fragile, individual narratives and "surmises," the threads of which will weave the tapestry of the whole. Most importantly, this assessment is driven by the *representation* of trauma and a self-conscious engagement with the act of narration itself.

The novel's awareness of its own wish fulfillment thus directly counters the suggestion that a naive happy ending or for that matter a simple and complete narrative is possible after a long history of omissions and silences. Nonetheless, the text does offer an alternative to the horrifying and paralyzing silences that previously marked its characters' lives. It also suggests that no one is untouched by the lives of women like Roseanne: Dr. Grene subconsciously knows Roseanne's story not because it is true or because he is psychic but because, as John Banville pointed out in his *New York Times* op-ed in 2009,[31] on some level all of Ireland *always* knew the story of these women—its "lost women"—but did not acknowledge that narrative or hear their stories. The novel thus presences such stories without stressing authenticity or "truthfulness." It is the act of acknowledgment itself that is potentially healing at the personal and communal levels; it is the act of creating a space for such silences to be broken that offers hope.

Ultimately, *The Secret Scripture* recognizes but complicates the contest for authority over life narratives between occluded histories and dominant narratives, the unreliability of traumatic memory as a consequence of self-protection and suffering, and the ways in which individual lives in Ireland are touched by such stories, directly and indirectly, consciously or unconsciously, through the very fabric of Irish society. The self-consciousness with which both Roseanne and Dr. Grene enact storytelling represents in some respects the trauma victim's need to *testify*, for, as Dori Laub notes, "the testimony is . . . the process by which the narrator (the survivor) reclaims his position as a witness: reconstitutes the internal 'thou,' and thus [claims] the possibility of a witness or a listener inside himself."[32]

The reliability of those memories is ultimately irrelevant to the value of the act of narration, just as the wished-for happy ending and total closure—which *The Secret Scripture* tellingly defers—is in reality unlikely to be achieved. The metanarrative awareness with which such a fairy tale ending is created rejects that possibility outright. Instead, it is through the acts of creation of witnessing and of authoring and sharing one's own history, as best one can organize and comprehend it, that a "ragged gospel" like Roseanne's can receive the respect and reverence owed it both by survivors of trauma and those who, as a society, have witnessed and shared it. In that respect, such a story, whatever its potential inaccuracies, does form a kind of "gospel truth" (216). In the interweaving and foregrounding of story over "truth," *The Secret Scripture* not only reflects on the curative powers of narrating trauma but also enacts the process of social acknowledgment and sharing that can move both societies and individuals forward from a silent and unspoken past. In the next chapter, on Emma Donoghue's *Room*, I consider how the stories that survivors sometimes tell to survive may subsequently need to shift to enable the process of recovery.

4

"Stories Are a Different Kind of True"

Narrative and the Space of Recovery in Emma Donoghue's Room

In *The Secret Scripture*, Roseanne Clear McNulty observes that at times one might "hold up a wall made of imaginary bricks and mortar against the horrors and cruel, dark tricks of time."[1] While that novel challenges us to consider the role of what is "true" in narrating a traumatic history, it also, as we have seen, gestures toward the stories people tell in order to survive a traumatic past or present or both. Emma Donoghue's painful and beautiful novel *Room* (2010) expands on this question by focusing on the ways in which the stories we tell must adapt to the reality of our (sometimes changing) situation. Pondering such questions from within the framework of its post–Celtic Tiger moment, Donoghue's novel juxtaposes the coping narratives employed within a traumatic situation to those subsequently employed without.

I focus here as much on what happens within "Room" as a negotiated traumatic space as on how that negotiation inflects Jack and Ma's reentry into the world once they leave Room. Both moving and experientially suffocating, the novel simultaneously represents a fantasy zone of coping forged by Ma and a re-creation of that zone narratively through its young narrator's observations. Ma's story rehabilitates for Jack what is, by any other account, a space of trauma and highlights how the narrative appropriation of traumatic space can be a coping strategy. Although recognizing the trauma written on Jack's young body, *Room* also captures the cost such strategies inflict on mother and child alike as they eventually must seek to revise the temporary and heavily conditioned readings in which they were so long protectively cocooned. The novel also offers a timely metanarrative critique of how this constructed narrative compares to contemporary social realities.

This analysis thus focuses not only on the novel's representation of the imaginative recourse available to victims of trauma but also on the metaphorical valences of Room as both emotional and psychological space. As is true for many victims of trauma, Ma's survival depends on the story she tells to herself and to Jack, which enables her to enter what one study calls "a phase of adaptation in which captives resort to a number of coping strategies."[2] Upon their release from captivity, Jack and his mother's challenge is to reconcile narratives of traumatic memory with the protective counternarrative Ma forged of and in the traumatic space of their confinement. For Jack, however, there is no conditioning history of trauma, for their recuperated traumatic space is all he has ever known. As a result, Ma's unraveling of a coping narrative from within Room necessarily involves rewriting Jack's narrative of an essentially happy childhood to mesh with the darker reality that shaped his life.

Room follows the experiences of a five-year-old child, Jack, and his mother, identified only as "Ma." Unbeknownst to Jack for half the novel, he and Ma live in captivity in a small, eleven-foot-square shed on the property of an older man, Ma's abductor, whom they call "Old Nick." This is the space in which Jack was born and that he knows intimately as "Room." Indeed, it is the only space he has ever known—until they effect a daring escape. For the rest of the novel, Jack and Ma struggle in different ways to reintegrate into society and a wider social network as well as to reimagine their own relationship in a broader and in some ways ironically more constricting world.

Room begins on Jack's fifth birthday, and for most of the first half of the text we watch as his days proceed through the strictly crafted routines not uncommon in childhood. We follow him as he eats and dresses; we see him watch television, monitored carefully by his mother under the proviso that too much TV "rots our brains."[3] We accompany him as he engages in imaginative play with cardboard boxes and eggshells, books and crayons. Most of all, we recognize the highly regulated nature of his day: for example, he notes, "It's 05:39 so we can have dinner" (33); "It's 12:13, so it can be lunch" (16); and "Monday is a laundry day" (39). In many respects, Jack's day proceeds in accord with the natural rhythms of childhood, complete with exercise, *Dora the Explorer*, naps, storybooks, and cuddle time with his mother.

Through Jack's naive and childlike narration, however, the reader quickly recognizes that only Ma's ingenuity provides these elements of safety, security, and imaginative play in an environment of sensory and material deprivation. She learns how to make paste from flour; she makes a "mobile from a long spaghetti and threads tied with things pasted on" (81). Cereal boxes become toys to make an "Ancient Egyptian Pyramid," which can be recycled to make a ruler (19). Ma makes beach balls out of pages of used paper (30), and they play "Telephone with toilet rolls" (56). Toilet paper itself becomes a toy: "good," as Jack notes, "for a drawing that goes on forever." But when he is "all done [he rolls] it again so [they] can use it" (40). In short, Ma spends almost every waking hour finding ways to entertain, teach, and imaginatively enrich her son despite the lack of toys, educational resources, and options in their space of confinement.

What passes for routine to Jack also embodies practical survival strategies for his mother—strategies crafted to be unthreatening and one might even say "normal." Thus, in Jack's innocent counting practices we see that his mother is rationing food to ensure sufficient sustenance between deliveries: "I count one hundred cereal" (6). Similarly, while Jack receives his mother's admonition about germs and cleanliness the way any child might on being told to clean his room, the reader understands Ma's underlying terror at the idea of sickness and germs. She warns that "germs could make you die" (4), fears spiders as "dirty" (8), and wards against mice, lest they come "stealing . . . food, bringing in germs on their filthy paws" (32). Ma introduces an exercise regimen within their cramped confines, having Jack do "Phys Ed" on a "Track" which she forms by stacking their furniture (15). Her obsession with health and cleanliness, guarding against infection and disease, makes sense in an environment where access to health care is severely restricted. Jack's observation one day that he and Ma "have a pretty busy morning" (39) signals how effectively she manages to create a healthy life and a sense of normalcy for her son in captivity, ameliorating the consequences of confinement as best she can.

Perhaps most importantly, Ma incorporates a variety of activities into Room that Jack understands simply as additional tasks but that the reader recognizes as ways that she continues to seek the means for escape. During one night, Jack notes, "Ma [is] standing beside Lamp and everything bright, then *snap* and dark again. Light again, she makes it last three seconds then dark, then light for just a second" (27, emphasis in original). Jack relays his experience of "play[ing] Keypad," where he stands on a chair and Ma tells him numbers to enter. "I press them on Keypad quick quick no mistakes" (57). Although the numbers "don't make Door beep open," Jack enjoys "the little clicks" when he pushes the button, receiving the practice as a game. Similarly, integrated among his list of daily activities is simply "Scream," which bears quoting at length:

> After nap we do Scream every day but not Saturdays or Sundays. We clear our throats and climb up on Table to be nearer Skylight, holding hands not to fall. We say "On your mark, get set, go," then we open wide our teeth and shout holler howl yowl shriek screech scream the loudest possible. . . . Then we shush with fingers on lips. I asked Ma once what we're listening for and she said just in case, you never know. (40)

It is evident here that through her flashing lights, the keypad combinations, and their cries, Ma is trying to get the attention of the outside world (except on the weekend, when Old Nick is presumably around) and to find the means to escape. Ma's ability to normalize her surroundings for Jack, who accepts these activities unquestioningly as games, recasts captivity as "play," thus giving him a chance to have at least a kind of childhood.

Although Ma's desire to create as normal a life as possible for Jack is to be expected, her actions cannot be read outside the interpretive field in which the story is set and thus bear, too, on her own psychological needs and responses to trauma. When in captivity, victims are subject to particular psychological forces that condition them to respond in certain predictable ways. As Judith Herman notes, "The psychology of the victim is shaped by the actions and beliefs of the perpetrator."[4] Accordingly, Ma is forced to accommodate Old Nick's whims and demands because doing so is literally an issue of life or death. Ma recognizes that she must not anger or upset Nick, which she explains to Jack when their electricity is cut as punishment: "It's my fault, I made him mad. . . . He can't stand it when I start screaming, I haven't done it in years" (79).[5] The need to be responsive to her captor is typical of such situations: as Anne Speckhard and her colleagues explain, "During any period of forced captivity, a captive suddenly finds that his will falls under the control of his captor, that he must control his emotions and that indeed his behavior must resemble, if not become, an act of submission."[6] *Room* vividly captures that element of captivity.

Ma's compliance with Old Nick is also conditioned by his expectations and demands for appreciation, despite his role as kidnapper. For example, when he clears the skylight, he expects her gratitude, mockingly complaining, "I'm just the grocery boy, take out your trash, trek around the kidswear aisles, up the ladder to deice [*sic*] your skylight, at your service ma'am." Ma, going along, replies, "Sorry. Thanks a lot" (36). As Herman notes, for a perpetrator such as Old Nick, "simple compliance rarely satisfies him; he appears to have a psychological need to justify his crimes, and for this he needs the victim's affirmation. Thus he relentlessly demands from his victim professions of respect, gratitude, or even love."[7] Nick's insinuation that he is somehow doing Ma a favor exemplifies this pattern. When Jack, learning all too well from his mother, asks her if they shouldn't thank Nick for bringing them necessities, Ma's sense of coercion is clear: "Why should we thank him?" she asks, later noting of her expression of gratitude, "It was a fake thank" (45).

Jack's birth, in some respects, serves as a liberating variable for Ma both imaginatively and emotionally. Having Jack mitigates Ma's sense of isolation because "as long as the victim maintains any other human connection, the perpetrator's power is limited."[8] Like a refocusing of attention onto "basic needs," which Ma clearly performs, "attachment" is one of the primary means by which captives self-sooth.[9] Thus, her ability to refocus on another person and on a child's basic needs is doubly compensatory for Ma.

As a result of their bond, Ma is able to create a fantasy space in captivity through narrative not only for herself but also for Jack by employing what George Orwell referred to as "doublethink": "The [person] knows in which direction his memories must be altered; he therefore knows that he is playing tricks with reality; but by the exercise of *doublethink* he also satisfies himself that reality is not violated."[10] It is through this process that Ma is able to construct the alternate world called "Room"—one that is self-contained, "real," whereas the Outside World is unreal and separated by a boundary that cannot be readily crossed, like the boundary between the atmosphere and outer space. Obviously, Ma does know there is an outside—and her separated construction begins to crumble as the sense of imminent threat from Old Nick wears away at her habituated responses, as we shall see. Nonetheless, the totalizing narrative in which Jack is immersed shows that his mother, too, has participated in this fiction, to a degree, through doublethink.

Jack has a highly elaborate sense of what is real and unreal: "Ships are just TV and so is the sea except when . . . our letters arrive. Or maybe they actually stop being real the minute they get there? . . . Forests are TV and also jungles and deserts and streets and skyscrapers and cars. Animals are TV except ants and Spider and Mouse, but he's gone back now" (54). He also differentiates himself and Ma from people on TV, noting that "the word for us was real. The persons in TV are made just of colors" (13). Ma narrates Room as a world constrained by a boundary that is permeable when necessary, such as to procure food or to explain away certain appearances and disappearances. This narration protects Jack, so he does not feel the impact of all he is missing, but it is also potentially what allows Ma to effect the kind of emotional constriction common to captives, who "develop the capacity voluntarily to restrict and suppress their thoughts" and to "exist simultaneously in two realities."[11] As Ma wisely tells Jack, "Stories are a different kind of true" (71).

Ma's ability to deny her reality also allows her to protect Jack imaginatively from her abuser. She implies to her son that Nick himself is a thing of nightmare, calling him "Old Nick" (a.k.a. the devil)—after "a cartoon about a guy that comes in the night" (12). (That "Nick" is not her captor's real name is confirmed when the police later acknowledge that the "owner's name doesn't match" [152].) Jack in turn actually doubts the reality of Nick, worrying that Nick might nurse from Ma and that "if he had some [milk] he might start getting realer" (47). Ultimately, then, the story Ma tells Jack about Room is a vehicle to craft an intelligible (if fictive) and less-threatening frame of normalcy for Jack, even as it also signals the workings of her own narrative coping mechanisms in captivity.

It is thus unsurprising that the narrative of Room begins to unravel for Ma—and thus for Jack—when her fragile illusion of safety begins to collapse. Ma has hidden Jack in Wardrobe during Nick's nighttime visits to assault her; as she tells Jack, "I just don't want him looking at you" (26). For his part, Jack knows that "the rule is, stay in Wardrobe till Ma comes for [him]" (73).

Two incidents shatter Ma's ability to believe in the fragile safety she has imagined in Room. In the first, Jack remotely moves the toy Jeep that Nick brought him for his birthday: it falls on Nick's head, and he chokes Ma in response, leaving what Jack uneasily observes are "marks" on her neck. As Ma explains, "He thought I was attacking him, dropping something heavy on his head" (53–54). This violence against Ma fractures her ability to maintain the illusion of normalcy: she complains that she "can't stand" reading one of their few books yet again, and "Scream goes on for ages because every time [Jack is] starting to stop Ma screeches more . . . her voice is nearly disappearing" (55–56). We see the weakening of Ma's ability to maintain her coping narrative when she tells Jack, "What we see on TV is . . . it's pictures of *real* things" (59, my emphasis). This statement violates the narrative integrity of the story that has shaped and driven Jack's life.

The second incident is when Nick sees Jack, and Ma shrieks, "Get away, get away from him!" (74). In retaliation, Nick cuts off their electric power, but Ma responds by beginning to engage narratives of past and family that she has until now carefully edited out. For captives, often "the past, like the future, becomes too painful to bear, for memory, like hope, brings back the yearning for all that has been lost."[12] Thus, shortly after this incident, Ma starts to tell Jack about her own history—that Nick "made" Room; that she had her own childhood, complete with mother and father; that she has a brother; and that "Room's only a tiny stinky piece" of the "real world" (81–84). This narrative understandably confuses Jack, who incredulously thinks that this history is "ridiculous, [because] Ma was never in Outside" and "Room just is" (83, 81). In contrast, in openly acknowledging that Room is not the whole story, as it were, Ma knows that she is engaging in an act of revision for herself and for Jack. As she tells him, "You have to let me tell this story" (94). Of course, as we saw in *The Secret Scripture*, such statements highlight not only the fiction Ma has woven but also the fictive nature and representative act of the novel *Room* itself, which metanarratively highlights the act of storytelling.

No longer able to maintain the illusions and story that have protected them for so long, Ma is thus catalyzed both to confront the true narrative of her trauma and to bring Jack into it as best she can (a process, not incidentally, that she calls "unlying"). By relaying to Jack the narrative of her past, her abduction, and even her prior efforts to escape, Ma breaks the fictive representation of safety and prepares Jack for the attempt to escape: "I figure it out," Jack says, "why Ma's telling me the terrible story" (97).

When Ma and Jack do at last successfully escape—a plan, interestingly, that is predicated on Jack remembering the story they will tell Nick to deceive him: "*Sick, Truck, Hospital, Police, Save Ma*" (112, emphasis in original)—both must face the consequences of the new narrative they now need to inhabit. In particular, this process involves Ma successfully helping Jack to understand what is and is not real and establishing a separate identity for the boy. At the same time, it requires that Jack engage Ma's history in a way that has never been accessible for him, which exposes the interpretive distance between their respective understandings of Room. Whereas Ma's engagement with her traumatic past serves as a kind of reclamatory narrativizing, Jack's engagement with it is different; he must come to terms with a traumatic past that was formerly unacknowledged by destabilizing what had been problematically normalized for him—and in a social context that, the novel suggests, is itself potentially problematic.

Within Room, as we have seen, Jack believes that only he and Ma are "real"—even Nick, the only other person he has seen, is debatably imaginary for Jack. As one scholar notes, "Jack's consciousness transforms his experiences into an uncanny universe in which boundaries between the real and the unreal become dangerously blurred."[13] Jack also must learn to differentiate himself from Ma. The conflation between them has always been at play in Room, no doubt in part because of Ma's need for Jack as an attachment but also because of her determination not to admit any claim by Nick on Jack.[14] Ma has told Jack he is "made of [her], like [her] spit is" (7), and Jack thinks that he and Ma are the same: he believes that "in books and TV all persons have things that belong just to them, it's complicated" (33), but he sees himself and Ma as a cohesive unit, so that "it's weird to have something that's mine-not-Ma's" (10).[15] Jack struggles to understand Ma as a separate entity: he doesn't like when Ma is "on" at the same time he is "off" (5) and feels uneasy at the idea that both Nick and Ma might be asleep when he is "on" (47).[16]

Finally, Jack think he "belongs to" Ma (10, 76, 209), and he comforts himself when away from her by telling himself he is "a bit of Ma" (137). Jack even develops an unnatural attachment to Ma's dead tooth, which he considers "a little bit of Ma's dead spit" (137). Indeed, in many ways his view of this tooth reflects his understanding of himself; he considers both himself and the tooth to be made of her "spit," and he sees separation from Ma as deadening for himself and the tooth alike: "He was a part of her a minute ago but now he's not. Just a thing" (70). Jack's tendency to carry Ma's dead tooth in his mouth, grotesque though it may be, reflects his inability to differentiate from her and his sense of physical and existential continuity with her.

Mary Grace Elliott has argued, I think rightly, that the extreme attachment between Ma and Jack is reflective of their delayed development out of the Mirror Stage.[17] As she argues, "In Room, Ma and Jack were one another's everything—they were, as Jack put it, 'Ma and me,' a cohesive unit, never separated from one another (170). After leaving Room, Ma begins to rediscover herself."[18] Ma's process of rewriting her own story involves editing her narrative—learning, as she tells Jack, to know herself again not only as "Ma" but also as her own distinct person. As she acknowledges, "I know you need me to be your ma but I'm having to remember how to be me as well at the same time" (221). Elliott argues, "With the onset of motherhood, Ma, in her captivity, gladly yields the split off part of herself in order to protect her child. . . . What is truly difficult for Ma is discovering the duality of her person five years into motherhood."[19]

This process of self-evolution requires that Ma continue to revise the temporary narrative that insulated her in captivity. Once freed, she thus continues the process of revision she began in Room prior to their escape. She tells Jack about the birth of his stillborn sister, responding to his aversion, "Let me finish [this story]" (204). She reflects on the need Jack filled for her in captivity, recognizing that having basic needs met are "no good if you don't have somebody to love as well," but her narrative about the importance of mother love frightens Jack, who calls it "a bad story" (221).

Ma's need to revisit and revise her story by integrating those parts she formerly had to cordon off reflects her attempt to regain mastery of her narrative and to scale her time in Room against the wider story of her life. As Dominick LaCapra explains, "When the past becomes accessible to recall in memory, and when language functions to provide some measure of conscious control, critical distance, and perspective, one has begun the arduous process of working over and through the trauma in a fashion that may never bring full transcendence . . . but which may enable processes of judgment and at least limited liability and ethically responsible agency."[20] This process is critical to trauma victims' movement from victim to survivor.

Such movement, however, is not possible for Jack in the same way, and this narrative divergence complicates the already difficult evolution both face in trying to differentiate from one another. Jack and Ma struggle to reconcile their competing histories and interpretive frames of Room. Once Ma begins to deconstruct the narrative coping strategy she employed in and for Room, maintained for seven years through "doublethink," she can no longer sustain the nurturing illusion of safety and "home" that insulated Jack and, arguably, herself. Yet because for him—unlike for Ma—Room is the only reality he has ever known, Jack's awareness of and then emergence into the outside world are disruptive and confusing. Jack doesn't like that Ma has different names—"I don't like her to have other names that I never even knowed" (117). Similarly, he does not like the idea that there are other Jacks in the world, grumbling, "I don't want to share my name" (117). This broadening of their connection and of his understanding of his place in the world is clearly a struggle.

Even more importantly, Jack has trouble scaling his grasp of reality to the larger world abstractly, which effectively leads him to have an existential crisis. While still in Room, he wonders, "We're the only ones [not in Outside]. Are we still real?" (71), and, alternatively, "I'm not in Room. Am I still me?" (138). Jack even asks, "Is Room still there when we're not in it?" (171).

In many respects, of course, the answer to these questions for Jack is "no." No longer uniquely Jack or the only other person in Ma's world, Jack also needs to recalibrate his understanding of himself as well as of his place in the wider reality. As Kinga Földváry notes, "Jack's sense of uniqueness, both of himself and of the phenomena of the universe, is shattered in the moment of contact with the outside world."[21] In the same way, "Room" is not Room once they are not in it, for the fiction his mother protectively created collapses upon their release. Thus, when they are rescued and Ma says, "Oh, Jack . . . we're never going back," her euphoria contrasts with his desolation: "I'm crying so much I can't stop" (155). For Jack, reality truly is altered: what for Ma is a temporary modification of her life history is, for Jack, a revision of his whole life story.

Perhaps not surprisingly, Ma's recovery is thus complicated by her impatience at Jack's inability to share in her loathing of Room. As indicated earlier, Ma refers to Room as a "tiny stinky piece" of the "real world" (84). When a nurse asks Jack if he isn't "homesick," Ma's anger is instantaneous and visceral: "It wasn't a *home*, it was a soundproofed cell" (207, emphasis in original).[22] Ma also recoils from any marker of her time in Room, refusing to indulge her mother's curiosity. As Laura Moss notes, her control of that narrative shows her growing empowerment: "As a patient who resists, Ma maintains tight control over her narrative. Within the novel, she refuses to have her story be viewed as a paradigmatic case of sexual abuse, confinement, and violence. . . . The extended interview scene . . . raises the question of . . . how to witness a painful story."[23] As a corollary to this desire for control, of course, Ma finds Jack's longing for Room intolerable. When Jack asks her whether they are locked into the hospital Room, she "nearly barks . . . Why, are you not liking it here?" (191). Her need to separate from Jack and to rewrite the terms of their relationship outside Room culminates in an encounter where she inadvertently pushes him away too forcefully, telling him, "Get off me" (230), and causing him to fall and hurt himself. Ma's struggle to relearn and reclaim her own identity, even as she seeks individually to reconcile her trauma with her larger life narrative, is complicated by Jack's resistance to her interpretive frame.

Of course, all of this stands in stark contrast to Jack's understanding and interpretation of Room. Whereas Ma's past includes all of her history, pre- and post-abduction, Jack's entire life has been spent in Room, so that space is for him not cathected with any feelings of sadness, loss, or pain in the same way. When Ma redefines Room as a "cell," Jack asks himself, "If Room wasn't our home, does that mean we don't have one?" (207). Similarly, lacking Ma's sense of imprisonment and restriction, Jack cannot understand her aversion: "We have to be in the world, we're not ever going back to Room, Ma says that's how it is and I should be glad. I don't know why we can't go back just to sleep even" (190). Ultimately, Room was the world Jack knew and could negotiate. Whereas Ma seeks to evade memories of her confinement, as we have seen, Jack continues to insist that "in Room I was safe and Outside is the scary" (219). He is confused and perhaps bitter over Ma's view of Room: "She says *remember* but she doesn't want to remember Room" (305, emphasis in original). For Jack, Room is a space of childhood: Ma's need to reclaim the space as brutal directly—and inevitably somewhat ruthlessly—undermines his life experience as one of security, safety, and comfort.[24]

Finally, for Jack, the objects in Room have constituted his childhood playmates and companions, and this understanding, too, poses a conflict between Ma and Jack's respective coping processes. As Dominique Hétu observes, Jack "behave[s] with objects as if these objects were alive and could allow [him] to live differently."[25] What are markers of a traumatic past to Ma are personified companions to Jack, carrying different historical meanings for him than they do for her. The space Room occupies for each of them—in their pasts, in their memories, in the narrative of their lives, and in their present—is fundamentally not the same.

Given Jack's relationship to things in the novel, critics often focus on his role as a child, reading him as a symbol of the "posthuman" and a reflection on "nonhuman relationality."[26] Such readings tend to concentrate on Jack's relationship to objects not only within Room before his escape but also outside Room afterward. His responses to the wider world and the objects in Room, whether seen as symptoms of "fears and anxieties contemporary European society feels about the future" or of his emplacement in "a largely hyperreal world,"[27] can be read in broadly philosophical terms.[28]

As we have seen throughout this study, however, novels written in the post–Celtic Tiger period are inflected not only by a sober-minded willingness to interrogate the past but also by a desire to confront directly the materialism and excesses of that era. Thus, Mary McGlynn notes that such novels offer "an explicit confrontation of the excesses shaping the crisis" and that, in particular, "women's fiction is frequently concerned with domestic space."[29] Against this backdrop, it is interesting to reconsider the role of "things" in the text and the manner in which the narrative construction of Room and of Jack's life shifts under the cold glare of post-Room society.

As others have noted, the markings of trauma written on Jack do not become evident until he emerges from Room: "the boy's small stature, which has been caused by malnutrition, and . . . deathly jail-pallor, a result of a seven-year-long deprivation of sunlight," mark the physical impact of trauma that neither Ma's narrative nor the novel's accommodated during their confinement.[30] As in the other texts discussed in this study, the subsequent descriptions of Jack as an embodied subject reflects the author's awareness of the somatic element of trauma as well as a self-conscious engagement with that act of traumatic representation.

Despite the self-deception and the dawning awareness of harm that these physical manifestations capture, however, *Room* also provides an alternate narrative that is, in some respects, strangely superior to the one Jack and Ma encounter on the outside. For example, despite their prior deprivation, only *outside* Room do questions of possession and want arise, as when Jack mistakes a copy of Dylan the Digger for his own (246). The novel implicitly contrasts the past Ma lived as a typical teenager, with "walls [that] were covered in posters, . . . a giant fan and a dreamcatcher" (255), with the sense of material lack but emotional and imaginative depth Jack enjoyed in Room. Finally, Jack's grandmother marvels at the idea that Jack could even have a childhood at all in the midst of such lack: "Grandma's staring at me again. 'Growing up without LEGO,' she tells [her husband] Steppa, 'I literally can't imagine it'" (273). Most importantly, of course, by having Ma agree to an interview—because "it's for Jack's college fund" (230)—the novel highlights the subordination of her revised, empowering life narrative to material societal demands rather than to the case for survival that her narrative in Room represented.

In this respect, even as the novel explores the very personal traumatic narrative that Ma and Jack must navigate, it also interrogates wider social narratives and their influence on Ma's attempts to control her own story. Jack's fictive reality of friendly "Things" in Room contrasts favorably to the realities of the coldly materialistic, acquisitional society they encounter on the Outside—an ironic juxtaposition that pointedly critiques the Celtic Tiger ethos of greed. Like *The Gathering*, *Room* thus positions its characters' narrative negotiations against the wider backdrop of a critiqued materialistic social milieu.

☼

As a result of their differing relationships to their traumatic past, Ma needs to reappropriate Room narratively as a space of suffering and deprivation and struggles to do so both personally and under the weight of social pressure, whereas Jack possesses neither the history nor the experience to engage this narrative of trauma, either personally or socially. Ma and Jack thus pursue parallel but disparate paths to recovery. It seems telling that the traumatic details of Ma's experience are incorporated only marginally within the narrative, as she speaks to Dr. Clay in the background or writes in her notebook—none of which is accessible to us through Jack. This suggests that Ma's process of reintegration and recovery is simply not directly accessible—or even applicable—to Jack. Of course, all of this also occurs in the tellingly *unheimlich* space of the hospital, which comes across as more sterile and unattached than Room according to Jack's warm and familiar descriptions of Room. The hospital, like the hotel in *The Gathering*, thus marks a neutral space, uncathected with emotional content or attachments, in which Ma and Jack can engage their evolving narratives of trauma and recovery.

Ma and Jack's common path toward healing ultimately involves not only a renegotiation of their relationship but also a compromise regarding the meaning of their shared history and the interpretive space of Room, both as past and as a part of their wider present. Jack's evolving sense of separation from his mother is reflected when he observes to Dr. Clay, "Maybe I'm a human but I'm a me-and-Ma as well" (274). As they continue to try to differentiate, Ma stops nursing Jack and notes that she needs a space "that's just mine, sometimes," in their new apartment (304).

Importantly, Ma also ultimately tries to accommodate both Jack's understanding of the past and her own simultaneously. Although her need to differentiate from Jack and to protect her own interpretation of the past causes her to demand angrily, "If for once in your life you thought about me," when Jack asks for Rug (305), she does allow him to have it, recognizing it means something different for him: "Tell you what, you can keep it in your own room, but rolled up in the wardrobe. OK? I don't want to have to see it" (305). Ma even agrees to take him back to see the shed in which they were confined, noting, "Let's get this over with, Jack, because I am not coming back again" (317). Her willingness to do this for her son shows that she is adapting to his worldview—not allowing it to obliterate her own but accommodating the differing valence Room carried for him. Ma thereby enables their respective histories to run parallel but distinct paths of healing while still narrativizing their common past.

As importantly, upon their return to the shed, Jack shows that his interpretation and negotiation of Room have shifted. Absent his mother's recuperative coping narrative and all the items that made the space within the shed his home, Room has reverted to a place instead of a space cathected with meaning: Jack observes, "It's not Room now," and then admits, "It's like a crater, a hole where something happened" (320–21). Tacitly recognizing that "*space is a practiced place*,"[31] Jack thus acknowledges that Room has been hollowed of its meaning, which detaches the value of his childhood from the space of Room. Jack shows that he has altered his understanding and accommodated some revision to his past, even as Ma acknowledges the important and different meaning this historical space holds for Jack.

Like many twenty-first-century Irish novels, then, *Room* does not focus solely on trauma or simply on the process of "telling." It examines the need to narrativize a traumatic past and to integrate that past into one's personal narrative, and it presents the challenging task of letting go of a coping strategy that, although effective in the moment of trauma, becomes a hindrance in the outside world. That effort is troubled by narratives of materialism and desire, which arguably hail from the novel's post–Celtic Tiger context, reflecting how such "doublethink" narratives can ironically represent a fantasy space in more ways than one. By contrasting the deprivation of Room favorably to the "Outside," even while recognizing the physical imprints of trauma on Jack, the novel suggests that Ma's alternative narrative offers an ironically favorable, because fantastic, alternative to the "normal" world they now inhabit. This seems to imply that the Celtic Tiger ethos is itself an alternate narrative that must be overcome. Ma's ultimate negotiation of those pressures as well as her surrender of her coping narrative and eventual identification of Room as traumatic space empower her and enable her to move on.

Jack's process is different. Unaware that Room *was* a traumatic space, Jack must renegotiate the terms by which he reads and understands the world in the first place in order to recover. His renegotiation is thus a subtle representation of the challenging process that children must undertake when traumatic conditions are all they have known. As Földváry notes, the consequences of Ma and Jack's captivity come to light in the text only indirectly: "we are introduced to the more far-reaching consequences of their imprisonment: Jack's inability to orient himself in the physical world, . . . oversensitivity to sunshine, germs, noises and light and, most of all, human society."[32] Jack's negotiation of trauma means recognizing not that his trauma must be presenced but that there was trauma at all. This, in turn, means acknowledging that the person with whom he shared confinement and captivity cannot interpret their experience in the same way he does.

Ultimately, *Room* testifies to the ability of the human spirit to overcome trauma, and it represents the variable and highly individualized processes by which such negotiation and recovery take place. As Donoghue noted in an interview, "I always knew that it was going to be a story in two halves. I didn't want people to think: they're out; now there will be a happy ending, like *Alice in Wonderland.* I wanted Jack to discover himself as independent from his mother. And I wanted her to have all those moments when she longed for some separation from him."[33] Jack and Ma's disparate paths to recovery highlight not only the temporary nature and effectiveness of a short-term strategy for coping with trauma but also the highly conditioned and subjective nature of narrativizing that trauma in the aftermath.

Perhaps because "stories are a different kind of true," individuals who have experienced trauma require distinct, personalized narrative remedies to incorporate and ultimately integrate such experiences into their lives. Not unlike *The Secret Scripture*, then, *Room* also creates space for disparate, even competing stories. By focusing on Jack's narrative and presenting Ma's only indirectly, the narrative structure gestures toward such variability.

At the same time, although *Room* is not engaged directly with the kinds of national allegory one might identify, for example, in *The Gathering*, it enacts a similar sort of praxis and clearly engages its social moment. Suggesting the need for negotiation between differing interpretations, an inclusive understanding of history, and a willingness to confront the reality of a painful or contested past, *Room* shares with the other novels in this study a self-conscious engagement with the potentially curative power of narrative as well as the potential to signal solutions applicable at a wider, even national level. The novel also interrogates the material culture that so recently characterized Irish society, using the fantasy space of Room as an ironic juxtaposition to the accepted materialistic norms of Celtic Tiger society. The novel models a strategy to recover and heal not only from a traumatic past but sometimes also from the very coping mechanisms that were enabling in their historical moments. In *Let the Great World Spin*, in contrast, Colum McCann explores whether society itself can sometimes offer a vehicle for recovery rather than exacerbating a post-traumatic moment.

5

"Nothing Is Entirely by Itself"

Recovery, the Individual, and the Solace of Community in Colum McCann's Let the Great World Spin

> Each story is shifted sideways by each day that unfolds. Nothing ends.
>
> —Colum McCann, *Let the Great World Spin*

Colum McCann's novel *Let the Great World Spin* (2009) has been noted for its ambitious narrative scope and McCann's characteristic engagement with an ethos of empathy. As McCann related in an interview with Joseph Lennon in 2012, "The greatest thing about fiction is that we become alive in bodies not our own. If it isn't about empathy, then I don't know what it's about."[1] As a result, "empathetic engagements" have become what one critic calls "a driving force in his work."[2]

Perhaps of greatest interest in McCann's latest novels, however, is the representation of solace they offer in response to the experience of suffering and loss. Such solace is predicated on an understanding of community as inherently curative; the idea that no one life truly occurs in isolated, unique suffering; and trust in the world as a smaller and therefore more comforting place than it many times may seem. *Let the Great World Spin* depicts the comforting smallness of the world in its very largeness as well as the interconnectedness of people to emphasize our shared understandings of hope, loss, love, and pain.

Although using the microcosm that is New York City and the symbolically freighted site of the Twin Towers as its setting, the novel employs a specifically Irish literary tendency to narrativize trauma, even as it simultaneously displays what Eóin Flannery has identified as McCann's own "aesthetics of redemption." In his study by that name, Flannery convincingly argues that the novel is "an allegory on human suffering," which "showcases the longevity and the breadth of human suffering and resilience across races, classes and nationalities in New York City."[3] Far from capturing only the horror and loss of the events of September 11, 2001 (9/11), *Let the Great World Spin* also performs the tension of life's joy and pain: it offers comfort and solidarity transcending the individual and the nation without dismissing the relevance of either, thus suggesting the possibility for recovery even when facing the most traumatic catastrophe or loss.

As important and in keeping with the focus of this study, Flannery also notes that "if the question of empathy is crucial to understanding McCann's work, then the relationship between empathy and narrative is essential to any engagement with his fiction."[4] In this chapter, I thus want to examine the ways in which the novel emphasizes the more abstract nature of human suffering and healing over and above the cost of that specific day, but by stressing the very bodily reality of John Corrigan, an Irish priest. As character Gloria notes, "Everything in New York is built upon another thing, nothing is entirely by itself, each thing as strange as the last, and connected."[5] The novel's Yeatsian inversion in claiming "things don't fall apart" (325) reflects McCann's ultimate reassertion of hope in the midst of suffering and a dogged declaration of the cyclical nature of good and evil, hope and despair. That lofty claim is counterbalanced by his emphasis on the very physical reality of Corrigan's life, suffering, and premature death.

In addition, this sense of hope is as grounded in New York grittiness as it is in the echoes of Irish silences, in the shadow of the World Trade Center attacks, as in the individual loss of a singular Irish priest. Whereas most of the novels in this study engage their post–Celtic Tiger moment directly or indirectly, *Let the Great World Spin* takes a broader approach even as it engages with its Irish literary milieu.

Taken together, all these juxtapositions acknowledge the scale of human suffering even as they offer a reassuring confirmation of the human ability to persevere and recover regardless of place, time, or creed. The novel thus proffers a panoramic affirmation of the universal ability to recover and endure, but it does so without negating the relevance of the individual. It is consistent not only with McCann's wider canon but also with the literary shift from a focus on silences and trauma, resonant with the wider Irish canon, to an emphasis on the possibility of healing and recovery.

☼

Let the Great World Spin has been lauded for its compassionate representation of New York City; it has been called the "first great novel about 9/11."[6] Set before the tragic events of that day in 2001, the novel balances the marvel and sense of community provoked by Philippe Petit's historic World Trade Center tightrope walk and the shadow of horrified solidarity evoked by knowledge of the Towers' inescapable future. McCann thus generates a sense of optimism and wonder at the interstices of a flawed but hopeful past and a looming, heartbreaking future.

As focused on New York sensibilities as the novel may be, however, it also hinges on much wider contexts. For some critics who have analyzed the text to date, the novel's international view signals McCann's rejection of the centering of American experience. For example, Flannery reads the text as "prompt[ing] the question: where can we divine non-American and non-contemporary moments of hope and despair?"[7] Similarly, Sinéad Moynihan claims that McCann's interrelation of "spatial and temporal dimensions of trauma offers a radical critique of the way in which much post-9/11 fiction and criticism leaves unchallenged trauma's temporal aspects."[8] In such readings, *Let the Great World Spin* counters American exceptionalism and regionalism with a more inclusive political understanding of the traumatic events of that September day.[9]

Such readings provide valuable insights into McCann's refusal of a narrower politicized use of the World Trade Center attacks. Despite the New York setting, other, specific geographical locations are not negated but rather are set in dialogue. This approach is reflective of McCann's wider, inclusive literary effort: "His renovation of 'literary Irishness' has more to do with an openness to foreign 'others,' to a celebration of empathy as a political and cultural force, and to a tendency that permits dialogue between Ireland and the world, the local and the global, and not [with] the supersession of one by the other."[10] Just as *Let the Great World Spin* collapses boundaries between high and low, subway and skyscraper, so too does it blur the divide between individual and national suffering, between different definitions of home, and between past and present.

As many reviewers note, *Let the Great World Spin* is also distinguished by its polyphonic, multilayered narrative structure—a structure that is, of course, even further evolved in McCann's subsequent novel, *TransAtlantic* (2013).[11] Not unlike that later novel, this story traces and ultimately weaves together multiple narrative threads. The central line of the story is usually considered to be the exploits of the tightrope walker Philippe Petit in that all events in the novel occur on the August day of his tightrope walk in 1974.

By juxtaposing a day of such community and wonder in 1974 against the readers' knowledge of the World Trade Center's fate in 2001, McCann is generally recognized to reclaim the space of the World Trade Center artistically and politically. He has acknowledged the intention behind this contrast: "Then—when the towers came down in 2001—the tightrope walk popped out of my memory, one of those eureka moments, and I thought, What a spectacular act of creation, to have a man walking in the sky, as opposed to the act of evil and destruction of the towers disintegrating."[12] As Flannery argues, "The 'walker's' gesture facilitates an instance of belonging and restores faith in the possibility of solidarity." Given that the novel addresses 9/11 "in elliptical ways," this juxtaposition clearly suggests the overlaying of a moment of communal hope over later communal despair.[13]

The narrative reinforces this allusion to future communal horror through its language. As New Yorkers watch Petit from the ground, "They found themselves in small groups together . . . [a]ll of them reassured by the presence of one another. . . . The watchers below pulled in their breath all at once" (4, 7). McCann's language emphasizes a sense of community ("all") among those on the sidewalk; although helpless to do anything but observe, they nonetheless are conscious that they are observing together. Superimposing the wonder and inspiration of that August day on the shadow of horror from early September twenty-seven years later, a time when other New Yorkers also watched with anxiety and breathlessness from below, McCann layers and effectively reclaims both moments of forged community in the streets of New York.[14]

As Sinéad Moynihan argues, "The novel challenges the notion of an easy opposition between creation and destruction."[15] It decenters the World Trade Center bombings and recuperates that trauma spatially, artistically, and politically.[16] Petit's tightrope walk catalyzes this deconstruction narratively, notes Alison Garden: "McCann redirects the energies surrounding the attacks on the World Trade Center to New York of the 1970s and in so doing, constructs a novel which is ultimately hopeful for the future."[17] Petit is clearly a central figure in the novel; he has been called "the focal point towards which manifold gazes from all perspectives and directions converge and in which disconnected individuals in the anonymous city become united."[18]

Less attended to but equally relevant to the core of *Let the Great World Spin*, however, are the life and death of a liberation-theology-inspired radical Irish priest, Father John Corrigan. As Elizabeth Cullingford notes, "McCann . . . insists that the hero of *Let the Great World Spin* is not the tightrope walker, but the Irish immigrant John Corrigan, who was originally the single focus of the book."[19] Despite dying only seventy pages into the novel, Corrigan, I would argue, is the thread that binds the novel together as much as—or perhaps even more than—Petit.

Growing up in Ireland with his brother, Ciaran, and his mother, all of whom were abandoned by their father and husband, Corrigan walks a reckless, tenuous line between selflessness and self-destruction.[20] Giving away blankets to the poor; consorting with the local alcoholic homeless; and later living among the prostitutes in the

Bronx, Corrigan, as his brother observes, "was some bright hallelujah in the shitbox of what the world really was" (15). Ciaran also later describes Corrigan as "a crack of light under the door" (67)—a thin line of hope to keep in sight in a dark and threatening world. Whereas Petit inspires confidence, joy, and wonder, Corrigan is a beacon in a world characterized by struggle, uncertainty, and doubt.

Throughout the story, Corrigan keeps company with prostitutes, in particular a mother and daughter tandem, Tillie and Jazzlyn. He allows the local prostitutes to use his apartment as a rest stop, despite the physical abuse it brings him from their pimps. Corrigan also works with a local nurse, Adelita, to care for elderly patients, driving them to various locales in a van. Corrigan falls in love with Adelita, which causes him both joy and a crisis of religious conscience because he has taken a vow of chastity. When Jazzlyn and Tillie are arrested in a prostitution crackdown, Corrigan takes the van to the courthouse for their sentencing. He leaves with Jazzlyn, who is freed through her mother's sacrifice (perhaps tellingly in this novel, Tillie takes the fall). Corrigan and Jazzlyn are in a serious car accident, however, that leaves Jazzlyn dead, thrown through the windshield, and Corrigan close to death from internal injuries.

Corrigan's death ignites a series of chain reactions. As a result of it, his brother meets Lara, an artist who was high on cocaine and a passenger in the car that struck Corrigan's van; the two later marry and return at least part-time to Ireland. Lara, because of her guilt, also visits Tillie in jail and arranges for her to see her grandchildren, whom Tillie calls "the babies." The judge, who adjudicates over Tillie and Jazzlyn's sentencing, Sol Soderberg, is also given the case of Philippe Petit when trespassing and other charges are filed against him after his stunt. Judge Soderberg's wife, Claire, is mourning the death of their son, Joshua, in Vietnam; her support group for mothers of dead soldiers includes Gloria, a neighbor to Corrigan who will eventually adopt Jazzlyn's orphans.

Thus, as much as Petit and his high wire, Corrigan is a sinuous link that threads these lives together. Whereas Petit's act is a moment of beauty and transcendence, however, Corrigan's binding of others is grounded in loss. But just as Petit is, as Judge Soderberg notes, "a monument in himself" (248), Corrigan serves as a beacon of sorts for others—as did the Towers—toward which they turn in projecting their grievances, desires, and fears.

Despite this central role, Corrigan ("Corrie") has been unevenly attended to in favor of Petit in assessments of the novel. Although Moynihan recognizes Corrie's "extraordinary . . . empathy for the marginalized and disaffected," for example, she mostly sidesteps the meaning of his death and considers another character's narrative relation to Petit.[21] Similarly, Regina Schober emphasizes the "image of the line" as pertaining to "the act of creating connections, of relating to others," and she thus stresses Petit's similarities to the computer hacker, noting that "both . . . act within a network."[22] In both cases, interestingly, a fairly minor character is viewed as paralleling Petit.

Yet it is Corrigan who provides both a parallel and a foil to Petit, and in this respect he not only creates tremendous narrative balance within the novel but also interrogates what Petit literally and metaphorically stands for. The contrast between skyscraper and subway has been much commented upon in the novel;[23] Corrigan and Petit provide another such pairing. Flannery has noted that "Corrigan and the wire walker are embodiments of spatial and hopeful extremes," and certainly, as he suggests, both force others to "think twice": "The wire walker halts his watchers, [and] Corrigan forces others to reflect on the value of the most worthless of discarded lives."[24] In many respects, those parallel effects are generated through polar opposition. Although Petit is "literally . . . in an elevated position that enables him to have full view of the city, [he] remains oblivious to the lives, experiences, or thoughts of the peripheral nodes";[25] in contrast, Corrigan's life is grounded—literally—in the lives of the people around him.

Corrigan's life is also an exercise in contradictions, and his own suffering and choices bind him to those around him as much as Petit's decision to walk the wire isolates him. Petit's peaceful determination is matched by his isolation: "There were times when he was so at ease that he could watch the elk, or trace the wisps of smoke from the forest fires, . . . but at his best his mind remained free of sight" (161). As one critic concisely notes, his walk has "no constructive end other than the outstanding beauty of the act itself."[26]

This sensibility stands in sharp contrast to Corrigan, who struggles constantly with indecision, unclarity, and doubt. When he was a child, for example, his fervent prayers would deteriorate in the middle: "The more rhythmic the prayers got, . . . in the middle of it all [his brother] could hear him curse, and they'd be lifted away from the sacred" (13). Similarly, whereas for Petit "it all came down to the wire. Him and the cable" (162), Corrigan's reality is all about connection. His view of Christ is telling:

> What Corrigan wanted was a fully believable God, one you could find in the grime of the everyday. The comfort he got from the hard, cold, truth—the filth, the war, the poverty—was that life could be capable of small beauties. . . . [H]e consoled himself with the fact that, . . . when he looked closely into the darkness he might find the presence of a light, damaged and bruised, but a little light all the same. (20)

If it is true that Petit's walk invokes "the numinous touching upon the banalities of the everyday,"[27] Corrigan does the opposite. His desire is to find the numinous *in* the banal. As Flannery notes, "*Let the Great World Spin* . . . refuses to accept the inability of the ordinary to inspire and to accept only despair without the possibility of recovery from grief."[28] Corrigan's gritty, realistic suffering counters the hopeful, almost ethereal beauty of Petit's tightrope walk, providing another balancing contrast.

It is important to note that Corrigan in fact speaks for—and replicates the suffering and sorrow of—most of the characters in the novel. He notes of his prostitute friends, "They're all throbbing with fear. We all are" (29). Whereas Petit becomes a projection of sorts to those who watch him—Marcia, for example, reads the loss of her son through his walk (98–99), and Soderberg reads him as "a statue, . . . a perfect New York one, a temporary one" (248)—Corrigan has what his brother describes as "an affinity with pain. If he couldn't cure it, he took it on" (42).

But rather than being separated by space and transcendent with ambition, like Petit, Corrigan is marked by his sameness to those around him—not only in his desire to join with the lowly (what Flannery calls his forcing of others to "reflect on the value of the most worthless of discarded lives"[29]) but also in his shared sense of loss. Ciaran notes that his brother never recovered from the abandonment by their father; he says, "I knew then that there'd be no more talk about our father. He had closed that path down, quick and hard. . . . Corrigan wanted other people's pain. He didn't want to deal with his own" (31). As a result, Corrigan is a Christ-like figure, "a martyred redeemer of the wretched of the earth," which creates "a further symmetry to the figure of the wire walker as a transcendent or resurrected cruciform figure."[30] Just as those watching Petit forge a community of reassurance and the novel offers an artistic counterbalance to the communal suffering of 9/11, Corrigan's willingness to share others' suffering offers solace, yet through identification and recognition.

This sense of personal trauma and internal struggle is echoed throughout the novel. And this sense of real suffering significantly differentiates Corrigan from Petit. In particular, just as Corrigan wishes to deny his own pain for the sake of those around him, others who suffer struggle to express their misery. In one of the most heartbreaking passages in the novel, Claire mourns her failure to speak to her son: "What was it I never said to Josh? . . . The only thing you need to know about war, son, is: Don't go" (86). Adelita keeps a picture of her hated ex-husband because he is her children's father, but Corrigan notes, "She doesn't talk about him" (54). Fernando, who photographs graffiti art underground, wishes to tell his stepfather, "You ain't my old man," but he is "never quite able to say it" (173). Sol notes that "silence was his way out" of grief (89). Tillie is crushed by the loss of her daughter, Jazzlyn, repeatedly mourning her failure as a mother and expressing in an internal meditation that no one hears a desire to hang herself from a pipe in prison. Whereas Corrigan says you "get to know [God] by His occasional absence" (27), Tillie claims that "God is due His ass-kicking" for the loss of her daughter and the incomprehensibly profound suffering of her life, which is essentially invisible to society (236).

I return later to the issue of silence, but here I would note that Corrigan's ability to hear and see the most invisible and silenced members of society and his almost Christological paralleling—and embodiment—of that suffering metaphorically capture the power of rendering such suffering valued and visible.[31] Just as the watchers of Petit's wire walk "pulled in their breath all at once," the parallel responses of McCann's characters to suffering narrows the distance between them, with Corrigan serving as a kind of touchstone for their pain (7). Yet, importantly, although Corrigan has been read as a parallel to Petit as "an edifice of altruistic humanity and hope in the novel,"[32] it is important not to devalue Corrigan's very real suffering—suffering that is not actually ever alleviated and that so profoundly parallels the hopelessness and pain of other characters in the novel.

Perhaps not surprisingly, Corrigan's is not an abstract, artistic, aesthetic life or death. Indeed, the very description of his end is marked by its physicality and gruesome detail: "Corrigan was smashed back by the steering wheel, which caught his chest and shattered his breastbone, his head rebounding off the spidery glass, bloody, and then he was whipped back into the seat with such force that the metal frame of the seat shattered, a thousand pounds of moving steel, the van still spinning from one side of the road to the other" (69). Corrigan's harsh, pained, doubt-riddled existence and physically violent death counterbalance the certainty, artistry, and transcendence of Petit's wire walk: "Within seconds he was pureness moving, and he could do anything he liked. He was inside and outside his body at the same time, indulging in what it meant to belong to the air, no future, no past, and this gave him an offhand vaunt to his walk. . . . The core reason for it all was beauty" (164). If the subway and the skyscraper certainly juxtapose two opposites as not opposite at all, then Petit and Corrigan balance out the ideal and the real—the triumph of human ambition with the lowly, the suffering, and even the doomed. Corrigan's contrast to Petit promises that the lovely must always be counterbalanced by the unlovely, the ethereal with the physical, the transcendent with the earthbound. As importantly, through Corrigan's premature (and oft-neglected) death, we are reminded that the mirror side of recovery is trauma. Relativizing both, McCann normalizes suffering and the traumatic as recuperable, as two sides of the natural human experience.

☼

The coexistence of these seeming opposites provides a larger, panoramic view of human existence that runs structurally at all levels throughout the novel.[33] Just as hope and pain coexist in this way—with the Towers of Petit's time and the Towers of September 11, 2001, being the ultimate such example of coexistence, as we have seen—the novel takes pains to show how many differences overlap yet maintain their distinction even in their combination. Perhaps not surprisingly, this paralleling at the level of the individual (Corrigan/Petit) also occurs at the level of the nation. Although it is true that McCann rejects the centering of American experience for a more-inclusive, less-bounded representation, this rejection of boundaries is more than only a political act, as I have suggested. Rather, it highlights the commonality of human experience as fundamentally healing and curative.

The novel is grounded emphatically in New York, but it also reaches out seamlessly and inclusively to other places and times in ways that privilege personal meaning over national hierarchies. For example, Ciaran Corrigan notes, "Distant cities are designed precisely so you can know where you came from," as he flees to New York after nearly falling prey to an IRA bomb (59). Indeed, a wider awareness of origins balanced by the blending of differing definitions of home runs throughout the text. In trying to dissuade Corrigan from the life with prostitutes he has chosen, for example, Ciaran avers, "They're not Magdalenes" (39). Corrigan himself notes that national boundaries are meaningless, observing, "I'll go back to Ireland, find a different poverty. But nothing made sense. The end of the country, man, but there was no revelation" (52). When Lara offers Ciaran a ride home after John's funeral, he laughingly asks, "Home? . . . Can your car swim?" (150)—but ultimately he and Lara live part-time in Ireland, where he sports "half an American accent" (341). Finally, Ciaran returns Corrigan's ashes to Ireland and scatters them so Corrigan can be "a part of many things" (154). Ireland and New York run parallel and yet intersect, their differences and overlaps blurring in the course of the novel. This pairing emphasizes the smallness and largeness of the world at once, again hollowing out differences in favor of a reassuring, wider sense of community.[34]

Ireland is not the only differing locale integrated into the novel. Gloria moves to Poughkeepsie; Jazzlyn works in New Orleans and buys a photo in San Francisco, but her connection to Claire brings her back to an origin she barely remembers. Her boyfriend is Italian; her sister is in the service in Baghdad. Gloria speaks of her mother's stories, "read in a high African singsong that . . . came down along the line from Ghana long ago, something that she made American, but [that] tied us to a home we'd never seen" (287). Finally, the entire chapter where "the Kid" uses the ARPANET to dial a pay phone to New York for a firsthand insight into the wire walker stresses simultaneous distance and proximity, the binding of lives across vast distances.

As Joshua told Claire before his death in Vietnam, "It was crazy how small the world truly was. It was a matter of opening up to it" (89). The novel enacts the very expanding and shrinking of distance that it describes and thus suggests—like the opposites Corrigan and Petit, high and low, terrestrial and ethereal—that perceived differences are reassuringly less significant than they may seem. McCann thus further explodes the idea of rapprochement from only the individual to national levels even as he maintains the importance of discrete lives and experiences.

For McCann, distances between people—high and low, foreign and domestic, suffering and comforting—are ultimately reconciled through empathy, as we have seen. And if it is empathy that ultimately offers recovery from suffering, that empathetic identification can best be found through narrative and communal sharing. McCann has argued, "With storytelling there need be no regard for borders, no regard for boundaries, no regard for wealth: everyone has a story. . . . We all have a need to tell it, a desire to tell it, a compulsion to tell it: we *have* to tell it."[35] As Flannery observes, "The simple act of telling one's story to a willing listener might constitute the redemptive act, but for McCann, there is currency in such acts of simple sharing."[36]

This focus on narrating and representing one's suffering is characteristic not just of McCann and his canon, however; it also supports the pattern I have traced throughout this study. I noted earlier that most of the characters suffering throughout *Let the Great World Spin* employ silence as an (inadequate) strategy to cope with pain. McCann's employment of silence in representing suffering illustrates the destructive force of such verbal and emotional isolation—a force best remediated through the community and connection that the novel espouses and models narratively.

Yet such an awareness of the possibility of silence is in itself paradigmatically characteristic of contemporary Irish fiction—one of the markers that enables McCann, rightly, to claim simply, "I'm a very Irish writer."[37] Just as contemporaries Anne Enright, Sebastian Barry, and, as we will see in the following chapter, Colm Tóibín have explored the painful valences of silence only to reject or overcome them in recent fiction, McCann's canon testifies to the importance of narrativizing trauma in order to transcend suffering.

Let the Great World Spin recognizes, though, that narrativizing trauma can be challenging. Richard Gray, following Cathy Caruth, claims that "perhaps the way to tell a story that cannot be told is to tell it aslant, to approach it by circuitous means, almost by stealth."[38] As we have seen, Flannery also suggests that this method is at play in *Let the Great World Spin*, where McCann confronts the events of September 11 indirectly.[39] Bertrand Cardin similarly notes that McCann was not interested in capturing the gruesome details of that apocalyptic trauma: "He rejected writing a detailed narrative about the catastrophe. . . . *Let the Great World Spin* does not recount the disaster as such. . . . Yet the temporal ellipsis between 1974 and 2006 passes the narrative of the World Trade Center collapse over in silence."[40]

Nonetheless, McCann *does* capture Corrigan's death in gruesome detail, as we have seen—and here, too, I think the narrative willingness to represent Corrigan's death in such detail while obscuring the losses of 9/11 reinforces both McCann's willingness to disrupt neat hierarchies and his emphasis on the importance of the pedestrian as curative and recuperative. In other words, by presencing the loss of an anonymous, indigent priest narratively more than the loss of a multitude, McCann speaks to the inherent value of each individual pain while not devaluing communal pain. Nor does he allow the narratives of recovery to overwrite the validity of that pain. Rather, his collapsing of such priorities reinforces the ubiquity of loss and thus normalizes it in a manner that is ultimately restorative. Like Corrigan's valuing of each individual life, McCann's narrative presencing of the loss of Corrigan stresses the ubiquity of suffering, individual and communal, and the equally ubiquitous potential to heal. In this respect, of course, the narrative structurally replicates Corrigan's worldview.

Unfortunately, McCann had his own cause to ponder such ideas after he was assaulted in New Haven, Connecticut, in 2014. In the writing of his recent collection of short stories, *Thirteen Ways of Looking* (2015), these questions of narrativizing trauma and what it means to heal became all the more pressing, and it seems that, for this author, the experience confirmed his understanding of the need to speak one's trauma in order to recover:

> What happens when we get hurt is not nearly as interesting as how we learn how to heal. I constantly buck this idea that my work is sentimental or soft because it embraces the possibility of healing. It is full of sentiment, absolutely—but I will fight for the muscularity of my sentences and ideas any day. I have said this sort of thing before, but it is very important to me; when I think of trauma and recovery, the ability to tell your story is profoundly necessary. *Listening* is at the core of so much of what I am doing. Basically, all those stories in *Thirteen Ways of Looking* were about recovery and grace.[41]

McCann's hopeful revisitation of trauma and loss in *Let the Great World Spin*—the assertion that the city "accepted whatever came its way . . . the little shocks of good that crawled out from underneath the everyday" (248)—reflects a willingness to engage traumatic events with an eye toward the future, a sense, as the novel claims, that ultimately things "*don't* fall apart" (325, emphasis added), that there is a "crack of light under the door" (67), a reassuring interconnection between individuals and nations, cities and places, that I have been tracing throughout this chapter and this study. This sense of interconnection is consistent with a broader tendency in more recent Irish works to look past trauma toward opportunity and thus to suggest that the capturing of trauma is of itself inherently reparative.

McCann has claimed that "each story is shifted sideways by each day that unfolds. Nothing ends."[42] If, as Sol Soderberg believes, "the city lived in a sort of everyday present," then *Let the Great World Spin* suggests we as human beings partake in a constant process of making anew. Whether in reference to the national or the international, the individual or the communal, American or Irish, past or present—*Let the Great World Spin* refuses to succumb to the demands of either paralyzing grief or transcendent beauty. The Petits and the Corrigans of the world are of a piece, and it is in that coherence of contradictions that recovery can be found.

Let the Great World Spin thus presents community more broadly as the light that dispenses the darkness, if only as a "line beneath the door." The novel speaks to what "endures"—and although what "endures" can be a question of an individual or a community in the face of loss, it also invokes the durability and resiliency of the past and the human spirit. This desire to presence not only loss but also the healing power of words is a constant thread through McCann's work, even as it has become an increasingly obvious aspect of the Irish literary canon in the twenty-first century. It is, then, perhaps best to let McCann speak for himself: "Stories are the most democratic things we have. They cross all sorts of borders. They cross gender boundaries, geography, issues of wealth and belonging. We all have a deep need to tell them and we also have a deep need to listen. They make us whole."[43] Our last novel, *Nora Webster*, crosses the boundaries of an individual text to explore trauma and recovery canonically, metanarratively enacting the same balance of hope and pain McCann signals here and suggesting that healing is both a process and an evolution.

6

Trauma, Recovery, and Intertextual Redemption in Colm Tóibín's *Nora Webster*

As discussed in the introduction, Colm Tóibín was one of the earliest Irish authors to engage not only trauma but also issues of recovery in his work. In particular, his novel *The Blackwater Lightship* (1999) examines the consequences of a family's failure to discuss the loss of their husband and father as well as the national cost of eliding segments of the Irish social fabric, allegorically captured in the traumatized body of Declan as he suffers from AIDS.[1] This concern with the need to disrupt painful silences and to *presence* suffering narratively is a fundamental aspect of this author's work.

Tóibín's novel *Nora Webster* (2014) continues a twenty-five-year pattern in the author's oeuvre in which he represents the familial impact of traumatic loss, often by drawing on his own personal history. Focusing on a widow and mother as she navigates parenthood and life alone, *Nora Webster* extends Tóibín's engagement with themes of small-town interference, pained silences, dysfunctional communication, emotionally neglected children, and disconnected or selfish mothers. Embedded in his customary Enniscorthy setting, the characters circulate in the familiar (if claustrophobic) fictional milieu of Tóibín's other novels. In these ways, *Nora Webster* adheres to an already well-established pattern.

What differentiates *Nora Webster* and makes it most suitable for the conclusion of this study, however, is the manner in which this later novel marks an evolution from Tóibín's earlier representations of traumatic loss. It focuses not on the impact of neglectful parenting on adult children but rather on the grieving perspective of the failing parent. By narratively giving voice to Nora's point of view, Tóibín creates a remarkably sympathetic portrait of a mother figure—a figure who in his other Irish texts is painfully limited or emotionally stunted. By stressing what the central character has lacked through her own neglect, through the restrictions imposed on her by her town and by widowhood, through her own failure of empathy, and through the loss of her husband—and by doing so consistently from her perspective—*Nora Webster* humanizes the figure of the flawed mother more than any of the author's previous works does.

More importantly, the novel thus serves as a kind of answer to Tóibín's earlier Irish texts. By constructing *Nora Webster* as a text in dialogue with prior novels, Tóibín makes clear that this novel does not merely re-create but also responds to these familiar thematic issues. For the main character's evolution and nature to be appreciated fully, *Nora Webster* thus must be read within the context of Tóibín's wider Irish oeuvre. *Nora Webster* portrays a character coming to terms with her grief; at the same time, it enacts a type of authorial peacemaking with the figure of the mother across Tóibín's canon. Although the other texts in this study represent a process of narrativizing trauma and recovery and scrutinize the act of narration itself as a vehicle for recovery, *Nora Webster* provides an important meditation on perspective in narratives of recovery and explores recovery from trauma intertextually across a canon. In this way, the metanarrative gesture of recovery responds to Tóibín's own canon of representation of trauma.

Nora Webster follows the experiences of a mother and widow in Enniscorthy during the late 1960s or early 1970s as she attempts to navigate life as a newly single parent after the sudden, early demise of her husband, Maurice. Trying to survive fiscally given her altered circumstances, to navigate small-town politics and wider familial dynamics, and to relate to and support her four children even as she struggles with her own disorientation, grief, and loss, Nora presents a portrait of endurance, psychological limitation, courage, and the boundaries of grief. In many ways, the novel is consistent with Tóibín's prior novels and short stories set in Enniscorthy. It redeploys many familiar elements: children abandoned at a relative's house during their father's illness and death; a remote and emotionally inaccessibly mother; and the emotional scarring of children from these experiences. This foundation reflects Tóibín's own history, just as his authorial practice reifies his stated belief that "you are always working out of some deep business of self."[2]

Nora Webster foregrounds its thematic consistencies with the earlier fiction and urges the reader to keep them in mind.[3] For example, Nora is painfully aware of her community's watchful eye, which she allows to influence the manner and modes of her grief. As she endures a parade of mourners in the months and weeks following Maurice's death, she is conscious of the almost voyeuristic intrusion their social calls represent: "Looking into the fire, Nora tried to think back, wondering if May Lacey had ever been in this house before. She thought not. She had known her all her life, like so many in the town, to greet and exchange pleasantries with, or to stop and talk to if there was news."[4] Nora's sense of community resonates with others' in Tóibín's canon. Her view of her society closely parallels Molly's perspective in Tóibín's earlier short story "A Priest in the Family" (2007), when Molly reflects on her relationship with the town: "She greeted people she met on the street by name, people she had known all her life. . . . She knew all about them, and they about her."[5]

Such references are not just oblique. May Lacey is a character directly out of Tóibín's novel *Brooklyn* (2009), who also registers a similar complaint about Dora Devereaux and her sister, Stacia, who are in turn characters from *The Blackwater Lightship* (1999). Such nested references highlight the claustrophobic nature of their shared society and demand that *Nora Webster* be read against Tóibín's other Irish novels. Nora is a mother in her own right as well as a character in a line of similar characters against whom she is measured.

Like Molly in "Priest" and Dora Devereaux in *The Blackwater Lightship*, Nora is also painfully aware of her neighbors' intrusive curiosity, which invokes direct intertextual references to Tóibín's earlier

Irish work. Nora notes as she leaves for her first day at work that "she felt that she was being closely observed" (111). She worries about how the town will react to her new hairdo; to her red coat; to her decision to sing because "people in the bar . . . would recognise her and would wonder why she was singing in a pub when Maurice was not even a year dead" (207); and even to her daughter's sense of London fashion: "You are not going to mass in this town dressed like that. . . . It might be wonderful in London, or in a magazine, but not down here" (130).[6] This self-consciousness evokes the familiar and complex relationship between a single, failing mother and her town that Tóibín frequently explores. Nora's resentment that everyone else knew about her sister Una's engagement is clear when she complains, "Oh, no hurry [to tell me about your engagement]. As I said, the whole town is talking about it" (155). This complaint directly echoes Molly's in "A Priest in the Family" when she avers that the "whole town knows" about her son being accused of pedophilia before she does.[7]

Such moments of excruciating self-awareness riddle Tóibín's other work but are multiply evoked in this novel. In *The Blackwater Lightship*, Dora Devereux obsesses over the intrusions of the neighbors—"Oh God Almighty, I'll have them all on top of me now. . . . I'll have them in droves."[8] Nancy in "The Name of the Game" (2007) warns her son, "Gerard, if anybody asks you any questions, you know, anyone from the town, tell them to talk to me. But tell them nothing."[9] Just as Molly asks her friend to have people talk to her, to "not be afraid to mention" what has occurred with her son, so, too, does Nora admit that "she would feel much worse if people began to avoid her" (8).[10] Dora finds society as irresistible as irritating: as noted earlier, she makes an appearance in *Brooklyn* as herself, the nosey neighbor who intrudes on May Lacey's grief.[11]

Cameos by other characters from Tóibín's Irish novels run throughout *Nora Webster*: they include Eamon and Carmel Redmond from *The Heather Blazing* (1992); May and Jack Lacey as well as Eilis and Tony from *Brooklyn*; and Nancy Sheridan from "The Name of the Game." Both repelled by and drawn to her societal connections and thoroughly entangled in the author's wider fictional milieu, Nora navigates the same limitations and characteristics of small-town society as others do in Tóibín's fictional Enniscorthy.

Given the novel's embrace of a familiar version of Irish life, its adherence to Tóibín's biographical history, and its aggressive foregrounding of intertextual resonances, it is not surprising that it also showcases the painful silences and dysfunctional families so common in Tóibín's work. Many critical studies explore what can be called "the denaturing effect of silence [on] the Irish family" in his work.[12] In the case of *Nora Webster*, this foregrounding both heightens our sense of Nora's failure through the novel's adoption of her perspective and reminds us through its intertextual evocations that this failure is all too familiar in Tóibín's mothers.

Nora Webster adheres clearly to this pattern. Like Nancy in "The Name of the Game" and Dora in *The Blackwater Lightship*, Nora is an exceptionally private person. She seeks to mask her emotions and to control her behavior—for example, behaving "strangely in closing the gates [to their house in Cush] when she had parked . . . , [and] in seeming almost furtive when Mrs. Darcy called" (15). A similar extreme tendency toward privacy and reticence is evident in her relatives. When Nora's sister Una feels slighted by Nora's response to her engagement, the conflict is met with a chorus of silences: Una says nothing; Nora's daughter Fiona merely stares; and Nora's other daughter, Aine, walks out. Yet Nora, despite recognizing that "she had gone too far" and trying "to think of something to say to relieve the situation quickly, . . . could think of nothing" (156).[13]

Nora also repeatedly fails to discern how to communicate with her loved ones: it in this respect that she is most evocative of Tóibín's other characters. Like Eamon Redmond in *The Heather Blazing*, who considers reaching out to his wife but "held back, and went instead into the bedroom and dressed himself,"[14] Nora often seems incapable of connecting emotionally to her children. When Fiona needs money, Nora hears the request as an indictment of her, Nora, yet when Nora considers speaking to Fiona about it, "she could not think what to say" (227). When she later realizes that Fiona thinks her mother is trying to steal her boyfriend, rather than discuss it with Fiona, Nora avers,

"I have more important things to do" (294). Similarly, when her son Donal is struggling in boarding school, Nora "did not know whether it was better for him to cry or not to cry" (307). Nora's interactions with her children can be awkward, to say the least.

Even when Nora is sympathetic to her children, she flounders. Trying to deal with Donal's turmoil, she concludes that saying "nothing was simpler, at least for the moment" (308). Recognizing the distress she causes Fiona by deciding to sell the house in Cush, "she felt helpless and regretted not having said something kind or special or consoling to Fiona before they left" (29).[15] Finally, rather than taking the lead as a parent, Nora often abdicates responsibility. Recognizing that her sister-in-law, Margaret, "seemed to have taken over the entire question of [Nora's daughter] Aine's education," Nora nonetheless concludes that "it was best not to think too much about it" (103). When Margaret later builds Donal a darkroom without consulting her (169–70), Nora nevertheless decides to say nothing. Once again, Tóibín creates a parent who does not quite understand how to connect with her children and who cedes responsibility for them.

Most important, Nora fails to grasp the impact of her decisions on her children and has limited insight into either her own motivations or the consequences of her actions. When she meets Donal at school, she realizes that he is looking for a sign he can come home, and her response is telling: "Her speaking about herself, her own needs, her own worry, made him appear even more alert. It occurred to her that he had thought more closely about her over the previous few years than she had about him. She wondered if that could be true" (310). In the same way, when Aine seems to be missing, Nora's impulse is to leave rather than to stay and search for her child—the "urge came to her again to walk out, find her car and drive home" (327)—a response that provokes resentment and even disgust in her other daughter. Like May Lacey in *Brooklyn* and Lily in *The Blackwater Lightship*, Nora in such moments seems to betray self-absorption at worst, cluelessness at best.

In its most pronounced moments, Nora's seeming disconnectedness can appear selfish or even heartless, leading one reviewer to call her "one of Mr. Tóibín's most distant and sealed-off central characters."[16] Katherine Proctor in *The South* (1990) thinks, "My son will look after himself. There is nothing more I can do for him."[17] Likewise, Nora often privileges her own needs and desires above those of her children—for example, leaving a vulnerable Donal home alone so she can finish her vacation. On occasion, she even imagines her children gone, thinking, "how easy it might have been to have been someone else, . . . having the boys at home waiting for her . . . [was] all a sort of accident" (256). Nora admits to herself that she has not always invested sufficiently in her children emotionally: "It was strange, she thought, that she had never before put a single thought into whether they were happy or not. . . . She had looked after them until the time came when that was difficult" (128). Tóibín has observed that some of his fictional mothers are "monstrous,"[18] and Nora fits this pattern well by consistently failing to consider her children's needs.

Perhaps the most powerful indictment of Nora's failure to understand her children or the consequences of her actions comes from her aunt Josie, who watched Donal and Conor when Maurice was in the hospital dying. When Nora's boys are home with her, Nora notes that they seem to be holding themselves apart, secretive and inaccessible: she observes that they greet Josie "warily" (36), and when Josie arrives, Nora sees that Donal's "stammer seemed more pronounced" (37). The boys' affect in seeing Josie seems to Nora "uneasy, almost scared" (46). Nora notices that the boys have apparently built a kind of bond that excludes her: she suspects that "something had happened to them . . . which they did not want her to know about" (25), and she vaguely recognizes that something has changed but cannot imagine what it could be: "In these months, she realised, something had changed in the clear, easy connection between her and them, and perhaps, for them, between each other. She felt that she would never be sure about them again" (21). Yet it does not occur to Nora that her own actions may have precipitated this distance. She leaps to the assumption that the boys were harmed in some way at Josie's, asking Josie, "What happened to them here?" (54). When her aunt replies that "they thought you might come and you never did. . . . I don't know what you were thinking of leaving them here all that time and never once coming to see them" (54), Nora is completely unprepared for this answer, simply responding, "Maurice was dying" (54).

Abandonment by the mother is nothing new in Tóibín's fiction. Silences, emotional stuntedness, and a failure to consider the needs of her children all place Nora in a long line of inadequate mothers captured in his work. From Katherine's abandonment of her son in *The South* to the death of Eamon's mother in *The Heather Blazing*, Lily Devereaux's emotional desertion of her children in *The Blackwater Lightship*, and Noel's mother's absence in the short story "A Song" (2007), the cost of the absent mother riddles his work.[19]

Yet having these familiar traits explored at length from the mother's perspective heightens our understanding of the degree of Nora's limitations and failings. In this respect, *Nora Webster* diverges significantly from the prior novels. Against the background of so many intertextual similarities, this pronounced change in perspective is brought all the more clearly into focus. As Roy Foster comments in his comprehensive and cogent review of the novel, the "subtly calibrated revelation of family patterns and pressures is classic Tóibín territory, but he has never mapped it better than here."[20]

Nonetheless, it would be a mistake to assume that Nora somehow stands as the apex of Tóibín's long string of failed mothers in his fiction. On the contrary: the extensive intertextual frameworks ultimately do not damn Nora but rather humanize and in some respects rehabilitate her through these very resonances. Ironically, the intertextual parallels that can place Nora among his "worst" mothers also make her the most relatable and the most sympathetic because we are finally, for the first time in Tóibín's fiction, given extended insight into the mother's motivations and a sense of her very human frailty. In this way, *Nora Webster* intervenes metanarratively into the silences that inhabit his prior Irish works, for the first time recovering the figure of the mother and offering a kind of canonical closure.

☼

Tóibín's characters, despite their flaws, are rarely one dimensional.[21] Some of the ways in which the author renders these characters more sympathetic as limited parents—such as presenting their personal histories or representing the pressures of their contemporary milieu—also appear in *Nora Webster*. By situating Nora within this broader context of his prior mother figures but telling the story from her perspective, Tóibín develops and explores potential that was only nascent in earlier texts. For example, Nora sees the proprietary assumptions and demands placed upon her as a widow in Enniscorthy society, but because this novel gives us her point of view narratively, we are better able to understand and sympathize with her dilemma. Nora notes that a neighbor "was speaking as though he had some authority over her" (1) when he pays her a condolence visit, and she hears in another neighbor's voice a "hectoring tone, as though she were a child, unable to make proper decisions" (12).

These scenes elaborate on Nancy's experience in "The Name of the Game." Nancy, who is condescended to by bank managers and monitored by the town, feels that "all her life she had been on display" and wishes to go "where no one would know anything about her."[22] Nora similarly recognizes that her society sees her future as already charted, regardless of her personal inclinations: "She did not have to get the train back to the town where everybody knew about her and all the years ahead were mapped out for her" (28–29). Tóibín has often written of the vulnerability of widows—or, as seen in *The South*, of single Irish women in general in the mid-twentieth century—but the fuller treatment given in the later novel softens our understanding of its main female character.[23]

Tóibín's decision to tell this story from Nora's point of view rather than from that of her grown children or through conversations between child and parent, as in his other novels, also alters our ability to understand and relate to this grieving mother. By keeping the cost to the children—the focus of most of his other Irish work—largely inaccessible and instead allowing us to struggle with what Nora can and cannot perceive, Tóibín tacitly reworks his prior critiques of the mother. By showing us a familiar world through Nora's eyes, *Nora Webster* offers a degree of redemption for the figure of the failing mother, and by narrating her own experience of trauma and loss, it recuperates her intertextually.

A few examples are telling. In *The South*, it is evident that as unsympathetic a mother as Katherine is, she is also a wounded product of her environment. Subject to the restrictive mores of Ireland of the 1950s and previously abandoned by her own mother, Katherine struggles to navigate her personal history—a dichotomy that configures her as both "victim and victimizer" in the novel.[24] Unlike Nora (whose mother is dead), Katherine is able to confront her mother about her abandonment and to reflect on the reasons why her mother left, even if she cannot process that event emotionally: "Please tell me what happened. How did you get out? How did I get out? How many of them came? Why did you leave and never come back?"[25] Similarly, although Katherine, too, abandoned her own son, Richard, her return to Ireland enables Richard to confront her and to air their differences: "You abandoned me. I remember how I felt then."[26] These encounters not only are cathartic but also force a reassessment on behalf of the culpable mother and enable both mother and offspring to come to terms despite their troubled histories.[27]

In *The Blackwater Lightship*, although Helen is profoundly and lastingly hurt by her abandonment by her mother, Lily, she is able to confront Lily, protesting, "When we settled back in together, the three of us, you were distant, you gave me no affection."[28] *The Blackwater Lightship* also allows us to recognize the mother's side, however. In response to Helen's statements, Lily explains that she felt she was doing what was best: "You don't know what happened to your father. . . . I had no choice. Is that what's been eating away at you all these years?"[29] Finally, in Lily's disillusionment around her childhood view of the local lighthouses as metaphors for a traditional family, we can hear the way in which her husband's death shook the foundations of her worldview. "I used to believe that Tuskar was a man and the Blackwater Lightship was a woman and they were both sending signals to each other and to other lighthouses, like mating calls. He was forceful and strong and she was weaker but more constant. . . . And all that turned out not to be true."[30]

From this intertextual grounding, *Nora Webster* picks up on but reverses the dynamic. In a photograph, Nora's mother holds her as a baby, sitting "stiffly as though the baby on her knee did not quite belong to her" (41). Aunt Josie also notes that Nora's mother did not particularly like Nora, observing, "She liked both her sons-in-law and both her other daughters better than Nora" (42). In her delirious dream about her mother during her crisis of grief, Nora acknowledges that "she had not loved her mother when she was alive" (341) and imagines that "she felt a closeness to her, a connection that she had in some ways always felt, but never acted on, or spoken about" (343).[31] She admits that she "had not bargained for this, had always felt that there would be time for herself and her mother to meet and talk with ease and warmth, or something like warmth" (342).

Such characters as Katherine, Richard, and Helen in Tóibín's other Irish novels are enabled to ask their mothers why they left; Nora cannot have that conversation.[32] She is thus deprived of the ability to voice her pain. In addition, as Foster notes, "not until 300 pages in do we [learn] . . . the way her sisters and mother saw Nora as a 'demon.'"[33] This position in her family differentiates Nora; it is not clear that she herself understands the implications of her family dynamics, and even if she does, there is no opportunity for redress.[34] As a result, Foster continues, one "might think we have been here before," but "the creation of Nora is something utterly new."[35] Nora has a painful childhood history but possesses no means to obtain closure.

Nora confronts a similar obstacle with her own children. In *The South*, Katherine speaks directly to Richard about the price he paid for her departure, and Helen in *The Blackwater Lightship* confronts Lily, but Nora is never quite able to have that conversation with her own children. Her proclivity to remain silent is only a partial reason the conversation never happens, however. There is also the fact that her boys are still relatively small. Unlike the grown children we meet in Tóibín's other Irish texts, Donal and Conor are not fully able to come to terms with what has happened. Nora reflects: "[Maurice's] body in a grave . . . must seem hidden and strange to the boys. . . . Every room, every sound, every piece of space, was filled not only with what had been lost, but with the years themselves, and the days. Now, in the silence, she could feel it and know it; for the boys it came as confusion"

(101). Nora can hear those silences and recognize her own grief, but the boys are not yet mature enough to process and recognize their own mourning.

Because the children, as children, cannot analyze or express their own feelings, and because *Nora Webster* approaches the children's grief from Nora's outside perspective, we can observe them only along with Nora, sharing in her sense of foreclosure, bewilderment, and limitation. The exclusion that the children feel is compounded by the expressive limitations on Nora arising from her emotional abandonment by and alienation from her own mother. Seeing the world from Nora's perspective allows readers to attribute her actions to her limited worldview and her lack of access to her children's thoughts rather than to more sinister motives. When Nora actually thinks about the fact that her daughter Aine is missing, for example, she is almost surprised to realize that "she was desperately worried" (327). A lack of self-awareness is a far cry from being wholly monstrous. Her emotional stuntedness could be the result not only of her emotionally deprived upbringing but also of her traumatized response to the loss of Maurice. As Judith Lewis Herman notes, "Traumatized people feel and act as though their nervous systems have been disconnected from the present."[36] Nora's occasional flashes of insight emphasize her limitations and her grief rather than her selfishness.

Emotionally limited as she is, Nora suffers the additional handicap of the children's unexpressed grief and her own loss, which also contribute to a more sympathetic portrait. This is clear in instances when Nora tries to assess how Donal and Conor truly are. In musing about her decision to leave the children after she notices their strange behavior, for example, she realizes that "the arrangements [she made] . . . had seemed natural at the time" (49) but that what "seemed reasonable then . . . did not seem reasonable now" (53). In the same way, when Donal is heartbroken at missing a chance to view the lunar walk, Nora only then realizes what the loss of his father has cost him: "She tried to remember what he was like before it all happened. It came to her now how attached he was to Maurice, how he would go over from the primary school to the secondary school and find Maurice's classroom and sit at the back. . . . He knew Maurice's timetable by heart" (221). The sense that Nora is unaware rather than wholly indifferent and that she is therefore emotionally limited, like Eamon in *The Heather Blazing*, reverses the pattern of children speculating about their parents' intentions that we have seen in *The Blackwater Lightship*, "A Song," and "One Minus One." The novel provides the moment of insight into the mother that is denied in "One Minus One"—for example, when the speaker wishes for a moment of connection with his mother that is never realized—and that is only briefly afforded to Helen and Declan in *The Blackwater Lightship* through their conversations with Lily. Against the backdrop of such a self-conscious intertextuality, we cannot but read Nora as a kind of narrative revision of the figure of the traumatizing—and traumatized—mother.

☼

Tóibín did not, of course, wholly overlook the mother's point of view in his earlier works, but *Nora Webster* marks a notable evolution in his representation of the mother. In a fine full-length study of Tóibín's work, Eibhear Walshe notes that in several of the stories in the collection *Mothers and Sons* (2007) Tóibín "is . . . viewing the maternal relation from the perspective of the mother" and that this view at times entails a more sympathetic portrait: "Many of these stories reflect on the inability of the son to understand the complex and constricting positions that these mothers find themselves caught in and these women are often powerless or choose silence in response to these dilemmas."[37] *Nora Webster* develops and elaborates the perspectival shift that is at times evidenced in the short stories or in brief flashes in earlier novels.

Because we see these experiences from Nora's point of view, we are also better able to understand her bewilderment and her own struggle to understand the new version of reality in which she finds herself. Rather than displaying simple dysfunction, this change in perspective characterizes some of Nora's silences as sheer helplessness in the face of her grief: Fiona "had not cried at Maurice's funeral, just remained silent . . . but Nora could sense what she [Fiona] felt all the more because she did nothing to show it. Nora did not know what she should say to her now" (27). At times, we realize, Nora is simply paralyzed.

Nora also expresses a profound sense of rupture, which reflects the likelihood that she is still in shock, still processing the loss of her husband and of her radically new reality. On a day trip with the boys, for example, she finds herself wishing "that what had happened could be erased, that the burden that was on her now could be lifted, that the past could be restored and could make its way effortlessly into a painless present" (38). When she considers returning to work, she recalls being employed in an office before her marriage as "a memory of being caged," and she longs for "the past year of her life to be wiped away and for him to return to them" (61–62). Her fury as she walks in the rain while visiting her sister signifies her profound sense of entrapment and loss: "This was what no one had told her about. She could not have ordinary feelings, ordinary desires. . . . [S]he felt a rage that she could not control" (87).[38]

At times, Nora engages in a sort of desperate daydreaming, such as her wish to be someone else or to be alone. Tóibín presents these fantasies in a sympathetic light; they reflect not distaste for her children or an abnegation of responsibility but rather her desperation to evade the fate that has befallen her. As Nora repeats more than once, "The problem for her was that she was on her own now and that she had no idea how to live" (86). Her sense of radical alienation—"no idea how to live"—reflects the shattering effect of trauma, whereby "the sense of connection between individual and community" is undermined.[39] By foregrounding Nora's perspective, Tóibín gives the reader access to a kind of understanding that has largely been absent or at least understated throughout his other works—insight into the mother's pain, isolation, and bewilderment.

Nora Webster privileges the wife and mother's attempt to process her grief, not the children's emotional process. Nora's meditations on Maurice can be sudden and devastating. When she walks out of work after a confrontation with Francie Kavanagh, in which the latter scornfully invokes Maurice, her despair is overwhelming: "She could barely see ahead of her as she walked. . . . It was the world filled with absences. . . . It was unlikely that Maurice was anywhere except buried in the graveyard where she had left him. . . . Maybe he could only imagine them all as vague presences, the ones he had loved, but love hardly mattered then, just as the haze here now meant that the line between things hardly mattered" (150–51). This scene, evocative of Helen's seaside meditations in *The Blackwater Lightship*, where the loss and suffering of the grown child is central, shifts emphasis to the grieving mother, exposing the profundity of her loss.[40]

In the same way, when Nora hurts her back while attempting to redecorate, her delirious belief that she sees Maurice reveals not only her mourning for her husband but also her fear for her children. In conversation with Josie, Nora says, "I don't know what I'm going to do. . . . And he said, Maurice said, when I asked him if Conor would be all right . . . he told me not to ask. What did that mean? . . . If I could be with him— . . . If I could be with him, that's what I said" (356–57). The depth of Nora's grief reminds us that although she has not helped her children sufficiently, she has failed to do so at least in part because of her own paralyzing sense of loss.[41]

In presenting the narrative from Nora's perspective, Tóibín does more than humanize her. By choosing to give the mother's sustained perspective in this novel, he for the first time offers an extended, cathartic response to the many traumatic representations of failed parents and abandoned children that fill his work, which he invokes and references along the way in *Nora Webster*. It is perhaps fitting, then, that Nora achieves some degree of peace after the dark night of the soul she experiences toward the novel's end. Although her hallucinations about Maurice lead her to an almost total collapse, so that "she could not imagine that she would ever return to normal" (360), she is saved by her family.

A remediation that comes through the family has not previously been seen in Tóibín's novels and stories—at least not to this extent. *The Heather Blazing* offers a tentative moment of connection between Eamon and his grandson, and *The Blackwater Lightship* offers a preliminary kind of reconciliation between Lily and Helen. But in *Nora Webster* the mother figure is embraced by her family, who rally to her support. When Nora appears at Josie's door, exhausted and pained, Josie takes care of her: "All you have to do is sleep, that's all you have to do. . . . That's what we are all for" (358). Similarly, when her sisters clean out her closets to remove Maurice's clothes—a metaphorical retaining that reflects Nora's emotional inability to let go—Una reassures her, "If we'd known [that you could not do this], we would have done it before" (372). *Nora Webster* offers a far less conditioned representation of the mother's pain than is usually provided in Tóibín's Irish novels.[42]

Nora's dawning awareness of her children's emotional life also offers some redemptive possibilities. Whereas other adult children throughout Tóibín's oeuvre come to terms with their histories, their parents, or their grief in only a limited way—as in Eamon's metaphorically loaded swim with his grandson, Michael, in *The Heather Blazing* and in Helen's cautious truce with Lily at the end of *The Blackwater Lightship*—Nora's evolution suggests the advent of a greater emotional awareness. Her belated recognition of the consequences of their father's loss for both Conor and Donal suggests not magical remediation but rather the possibility that she will better attend to her children's needs going forward. Thus, although she is partly responsible for causing the children's pain because they are too young to fend for themselves, her ability to see those errors and gradually to intuit their needs is correspondingly more redemptive because she carries that burden alone. The key narrative shift to representing younger children enables this greater sympathy for and understanding of Nora.

In *Nora Webster*, we see Nora begin to "learn how to live." Her growing interest in music and her willingness to do things that offer her comfort, such as purchasing a stereo, remind us that she is a woman learning to be single in her own right. She starts to navigate but not to be beholden to the pressures of external observations and expectations. In particular, when Conor is moved to "B-class," Nora recognizes that "this would not have happened were his father still alive" (273), but she does not succumb to the pressures of clergy and tradition. Rather, she threatens to picket the entire school and in a passage that is unexpected and funny threatens anyone who passes her picket with "a widow's curse" (276). We see something of this kind of strength in the characters Nancy in "The Name of the Game" and Molly in "A Priest in the Family," but Nora takes her independence to a new level, an assessment we can make in part owing to our extended access to her perspective: her moment of strength is less selfish than that of the other two women and less engaged with concerns about the town's views and opinions. Such moments—which are as much embedded in a critique of changing Irish society as in the study of Nora herself, a doubling of the personal and political that recurs throughout Tóibín's work—reflect Nora's slow, painful process of recovery.

Nora Webster thus offers a new direction in Tóibín's representation of the mother-and-family trauma. Whereas his earlier Irish novels focus predominantly on the impact of silences and neglect on the children, this novel takes the failing parent's point of view and enables us to balance her all too familiar mistakes with her weaknesses, to contextualize her flaws against her challenges and limitations. In light of Tóibín's previous representations of "monstrous" mothers, one might expect this exploration would not end favorably for Nora. As Ron Charles observes, "An autobiographical novel about one's emotionally rigid mother sounds like an opportunity for psychic revenge."[43] Yet this is not the case in *Nora Webster*—and herein lies the key respect in which this novel marks an evolution in Tóibín's canon that shifts his work from solely the representation of trauma to the language of and metanarrative engagement with recovery. As Charles notes, "There's nothing like that [revenge] in this story, which portrays Nora with tremendous sympathy and understanding."[44] Whereas semiautobiographical texts such "One Minus One" reflect the failure to engage, a sense of lost opportunity, and unresolved conflict, *Nora Webster* provides the imaginative resolution that previous characters never attain by offering narrative insight into the mother that was previously denied.

Tóibín's portrait of Nora reflects tremendous personal generosity as well as creative imagination. It provides an unflinching recognition of Nora's failures tempered by the recognition of her flawed humanity. Readers who are aware of the personal valences of Tóibín's work might well theorize how such an imaginative reconciliation could have personal resonances for him. If, as the author claims, "you are always working out of some deep business of self,"[45] then this novel may suggest a shift in his use of and perhaps relationship to his own history.

Considered in this light, we can look at *Nora Webster* as in many respects a recuperative capstone to Tóibín's Irish oeuvre. Capturing the elements of neglected children, selfish or insufficient mothers, interfering small-town society, and dysfunctional silences that run throughout his work, the novel nevertheless shifts narrative perspective from damaged child to suffering parent, from inscrutable mother to struggling widow, emphasizing intertextual parallels in such a way that the variations are unavoidably evident. Firm in holding Nora accountable for her failures, the novel nonetheless offers the explanation and insight that Tóibín's characters so often desire but lack.

In this way, Tóibín not only offers some degree of redemption for the flawed character of Nora but also suggests that he has made some peace with the figure of the failing mother more broadly and can remediate the canonical representations of trauma and loss that characterize his Irish canon. Perhaps this change signals Tóibín's evolving relationship with his own personal history—an evolution not unlike the literary evolution with trauma that we saw in John Banville's work. Either way, *Nora Webster* signals a hopeful gesture toward emotional recovery from grief and, like the other novels in this study, suggests that although twenty-first-century Irish authors continue to represent painful pasts and traumas, they are now doing so with an eye toward narrative's ability to capture and perhaps to lead toward recovery.

Notes

Works Cited

Index

Notes

Introduction

1. Denise McNamara, "Campaign to Recognise 800 Dead Tuam Babies," *Connaght Tribune*, Feb. 12, 2014, at http://connachttribune.ie/campaign-recognise-800-dead-tuam-babies/. Later reports modified the child body count to 796.

2. Subsequent reports cast doubt on the accuracy of the earliest reporting. The *Irish Times* offered various clarifications, and the Associated Press eventually issued a correction to address inaccuracies in its reporting. See Rosita Boland, "Tuam Mother and Baby Home: The Trouble with the Septic Tank Story," *Irish Times*, June 7, 2014, at http://www.irishtimes.com/news/social-affairs/tuam-mother-and-baby-home-the-trouble-with-the-septic-tank-story-1.1823393?page=3, and Associated Press, "Correction: Ireland—Children's Mass Graves Story," June 20, 2014, at http://news.yahoo.com/correction-ireland-childrens-mass-graves-story-184828902.html.

3. Ronan McGreevey, "Tuam Case 'Reminder of a Darker Past in Ireland,'" *Irish Times*, June 4, 2014, at http://www.irishtimes.com/news/social-affairs/tuam-case-reminder-of-a-darker-past-in-ireland-1.1820349.

4. Carl O'Brien, "Call to Extend Mother and Baby Homes Inquiry to Mental Homes," *Irish Times*, June 16, 2014, at http://www.irishtimes.com/news/social-affairs/call-to-extend-mother-and-baby-homes-inquiry-to-mental-homes-1.1833367.

5. Fintan O'Toole, "If Shame Has Gone, Why Do We Use Secret Abortions in England to Preserve the Myth of Holy Ireland?" *Irish Times*, June 10, 2014, at http://www.irishtimes.com/news/social-affairs/if-shame-has-gone-why-do-we-use-secret-abortions-in-england-to-preserve-the-myth-of-holy-ireland-1.1826199?page=2.

6. The examples of such soul searching one might proffer are many, but for a representative instance see John Banville, "A Century of Looking the Other Way," *New York Times*, May 22, 2009, at http://www.nytimes.com/2009/05/23/opinion/23banville.html.

7. Oona Frawley, introduction to *History and Modernity*, vol. 1 of *Memory Ireland*, ed. Oona Frawley (Syracuse, NY: Syracuse Univ. Press, 2011), xiii. For an analysis of the ways in which revisionism may propagate a false binary between "mythic falsehood

and scientific truth," see Graham Dawson, *Making Peace with the Past? Memory, Trauma, and the Irish Troubles* (Manchester: Manchester Univ. Press, 2007), 37.

8. Joe Cleary, "'Misplaced Ideas?': Colonialism, Location, and Dislocation in Irish Studies," in *Ireland and Postcolonial Theory*, ed. Clare Carroll and Patricia King (Notre Dame, IN: Univ. of Notre Dame Press, 2003), 20. Cleary observes, "Where both modernization discourse and Irish revisionist historiography stress the reactionary nature of Irish nationalism, postcolonial discourse has suggested that Irish nationalism can only be understood contextually, as the complex outcome of local interactions with an aggressively expanding imperialist world economy" (20). This attention to context clearly set the stage for later cultural explorations, such as memory studies, as Frawley suggests (introduction to *History and Modernity*, xiii–xvii).

9. On the hazard of allowing respect for "cultural traditions" to introduce "a postmodern world of relativism in which any notion of historical truth or ethical discrimination has been abandoned," see Dawson, *Making Peace with the Past?* 47.

10. Frawley, introduction to *History and Modernity*, xiv.

11. Frawley, introduction to *History and Modernity*, xvii. Frawley recognizes the hazards of reinscribing a unitary model of cultural memory when she demurs, "I do not suggest that there is, after all, a monolithic, unitary, and unified body of memories shared by all who might identify with or be associated with Irish culture" (xvii).

12. Robert F. Garratt, *Trauma and History in the Irish Novel: The Return of the Dead* (London: Palgrave Macmillan, 2011), 5.

13. "One of the ways of working through trauma implies narrating it, whatever form this takes" (Anne Goarzin, "Articulating Trauma," in "Trauma et mémoire en Irlande: Perspectives on Trauma in Irish History, Literature, and Culture," ed. Anne Goarzin, special issue of *Études Irlandaises* 36, no. 1 [Spring–Summer 2011]: 5, at https://etudesirlandaises.revues.org/2116).

14. Judith Lewis Herman, *Trauma and Recovery: The Aftermath of Violence—from Domestic Abuse to Political Terror* (New York: Basic Books, 1992).

15. Herman, *Trauma and Recovery*, 51. Ulrike Tancke's critique of trauma fiction draws from this sense of isolation; as she protests, "traumatic experience shatters a person's identity. . . . Applied to literary criticism, this destructive effect on the self ties in with the postmodernist belief in the instability of identity and meaning, and the inadequacies of textual renditions of reality" ("Trauma and Violence: Theorising Narrative Deception and Narrative Complicity," in *Deceptive Fictions: Narrating Trauma and Violence in Contemporary Writing* [Newcastle upon Tyne, UK: Cambridge Scholars, 2015], 7).

16. Herman, *Trauma and Recovery*, 174.

17. Shoshana Felman and Dori Laub, *Testimony: Crisis of Witnessing in Literature, Psychoanalysis, and History* (New York: Routledge, 1992); Cathy Caruth, ed., *Trauma: Explorations in Memory* (Baltimore: Johns Hopkins Univ. Press, 1995).

18. Dori Laub, "Truth and Testimony: The Process and the Struggle," in *Trauma*, ed. Caruth, 67, emphasis in original.

19. Cathy Caruth, "Trauma and Experience: Introduction," in *Trauma*, ed. Caruth, 5.

20. Bessel A. van der Kolk and Onno van der Hart, "The Intrusive Past: The Flexibility of Memory and the Engraving of Trauma," in *Trauma*, ed. Caruth, 163. For a concise review of traumatic memory as "unassimilated," see Garratt, *Trauma and History in the Irish Novel*, 7–8.

21. Dominick LaCapra, *Writing History, Writing Trauma: Parallax Re-visions of Culture and Society* (Baltimore: Johns Hopkins Univ. Press, 2001), ix, 88–89.

22. Felman and Laub, *Testimony*, quoted in James M. Smith, *Ireland's Magdalen Laundries and the Nation's Architecture of Containment* (Notre Dame, IN: Univ. of Notre Dame Press, 2007), 119–20.

23. Guy Beiner, *Remembering the Year of the French: Irish Folk History and Social Memory* (Madison: Univ. of Wisconsin Press, 2007), 25.

24. Beiner, *Remembering the Year of the French*, 28.

25. Garratt, *Trauma and History in the Irish Novel*, 12, my emphasis.

26. Frawley, introduction to *History and Modernity*, xv.

27. Frawley, introduction to *History and Modernity*. On the ethics of both remembering and forgetting, see Paul Ricoeur, "Memory and Forgetting," in *Questioning Ethics: Debates in Contemporary Philosophy*, ed. Richard Kearney and Mark Dooley (London: Routledge, 1999), 5–11.

28. Dawson, *Making Peace with the Past?* 13, 47–56, 62, 68–77, emphasis in original. In a recent article in the *Irish University Review*, Dawson revisits his earlier concern that "'collective trauma,' held to affect entire communities or nations and to have transgenerational impact, might be conceptualised 'while avoiding the danger of ascribing to that group a collective psyche . . . as if it were *like* an individual'" ("The Meaning of 'Moving On': From Trauma to the History and Memories of Emotions in 'Post-conflict' Northern Ireland," in "Moving Memory: The Dynamics of the Past in Irish Culture," ed. Emilie Pine, special issue of *Irish University Review* 47, no. 1 [Spring–Summer 2017]: 86, emphasis in original, quoting *Making Peace with the Past?*).

29. Smith, *Ireland's Magdalen Laundries*, 138; Maria Luddy, *Women and Philanthropy in Nineteenth-Century Ireland* (Cambridge: Cambridge Univ. Press, 1995).

30. Smith, *Ireland's Magdalen Laundries*, 188.

31. Goarzin, "Articulating Trauma," 2.

32. Garratt, *Trauma and History in the Irish Novel*, 3, 13.

33. Margaret Kelleher, *The Feminization of the Famine: Expressions of the Inexpressible?* (Cork: Cork Univ. Press, 1997), 2, 4. Kelleher does go on to condition the nature of literary silences about the Famine as at "risk of being overstated," but her

recognition of the dynamics of representation—or the lack thereof—nonetheless gestures toward the dynamics of trauma and a traumatized society.

34. LaCapra, *Writing History, Writing Trauma*, 23.

35. Dawson, *Making Peace with the Past?* 58.

36. For one reading of the use of social silencing in Anglo-Irish women's fiction, see Kathleen Costello-Sullivan, "Silence and Power in Anglo-Irish Women's Fiction," in *Back to the Present, Forward to the Past: Irish Writing and History since 1798*, vol. 1, ed. Patricia A. Lynch, Joachim Fischer, and Brian Coates (Amsterdam: Rodopi, 2006), 279–88.

37. Beiner, *Remembering the Year of the French*, 201. For a brief consideration of Irish folk studies and its relation to communal memory, see Dawson, *Making Peace with the Past?* 48.

38. Garratt, *Trauma and History in the Irish Novel*, 113.

39. Fintan O'Toole, introductory remarks, launch of *Digital Dubliners*, a multimedia guide created by students at Boston College, Ireland House, Dublin, June 11, 2014, comments paraphrased by the author.

40. John McGahern, essay on James Joyce's "Dubliners," typescript draft, n.d., P71/4.1.5. 837, p. 3, John McGahern Archive, James Hardiman Library, National University of Ireland (NUI), Galway, my emphasis. This essay was later published in the *Canadian Journal of Irish Studies* in 1991. In an article published in *Catholic World*, Bruce Cook writes, "The only thing I can recall like it [*The Dark*] for domestic brutality is James Joyce's story, 'A Little Cloud,' in *Dubliners*" ("Irish Censorship: The Case of John McGahern," *Catholic World* 206 [1967]: 178, photocopy, P71/6.3.1219, James Hardiman Library, NUI Galway).

41. Fergus Fahey, "Introduction," in "Descriptive List of the John McGahern Papers Compiled for James Hardiman Library," NUI Galway, Nov. 2007, i, also 1.

42. This is of course not to suggest that authors do not plumb their experiences all the time or to reduce McGahern's fictive appropriations to mere autobiography; rather, I suggest that McGahern was among the first to model narrativizing trauma, both personal and societal, fictionally in this way.

43. John McGahern, handwritten fragments from early drafts of "The End of the Beginning of Love," n.d., P71/1.1.2, John McGahern Archive, James Hardiman Library, NUI Galway.

44. John McGahern, handwritten fragments from early drafts of "The End of the Beginning of Love," n.d., P71/1.3.13, John McGahern Archive, James Hardiman Library, NUI Galway. It is interesting as well that McGahern elects to change the protagonist's name from "Jude" to "Hugh" in later versions of the novel.

45. John McGahern, handwritten fragments from early drafts of "The End of the Beginning of Love," 1957–61, n.d., P71/7.4, John McGahern Archive, James Hardiman Library, NUI Galway.

46. John McGahern, "What Ever you Say, Say Nothing: Ireland 1950–1959," *Irish Times*, Oct. 26, 1999, P71/4.1.16.906, John McGahern Archive, James Hardiman Library, NUI Galway.

47. John McGahern, "The Church and Its Spire," faircopy, n.d. (May 1, 1992), p. 14, P71/4.1.10/867, John McGahern Archive, James Hardiman Library, NUI Galway. For a valuable book-length study on McGahern's relationship specifically to the Catholic Church, see Eamon Maher, *"The Church and Its Spire": John McGahern and the Catholic Question* (Dublin: Columba Press, 2011).

48. Joseph O'Neill, "A Heartening Way with the Big Things," interview, *Guardian*, May 6, 1990, P71/6.2/1209, John McGahern Archive, James Hardiman Library, NUI Galway.

49. Indeed, an unpublished short story, "The Going," which was incorporated into *The Leavetaking*, effectively borrows the beginning of "The End of the Beginning of Love" while changing the character's name and increasing the number of children. See John McGahern, handwritten draft of "The Going," n.d., P71.1.4/64, John McGahern Archive, James Hardiman Library, NUI Galway.

50. John McGahern, *The Dark* (New York: Penguin Books, 1965), 7–10. On the title change for this novel, see John McGahern, "Typescript of 'The Dark,'" P71/1.3.50, John McGahern Archive, James Hardiman Library, NUI Galway.

51. John McGahern, typescript draft of "The End of the Beginning of Love," n.d., P71/1.1/9, p. 143, John McGahern Archive, James Hardiman Library, NUI Galway. In *Memoir*, McGahern acknowledges the autobiographical element in this scene: "I've always thought there was something sexual at their [his father's blows'] base, since they could flare up on nothing, and afterwards it was even hard to trace how exactly they began" (typescript draft of part of *Memoir*, P4.5.1112, p. 370, John McGahern Archive, James Hardiman Library, NUI Galway).

52. John McGahern, typescript draft of "The End of the Beginning of Love," P71/1.1/9, p. 56, John McGahern Archive, James Hardiman Library, NUI Galway; McGahern, *The Dark*, 18–21.

53. John McGahern, typescript draft of "The End of the Beginning of Love," pp. 37–39, John McGahern Archive, James Hardiman Library, NUI Galway. The sense of the children's alliance against their father recurs, for example, in *Amongst Women*.

54. John McGahern, typescript draft of "The Image," n.d., P71/4.1.1.804, John McGahern Archive, James Hardiman Library, NUI Galway.

55. John McGahern, typewritten transcript of an interview by Mike Murphy, Sept. 10, 2000, P71/6.2/1214, pp. 2–3, John McGahern Archive, James Hardiman Library, NUI Galway.

56. Ronan Bennett, "*The Country Girls*' Home Truths," *Guardian*, May 3, 2002, at https://www.theguardian.com/books/2002/may/04/fiction.reviews1.

57. Edna O'Brien, *Down by the River* (New York: Plume, 1997), 5, 261.

58. Bennett, "*The Country Girls*' Home Truths."

59. In her consideration of twentieth-century Irish literature "by Irish women writers aimed at girl readers," Susan Cahill unsurprisingly cites *The Country Girls* and *Down by the River* as examples of "representations of the teenage girl . . . generally characterized by crisis and trauma" ("A Girl Is a Half-Formed Thing? Girlhood, Trauma, and Resistance in Post-Tiger Irish Literature," *LIT: Literature, Interpretation, Theory* 28, no. 2 [2017]: 156–57).

60. Obviously, this list is not exhaustive. For a more comprehensive review of twentieth-century trauma novels, see Garratt, *Trauma and History in the Irish Novel*.

61. Herman, *Trauma and Recovery*, 175.

62. Laub, "Truth and Testimony," 61, my emphasis.

63. Garratt, *Trauma and History in the Irish Novel*, 8.

64. On *An Crann* and similar efforts to employ storytelling as a vehicle toward healing or reconciliation, see Dawson, *Making Peace*, 67–77. Colum McCann's investment in empathy and storytelling is well known; in recently discussing the Forgiveness Project, he noted, "It's an incredible organization of people all over the world who confront what it means to forgive. They tell their own stories in the most profound, direct ways. In forgiving, they embrace reason and contradiction. They forgive others, and in so doing, they forgive themselves" (in Kathleen Costello-Sullivan, "An Interview with Colum McCann," *TriQuarterly*, Apr. 25, 2017, at http://www.triquarterly.org/interviews/interview-colum-mccann).

65. Tancke, "Trauma and Violence in Contemporary Fiction," 10, 7. Tancke suggests that the use of trauma studies betrays a wider ideological purpose where "the postmodernist perspective . . . effectively covers over the pain, violence and corporeal immediacy of the traumatic experience, turning an exceptional, and exceptionally destructive event into a constitutive critical paradigm" (8).

66. Frawley, introduction to *History and Modernity*, 5, emphasis in original.

67. Dawson, *Making Peace with the Past?* 62.

68. Dawson, "Meaning of 'Moving On,'" 82, 84–85, 87–89.

69. For another critique of the concept of trauma as a result of "a colonial discourse of temporal disruption and contemporary political exigencies," see Conor Carville, "'Keeping That Wound Green': Irish Studies and Traumaculture," in *What Rough Beasts? Irish and Scottish Studies in the New Millennium*, ed. Shane Alcobia-Murphy (Newcastle, UK: Cambridge Scholars, 2008), 53. Like Dawson, Carville focuses on the use of trauma in history; I am focused on its use in literary representation.

70. Richard Kearney, quoted in Eóin Flannery, *Colum McCann and the Aesthetics of Redemption* (Dublin: Irish Academic Press, 2011), 202, emphasis in original. Flannery cites this passage in the context of his argument that literature is enabling for redemptive representations of the terrorist attacks in New York and Washington,

DC, on September 11, 2001, within the context of his focused engagement with McCann's specific intervention through *Let the Great World Spin*.

71. Colm Tóibín, *The Blackwater Lightship: A Novel* (New York: Scribner, 1999). For a reading of how this novel seeks to redress the individual and national elision of homosexuality and to recover from such traumatic omissions, see Kathleen Costello-Sullivan, *Mother/Country: Politics of the Personal in the Fiction of Colm Tóibín* (Oxford: Peter Lang, 2012), 123–54. For a reading of the novel as "deal[ing] directly with the trauma [that] death inflicts on a family where mourning is repressed," see Bridget English, "Laying Out the Bones: Death, Trauma, and the Irish Family in Colm Tóibín's *The Blackwater Lightship* and Anne Enright's *The Gathering*," in *New Voices, Inherited Lines: Literary and Cultural Representations of the Irish Family*, ed. Yvonne O'Keeffe and Claudia Reese (Oxford: Peter Lang, 2013), 204.

72. Edna O'Brien, *The Little Red Chairs: A Novel* (New York: Little, Brown, 2016).

73. Fidelma does ultimately speak her history relatively late in *The Little Red Chairs*, and her attendance at the trial certainly suggests that she confronts her past. Nonetheless, the bulk of the text concentrates on the consequences of trauma rather than on the process of narrativizing or recovering from that suffering or both. For another example of a twentieth-century use of trauma, see Garratt's reading of McCabe's novel *The Dead School* (1995) in *Trauma and History in the Irish Novel*, 115–20.

74. James Ryan, *Seeds of Doubt* (London: Weidenfeld & Nicholson, 2001), 242.

75. Eimear McBride's novel *A Girl Is a Half-Formed Thing* (Norwich, UK: Faber and Faber, 2013) took nine years to publish, so in some ways it dates more accurately to 2004.

76. Anne Enright, review of *A Girl Is a Half-Formed Thing*, by Eimear McBride, *Guardian*, Sept. 20, 2013, at https://www.theguardian.com/books/2013/sep/20/girl-half-formed-thing-review.

77. For a reading of *A Girl Is a Half-Formed Thing* as one of the "post-Tiger texts" that "explicitly link girlhood, trauma, language, and resistance in ways that challenge dominant representations of the girl in the Tiger period," see Cahill, "A Girl Is a Half-Formed Thing?" 155.

78. Garratt, *Trauma and History in the Irish Novel*, 114.

79. Maria Edgeworth to Michael Pakenham Edgeworth, Esq., Edgeworthstown, Feb. 10, 1834, in *Maria Edgeworth's Letters from Ireland*, ed. Valerie Pakenham (Dublin: Lilliput Press, 2018), 334–36, quoted in Declan Kiberd, "Irish Literature and History," appendix in R. F. Foster, *Illustrated History of Ireland* (Oxford: Oxford Univ. Press, 1989), 306–7, at http://www.ricorso.net/rx/az-data/authors/e/Edgeworth_M/quots.htm.

80. Quoted in Kersti Tarien Powell, *Irish Fiction: An Introduction*, annotated ed. (London: Bloomsbury Academic, 2004), 8.

81. Dawson, *Making Peace with the Past?* 5.

82. For a helpful timeline relevant to this period, see Susan Cahill, *Irish Literature in the Celtic Tiger Years 1990–2008: Gender, Bodies, Memory* (London: Continuum International, 2011), ix–xv.

83. Cahill, *Irish Literature in the Celtic Tiger Years*, 1.

84. Cahill, *Irish Literature in the Celtic Tiger Years*, 4.

85. Mary McGlynn, "'No Difference between the Different Kinds of Yesterday': The Neoliberal Present in *The Green Road*, *The Devil I Know*, and *The Lives of Women*," *LIT: Literature, Interpretation, Theory* 28, no. 1 (2017): 34–36.

86. McGlynn, "'No Difference,'" 45.

87. McGlynn, "'No Difference,'" 38.

88. Cahill, "A Girl Is a Half-Formed Thing?" 158.

89. McGlynn, "'No Difference,'" 37.

90. Colum McCann, *Let the Great World Spin* (New York: Random House, 2009), 325.

1. "My Memory Gropes in Search of Details"

1. Banville, "A Century of Looking the Other Way," emphasis in original.

2. Belinda McKeon, "John Banville, the Art of Fiction No. 200," *Paris Review* 188 (Spring 2009), at https://www.theparisreview.org/interviews/5907/john-banville-the-art-of-fiction-no-200-john-banville.

3. On the controversy over *The Sea*'s literary merits as centered on the novel's style, see John Kenny, *John Banville* (Dublin: Irish Academic Press, 2009), 1–7. Also see Carmen Zamorano Llena, "'The Figures of the Far Past Come Back at the End': Unmasking the Desired Self through Reminiscence in Late Adulthood in John Banville's *The Sea*," in *Flaming Embers: Literary Testimonies on Ageing and Desire*, ed. Nela Bureu Ramos (Bern: Peter Lang, 2010), 87–91.

4. Quoted in Kenny, *John Banville*, 21.

5. Herman, *Trauma and Recovery*, 1.

6. On discursive style and metanarrative devices, see Monica Facchinello, "'The Old Illusion of Belonging': Distinctive Style, Bad Faith, and John Banville's *The Sea*," *Estudios Irlandeses* 5, no. 10 (2010): 33–44, and Lieven Vandelanotte, "'Where Am I, Lurking in What Place of Vantage?': The Discourse of Distance in John Banville's Fiction," *English Text Construction* 3, no. 2 (2010): 203–25. On Banville's modernist/postmodernist proclivities, see Derek Hand, *John Banville: Exploring Fictions* (Dublin: Liffey Press, 2002), 1–21; Joseph McMinn, *John Banville: A Critical Study* (Dublin: Gill and Macmillan, 1991), 2–12; and Kenny, *John Banville*, 12–18.

7. As discussed later in the chapter, "Max" is not this character's real name: Max's mother asks, "Why does she keep calling you Max? . . . Your name is not Max"

(John Banville, *The Sea* [New York: Vintage, 2005], 156; all references are to this edition). I address this issue later in this chapter.

8. For a reading of *The Sea* that suggests that "place instigates mourning and mourning instigates place," see Joanne Watkiss, "Ghosts in the Head: Mourning, Memory, and Derridean 'Trace' in John Banville's *The Sea*," *Irish Journal of Gothic and Horror Studies* 2 (Mar. 2007), at http://irishgothichorrorjournal.homestead.com/theseabanville.html.

9. Monica Facchinello claims that the "features, tics and tropes in *The Sea* . . . sanction the writer's distinctive voice and go on clarifying the image of the kind of writer John Banville has become known to be" ("'The Old Illusion of Belonging,'" 40). By attributing this self-consciousness with style to the author, critics neglect its import as a trait of the character.

10. Derek Hand, quoted in Vandelanotte, "'Where Am I?'" 204. Carmen Zamorano Llena counters this view, arguing that Banville "brings [plot, character, pacing, suspense] together in his novel and makes them interdependent, so that all these elements are present" ("'The Figures of the Far Past,'" 104 n. 42). For another discussion of plot in Banville's canon, see Hand, *John Banville*, 165.

11. Rüdiger Imhof, "*The Sea*: 'Was't Well Done?'" in "John Banville," special issue of *Irish University Review* 36, no. 1 (Spring–Summer 2006): 165.

12. John Kenny notes that Banville "gained a reputation for incorrigible seriousness" and that this reputation led to a collapsing of the boundary between Banville and his prose style: "The same terms of personal description had been used so repetitively to fatten copy that Banville's deportment often seemed a caricatured extension of his own prose style" (*John Banville*, 1–2). An exception is Tomas Dobrogoszcz, who emphasizes "the novel itself [rather than placing] it in a specific literary context of Banville's oeuvre." Dobrogoszcz nonetheless reads Banville's use of language and "naming" as a means to attain a "lightness of approach" and as reflecting "the real problem of Max and his identity" ("The Eerie Re-visioning of Airy Past in John Banville's *The Sea*," in *The Playful Air/Light(ness) in Irish Literature and Culture*, ed. Marta Goszczyńska and Katarzyna Poloczek [Newcastle upon Tyne, UK: Cambridge Scholars, 2011], 57, 59, 65).

13. On Banville's tendency to focus on language and to foreground his characters' insecurities linguistically, see Kenny, *John Banville*, 34–35, 150–51, 170–71, and Vandelanotte, "'Where Am I?,'" esp. 210–14.

14. Banville, *The Sea*, 95; subsequent references are given parenthetically by page number in the text.

15. Imhof, "*The Sea*," 167.

16. John Banville, *Shroud* (2002; reprint, New York: Vintage International, 2004), 9, emphasis in original.

17. John Banville, *The Untouchable* (1997; reprint, New York: Vintage, 1998), 5, 44. As early as *Birchwood*, we see this concern with identity as Gabriel Godkin fears "a phantom of [himself] who mimicked [his] every movement" (John Banville, *Birchwood* [1973; reprint, London: Minerva, 1992], 99).

18. Facchinello, "'The Old Illusion of Belonging,'" 34. Kenny similarly observes that Banville's "oeuvre can be said particularly to constitute an organic whole" (*John Banville*, xi). More recent Banville novels such as *The Infinities* (New York: Knopf, 2010) also employ elaborate, lyrical prose and a sometimes self-indulgent revelry in language.

19. Imhof claims that "Morden is a chronicler who perceives reality, the world, in terms of art" ("*The Sea*," 166).

20. On the "compositional and thematic implications" of Banville's use of "painting and the pictorial generally," see Kenny, *John Banville*, 147–82, quotes on 147. For an analysis of *The Sea* in terms of "pictorial memory" as exposing "a particular narrative function of images," see Elisabeth Siegel, "'Another Fleeting Image': Pictorial Memory in John Banville's *The Sea*," in *Intermedialities*, ed. Warner Huber, Evelyne Keitel, and Gunter Süß (Trier, Germany: Wissenshaftlicher Verlag Trier, 2007), 107–17, quotes on 108–9. Dobrogoszcz reads the novel's use of pictures in terms of "the re-cognitive [*sic*] mind work involved in the process of recalling" and in reference to the Lacanian gaze ("The Erie Re-visioning of Airy Past," 60–64, quote on 60).

21. Banville, *The Untouchable*, 13.

22. "A chief component of the radical doubt about the claims of language and literature Banville has always expressed . . . is his increasing ridicule of the solemn author or artist, . . . who presumes in his megalomania that his endeavours at explaining both himself and the world have some claim to originality, authenticity or truth" (Kenny, *John Banville*, 150).

23. Banville, *Birchwood*, 12, 37.

24. Banville, *Shroud*, 39.

25. Kenny, *John Banville*, 170.

26. Patricia Coughlan, "Banville, the Feminine, and the Scenes of Eros," in "John Banville," special issue of *Irish University Review* 36, no. 1 (Spring–Summer 2006): 84.

27. This moment is of course evocative of Prufrock:

No! I am not Prince Hamlet, nor was meant to be;
Am an attendant lord, one that will do
To swell a progress, start a scene or two,
Advise the prince; no doubt, an easy tool,
Deferential, glad to be of use,
Politic, cautious, and meticulous;
Full of high sentence, but a bit obtuse;

At times, indeed, almost ridiculous—
Almost, at times, the Fool.
(T. S. Eliot, "The Lovesong of J. Alfred Prufrock," in *The Norton Anthology of Poetry*, shorter 5th ed., ed. Margaret Ferguson, Mary Jo Salter, and Jon Saltworthy [New York: Norton, 2005], 865)

This association is explicit when Morden remembers Anna responding as if to say, "*No, you're wrong, that is not it at all!*" (*The Sea*, 176, emphasis in original).

28. Vander's expertise is as much linguistic performance as any real expertise, and Maskell describes himself as a "failed artist." Nonetheless, the former has a successful academic career, and the latter is a respected art authority (Banville, *The Untouchable*, 23).

29. LaCapra, *Writing History, Writing Trauma*, 23, my emphasis.

30. Children who are harnessed with responsibility for events beyond their control often exhibit traits of both self-blame and alienation. For a reading of this tendency in children in dysfunctional settings, see Herman, *Trauma and Recovery*, 103–5.

31. For a reading of Morden's parents in terms of fantasy and desire, see Facchinello, "'The Old Illusion of Belonging,'" 38–39.

32. Morden's claim that he "did not hate them" but rather "loved them, probably" (26) reflects what Herman calls a child's ability to love and loathe his parents at the same time (*Trauma and Recovery*, 101–3).

33. Herman, *Trauma and Recovery*, 43. See also Imhof, "*The Sea*," 170.

34. For a reading of naming in terms of metafiction and "a kind of desubjectification attempt," see Vandelanotte, "'Where Am I?'" 212–14, 218–21, quote on 221. For a reading of "Max" through intertextual resonances in Banville's canon and of Max's new identity as a sign of "bad faith," see Facchinello, "'The Old Illusion of Belonging,'" esp. 35–37.

35. Imhof notes that the "death of the twins and of Anna have had the most shattering impact on Morden" ("*The Sea*," 171).

36. The phrases "a thing of air" and "Ariel set free" allude to Shakespeare's Ariel in *The Tempest*. Morden problematically imagines Ariel's freedom as a kind of entrapment, however, as if he, like Ariel, is now "at a loss" and as if, implicitly, his delivery of the news to the Graces makes him a pawn to forces beyond his control.

37. Herman, *Trauma and Recovery*, 43. For a reading of Morden as melancholic, see Anne-Julia Zwierlein, "Lost at Sea: Melancholia and Maritime Mindscapes in Early 21st-Century British and Irish Fiction," in *Narrating Loss: Representations of Mourning, Nostalgia, and Melancholia in Contemporary Anglophone Fictions*, ed. Brigitte Johanna Glaser and Barbara Puschmann-Nalenz (Trier, Germany: Wissenschaftlicher Verlag Trier, 2014), 161–77, esp. 161–67.

38. Anne Enright, *The Gathering* (London: Jonathan Cape, 2007), 97.

39. Caruth, "Trauma and Experience," 9. For a reading of the Cedars as "a monumental/architectural site of memory," see Hedda Friberg-Hanesk, "Waters and Memories Always Divide: Sites of Memory in John Banville's *The Sea*," in *Recovering Memory: Irish Representations of Past and Present*, ed. Hedda Friberg-Hanesk, Irense Gilsenan Nordin, and Lene Yding Pedersen (Newcastle, UK: Cambridge Scholars, 2007), 251–54.

40. Friberg-Harnesk, "Waters and Memories Always Divide," 250–51.

41. Hedda Friberg, "'In the Murky Sea of Memory': Memory's Miscues in John Banville's *The Sea*," *An Sionnach* 1, no. 2 (Fall 2005): 111.

42. See Friberg, "'In the Murky Sea of Memory,'" esp. 112, 116, 119–20. For a reading of the novel's focus on unreliable memory, see Dobrogoszcz, "The Eerie Revisioning of Airy Past," 59–62.

43. This passage, when "the image of her [Mrs. Grace] would spring up in [him] unbidden" and he sobs as if in a religious passion (*The Sea*, 65), clearly invokes James Joyce's story "Araby" (in *Dubliners*, rev. ed. [New York: Penguin Books, 1996], 31). The intertextual reference signals that the narrator is maintaining a critical distance from his younger self and gives weight to some critics' sense that the novel offers a commentary on aging (e.g., Llena, "'The Figures of the Far Past'"). However, the attempt to separate from one's younger self is also characteristic of traumatic dissociation.

44. Laub, "Truth and Testimony," 62.

45. Caruth, "Trauma and Experience," 8.

46. Herman, *Trauma and Recovery*, 38.

47. Van der Kolk and van der Hart, "The Intrusive Past," 176.

48. Van der Kolk and van der Hart, "The Intrusive Past," 172. Herman refers to the "frozen and wordless quality of traumatic memories" (*Trauma and Recovery*, 37). Elisabeth Siegel notes that "the past only seems to be definite and unchanging because Max turns it into images" ("'Another Fleeting Image,'" 111).

49. "The intense focus on fragmentary sensation, on image without context, gives the traumatic memory a heightened reality" (Herman, *Trauma and Recovery*, 38).

50. "Many people have [difficulty] in believing memories that seem to them to be false simply because they do not appear in easily recognizable forms" (Cathy Caruth, preface to *Trauma*, ed. Caruth, viii).

51. This resonates with a line from Tóibín's later short story "One Minus One," where the narrator avers that the past can "come back . . . with a force that feels like violence" (in *The Empty Family: Stories* [New York: Scribner, 2011], 70).

52. Friberg concludes that "the portrait of Chloe says as much, or more, about the present as it does about the past" ("'In the Murky Sea of Memory,'" 119). Because of the layered nature of traumatic memories, past and present are entangled and therefore difficult to differentiate.

53. LaCapra, *Writing History, Writing Trauma*, 21, 66. On the collapsing of past and present, see LaCapra, 46, 89.

54. Herman, *Trauma and Recovery*, 52.

55. Danielle C. Brousseau, Marvin J. McDonald, and Joanne E. Stephen, "The Moderating Effect of Relationship Quality on Partner Secondary Traumatic Stress among Couples Coping with Cancer," *Families, Systems, and Health* 29, no. 2 (2011): 114; 115 quoting C. R. Figley.

56. Brousseau, McDonald, and Stephen, "Moderating Effect," 122.

57. Herman, *Trauma and Recovery*, 33.

58. Herman, *Trauma and Recovery*, 42.

59. I privilege Chloe's death over Myles's because of the budding romantic attachment between Max and Chloe: as a vulnerable and emotionally limited child, Max would have been doubly invested in this new romance. For a reading of the "triangle" of "Max, Chloe, and Chloe's mute brother Myles," see Coughlan, "Banville, the Feminine, and the Scenes of Eros," 86–87.

60. Kenny, *John Banville*, 9.

61. Herman, *Trauma and Recovery*, 44.

62. LaCapra, *Writing History, Writing Trauma*, 22.

63. Banville, *Birchwood*, 12.

64. Kenny, *John Banville*, 67–70.

65. Banville, *Birchwood*, 174.

66. Kenny, *John Banville*, 70.

67. Banville, *The Untouchable*, 311, 229, 47.

68. Banville, *The Untouchable*, 309, emphasis in original.

69. Although Maskell lost his mother at a young age, he accepted his stepmother as his mother's substitute: he notes that "she had not a trace of wickedness in her" (*The Untouchable*, 63).

70. Banville, *The Untouchable*, 288.

71. Banville, *Shroud*, 187–88.

72. Banville, *Shroud*, 116.

73. Banville, *Shroud*, 153, 11, 13.

74. Banville, *Shroud*, 240.

75. Banville, *Shroud*, 254.

76. Kenny, *John Banville*, 170.

77. Kenny, *John Banville*, 177, emphasis in original.

78. Llena, "'The Figures of the Far Past Come Back at the End,'" 90.

79. On the narrator's unreliability, see Vandelanotte, "'Where Am I?'" 211.

80. Herman, *Trauma and Recovery*, 1, my emphasis.

81. Laub, "Truth and Testimony," 63, emphasis in original.

82. LaCapra, *Writing History, Writing Trauma*, 88–89, my emphasis.

83. Laub, "Truth and Testimony," 70.

84. Banville, "A Century of Looking the Other Way."

85. In this respect, these novels also present an interesting counterpoint to the extremity of austerity measures enacted by the Irish state.

2. "A Whole Fucking Country—Drowning in Shame"

1. Liam Harte, "Mourning Remains Unresolved: Trauma and Survival in Anne Enright's *The Gathering*," *LIT: Literature, Interpretation, Theory* 21 (2010): 189.

2. Caruth, "Trauma and Experience," 8.

3. Enright, *The Gathering*, 1; all references are to the 2007 Jonathan Cape edition and are subsequently given parenthetically by page number in the text.

4. Susan Cahill reads Veronica's proclivity toward self-harm as revealing "the repercussions of her relationship to touch and her own body . . . as receptacle for the traumatic knowledge" (*Irish Literature in the Celtic Tiger Years*, 179).

5. Herman, *Trauma and Recovery*, 109, 44.

6. Harte, "Mourning Remains Unresolved," 190.

7. Carole Dell'Amico, "Anne Enright's *The Gathering*: Trauma, Testimony, Memory," *New Hibernia Review* 14, no. 3 (Fómhar/Autumn 2010): 64.

8. Garratt, *Trauma and History in the Irish Novel*, 12. For a different reading of the novel not as a "mere therapeutic narrative" but rather as "an investigation of the inevitable human trauma of the split subject," see Sarah C. Gardam, "'Default[ing] to the Oldest Scar': A Psychoanalytic Investigation of Subjectivity in Anne Enright's *The Gathering*," *Études Irlandaises* 34, no. 1 (Spring 2009): 99–100.

9. Herman, *Trauma and Recovery*, 40–41, my emphasis.

10. Dori Laub, "Bearing Witness, or the Vicissitudes of Listening," in *Testimony*, ed. Felman and Laub, 57.

11. Veronica's use of the term *romance* is ironic: in contrast to how *romance* evokes courtship and love, she describes Nugent as "a gobdaw with a lump in his pants" (20). Her recurrent reference to "romance" (for instance, "history [as] such a romantic place" [13]) suggests that Enright is juxtaposing "true" history and a "romance" of history. Not only does this juxtaposition reflect what "romance" means to Veronica, but it also suggests the realist/romantic literary divide with which she toys. Ian Watt explains this implicit duality in another context: "If the novel were realistic merely because it saw life from the seamy side, it would only be an inverted romance" (*The Rise of the Novel: Studies in Dafoe, Richardson, and Fielding* [Berkeley: Univ. of California Press, 2000], 11). For one reading of "romance" as "a broadly epistemological . . . category whose meaning is overwhelmingly trivializing or pejorative," see Michael McKeon, *The Origins of the English Novel 1600–1740* (Baltimore: Johns Hopkins Univ. Press, 1987), 26–28, here 27.

12. Harte, "Mourning Remains Unresolved," 191. See pages 192–94 for Harte's excellent analysis of how the novel re-creates the modes of traumatic memory. Dell'Amico also notes that there is a "teasing process in this novel, providing a simultaneous assertion and undermining of certainty" ("Anne Enright's *The Gathering*," 60). On the "trauma novel" as a text that seeks to employ "a narrative strategy in which a reconstruction of events through memories, flashbacks, dreams, and hauntings is as important as the events themselves," see Garratt, *Trauma and History in the Irish Novel*, esp. 5–8, quote here on 5.

13. Dell'Amico, "Anne Enright's *The Gathering*," 60.

14. Herman, *Trauma and Recovery*, 38; Van der Kolk and van der Hart, "The Intrusive Past," 176. For a reading of *The Gathering* that "seeks to connect [the] testimonial model of telling to the way that death shapes narrative, in turn, revealing the ways in which death and mourning have been altered by modern fear of death and desire to prolong life," see English, "Laying Out the Bones," 203–23, quote here on 204–5.

15. Laub, "Bearing Witness," 62, my emphasis.

16. Claire Bracken and Susan Cahill, "An Interview with Anne Enright, August 2009," in *Anne Enright*, ed. Claire Bracken and Susan Cahill (Dublin: Irish Academic Press, 2011), 29–30.

17. For a reading of the novel that situates Veronica as "enact[ing] the role of the archetypal *bean chaointe* [keening woman]" and the story as "a lament, testifying to a widespread account of sexual abuse in families and institutions in Ireland," see Margaret O'Neill, "The *Caoineadh*, Psychoanalytic Theory, and Contemporary Irish Writing: Anne Enright's *The Gathering*," in *Folklore and Modern Irish Writing*, ed. Anne Markey and Anne O'Connor (Dublin: Irish Academic Press, 2014), 191–203, quotation on 194.

18. Veronica's remark interestingly echoes Banville's comments regarding "his own traumas" and the views he expresses in his *New York Times* op-ed ("A Century of Looking the Other Way"); see chapter 1. For an excellent and concise summary of Ireland's own culpability in forgetting, including a review of Banville's *New York Times* editorial, see Dell'Amico, "Anne Enright's *The Gathering*," 74 n. 21.

19. Dell'Amico, "Anne Enright's *The Gathering*," 63, 66–67.

20. Harte, "Mourning Remains Unresolved," 199.

21. The phrase "architecture of containment," of course, belongs to James M. Smith and his analysis of Ireland's "assortment of interconnected institutions, including mother and baby homes, industrial and reformatory schools, mental asylums, adoption agencies, and Magdalen laundries," which served to "[conceal] citizens already marginalized by a number of interrelated social phenomena" (preface to *Ireland's Magdalen Laundries*, xiii).

22. Harte, "Mourning Remains Unresolved," 196.

23. Dell'Amico, "Anne Enright's *The Gathering*," 67.

24. Laura Sydora, "'Everyone Wants a Bit of Me': Historicizing Motherhood in Anne Enright's *The Gathering*," *Women's Studies* 44 (Mar. 2015): 239.

25. Harte, "Mourning Remains Unresolved," 201, my emphasis.

26. Harte, "Mourning Remains Unresolved," 195.

27. Dell'Amico, "Anne Enright's *The Gathering*," 69–70, 72, my emphasis.

28. Harte notes a similar moment, claiming that "it is clear . . . that [Veronica's] perspective on the most socially sanctioned form of sex—that which takes place between a married couple—is disturbed by the latent dissonances of the most culturally forbidden kind, that between an adult and a child" ("Mourning Remains Unresolved," 196). Harte is stressing the latent impact of trauma, whereas I am emphasizing the space of the encounters themselves and how Veronica uses them.

29. Sydora makes a similar observation when she notes, "From an objective, feminine perspective, Veronica is writing her grandmother's physicality into existence, individualizing it as an independent physical structure" ("'Everyone Wants a Bit of Me,'" 260). I am suggesting that it is not just her grandmother's physical presencing but rather the *grotesque* physical presencing that is telling here.

30. Anne Mulhall, "'Now the Blood Is in the Room': The Spectral Feminine in the Work of Anne Enright," in *Anne Enright*, ed. Bracken and Cahill, 68.

31. Sydora, "'Everyone Wants a Bit of Me,'" 252.

32. For a reading of the house as "mirror[ing] the messy relationships at stake in the novel," evidencing that "the imagery of invaded spaces is all-pervasive," see Cahill, *Irish Literature in the Celtic Tiger Years*, 177.

33. Of course, this moment is also an echo of an earlier reference to her brother, who, Veronica notes, "was always a great man for people's *holes*" (76, emphasis in original). This emphasis on the body associates her with him in their shared physical humanity and also as victims suffering from a similar dehumanizing history of the molested body.

34. Dell'Amico, "Anne Enright's *The Gathering*," 64–72.

35. For a reading of Veronica as embedded in a "multi-generational scheme" within a commentary on the "division of investment . . . [in] child rearing," see Candis P. Pizzetta, "Division of Maternal Effort in Anne Enright's *The Gathering*," in *Constructing the Literary Self: Race and Gender in Twentieth-Century Literature*, ed. Patsy J. Daniels (Newcastle upon Tyne, UK: Cambridge Scholars, 2013), 199–212, quotes here on 200, 210. For a reading of "Veronica's feminist interrogation into the microcosmic history of Irish women in her family . . . as a large-scale exposition of the patriarchal, political, social, and familial structures responsible for the national victimization of Irish women," see Sydora, "'Everyone Wants a Bit of Me,'" 243.

36. Dell'Amico, "Anne Enright's *The Gathering*," 61. For a reading that suggests that "the inability to cultivate a safe domestic space points to a crisis in maternity," see Sydora, "'Everyone Wants a Bit of Me,'" 248.

37. Mulhall, "'Now the Blood Is in the Room,'" 68–69.

38. Cahill, *Irish Literature in the Celtic Tiger Years*, 180.

39. Harte, "Mourning Remains Unresolved," 198.

40. For a reading of the color scheme as related to "the context of persons who have been insufficiently mourned and belong to marginalized groups," see Dell'Amico, "Anne Enright's *The Gathering*," 65. We also see here Veronica's fear that a similar fate, of becoming like a ghost, something "vague" or something "faded," awaits her daughters through the matrilineal line. On "the erasure of the maternal" in Enright's fiction, see Susan Cahill, "'Dreaming of Upholstered Breasts,' or, How to Find Your Way back Home: Dislocation in *What Are You Like*?" in *Anne Enright*, ed. Bracken and Cahill, 87–106, quote here on 89.

41. Mulhall quoted in O'Neill, "The *Caoineadh*," 196. Sydora notes, "As exemplified in three generations of Hegarty women, . . . women are never really anything but prisoners within their own home" ("'Everyone Wants a Bit of Me,'" 249).

42. Cahill, *Irish Literature in the Celtic Tiger Years*, 178.

43. Margaret O'Neill argues that, "as in the keen, Veronica's anger is both personal and communal, as it is directed outwardly, against her family, as well as inwardly, against herself" ("The *Caoineadh*," 197).

44. Bracken and Cahill, "An Interview," 22.

45. See Cahill, "'Dreaming of Upholstered Breasts,'" and Mulhall, "'Now the Blood Is in the Room.'"

46. For a reading of "maternal subjectivity" as "part of the abject . . . attributed to Ireland's history as a colonised country," see Hannelore Fasching, "'The New Drama of Being a Mother about Which so Little Has Been Written': Maternal Subjectivity and the Mother Icon in Anne Enright's Writing," in *New Voices, Inherited Lines*, ed. O'Keeffe and Reese, 183–201, quote here on 199. For a reading of the novel's use of abjection in terms of both bodily and domestic borders, see Cahill, *Irish Literature in the Celtic Tiger Years*, esp. 177–78, 180–82. Cahill claims that in *The Gathering* "this is the abject body, turning itself into meat" (*Irish Literature in the Celtic Tiger Years*, 181). Sydora similarly argues that Veronica "realize[s] her own corporeal subjugation" ("'Everyone Wants a Bit of Me,'" 253). In contrast, I see Enright's use as reclamatory because it presences the traumatized body and Veronica's subjectivity.

47. For a psychoanalytic reading of Veronica in relation to motherhood and mourning, see O'Neill, "The *Caoineadh*."

48. Tancke, "Trauma and Violence in Contemporary Fiction," 6.

49. Claire Bracken and Susan Cahill, introduction to *Anne Enright*, ed. Bracken and Cahill, 7.

50. For a broader overview of Enright's recuperative use of the maternal in her canon, see Fasching, "'The New Drama of Being a Mother.'"

51. For a reading of the airport as symptomatic of a wider engagement with liminality and mourning in the novel, see Ana-Karina Schneider, "Skin as a Trope of Liminality in Anne Enright's *The Gathering*," *Contemporary Women's Writing* 8, no. 2 (July 2014): 206–22, esp. 211.

52. For a reading of Rowan as "embody[ing] the trauma of the past and also hope for the future," see O'Neill, "The *Caoineadh*," 201. Rowan is also, as Harte notes, potentially a sign of "the anointed future, a new child for the new millennium—innocent, inviolable, and wholly without stain or stigma" ("Mourning Remains Unresolved," 202).

3. "Surmises Held Up against the Truth"

1. LaCapra, *Writing History, Writing Trauma*, 88–89.

2. On more than one occasion, Father Gaunt lingers on the topic of Roseanne's beauty, and Dr. Grene notes that the priest "is almost clinical in his anatomising of Roseanne's sexuality" (Sebastian Barry, *The Secret Scripture* [London: Viking, 2008], 93–95, 230; all references are to this edition).

3. For a detailed reading of the novel's commentary on gendered and church politics after the founding of the Free State as well as its presencing of those elided by dominant history, see Gülden Hatipoğlu, "Palimpsests of History in Sebastian Barry's *The Secret Scripture*," in *The Adaptation of History: Essays on Ways of Telling the Past*, ed. Lawrence Raw and Defne Ersin Tutan (Jefferson, NC: McFarland, 2013), 153–60, esp. 155–57.

4. Barry, *The Secret Scripture*, 226; subsequent references are given parenthetically by page number in the text.

5. Linda Hogan, "Clerical and Religious Child Abuse: Ireland and Beyond," *Theological Studies* 72 (2011): 182.

6. *The Secret Scripture* is particularly notable for its address of Dissenters (and thereby its accurate complication of the more standard "Catholic/Protestant" Nationalist dichotomy), but that element falls beyond the bounds of this study.

7. The containment and construction of women in the Irish state have been exhaustively detailed elsewhere. For two foundational readings, see Kathryn A. Conrad, *Locked in the Family Cell: Gender, Sexuality, and Political Agency in Irish National Discourse* (Wisconsin: Univ. of Wisconsin Press, 2004), and Smith, *Ireland's Magdalen Laundries*.

8. Probably the most comprehensive study of this phenomenon is found in Smith, *Ireland's Magdalen Laundries*.

9. For one discussion of the nature of and problems with Irish insane asylums in the nineteenth and twentieth centuries, including those of involuntary institutionalization and overcrowding, see Mark Finnane, *Insanity and the Insane in Post-Famine Ireland* (London: Croom Helm; Totowa, N.J.: Barnes & Noble Books, 1981).

10. Tara Harney-Mahajan, "Provoking Forgiveness in Sebastian Barry's *The Secret Scripture*," *New Hibernia Review/Iris Éireannach Nua* 16, no. 2 (Summer 2012): 60.

11. On the perception of those outside the Nationalist ideal as "aberrant," see Smith, *Ireland's Magdalen Laundries*, esp. 1–20.

12. Roseanne's view of herself as a ghost echoes interestingly Max Morden's perception of himself as a "thing of air" rather than of substance (Banville, *The Sea*, 182).

13. As Robert F. Garratt observes, this interest in "individuals whose lives and stories have been underrepresented or even written out of standard histories of Ireland" is common in Barry's canon overall (*Trauma and History in the Irish Novel*, 136). For a reading of the novel that argues that "Barry sides with those revisionist historians who offer alternative adaptations of Ireland's past," see Hatipoğlu, "Palimpsests of History," 159.

14. For an insightful analysis of how Barry self-consciously invokes the forgotten histories of his own relatives in his canon and in this novel, see Harney-Mahajan, "Provoking Forgiveness," 57–58.

15. Harney-Mahajan, "Provoking Forgiveness," 63, 71.

16. Herman, *Trauma and Recovery*, 93.

17. For a reading of the novel as "borrow[ing] elements from trauma memoirs" and as a "commentary" on "life writing," see Sarah Herbe, "Memory, Reliability, and Old Age in Sebastian Barry's *The Secret Scripture*: A Reading of the Novel as Fictional Life Writing," *EnterText* 11 (2014): 24–41, quotes here on 30, 25.

18. Caruth, "Trauma and Experience," 5.

19. Laub, "Truth and Testimony," 62.

20. Herman, *Trauma and Recovery*, 38.

21. Caruth, "Trauma and Experience," 8; see also Caruth, preface to *Trauma*, viii.

22. Garratt, *Trauma and History in the Irish Novel*, 139.

23. For a reading of Dr. Grene's narrative as creating a "double narrative perspective" that provides a commentary on aging, see Herbe, "Memory, Reliability, and Old Age," 32.

24. Garratt reads Roseanne's and Dr. Grene's narratives as essentially different kinds of narrative that together "reflect on the difficulties of recalling traumatic experience, especially the unreliability of memory to sort out the details of the past" (*Trauma and History in the Irish Novel*, 140). I see the boundary of their stories as less defined in that Grene, too, engages in an unreliable narration of not only Roseanne's trauma but also his own.

25. A *cailleach* in Irish mythology is an "old woman or hag." In one of her most common Irish mythological iterations as the Cailleach Béire, she is "a revenant who enjoyed extraordinary longevity and survived serial epochs and historical ruptures" ("Digde: Aithbe Damsa Bés Mara [Digde's Lament] [c. 900]," in *Irish Women's Writing and Traditions*, vol. 4 of in *The Field Day Anthology of Irish Writing*, ed. Angela Bourke,

Siobhán Kilfeather, Maria Luddy, Margaret Mac Curtain, Gerardine Meaney, Máirín Ní Dhonnchadha, Mary O'Dowd, and Clair Wills [New York: New York Univ. Press, 2002], 111).

26. Harney-Mahajan, "Provoking Forgiveness," 55; 55n4, Chair of Panel cited in Jeffries.

27. Of course, by hiding the story in the floorboards, the novel both literalizes the story's occlusion through what the asylum metonymically represents and undermines that occlusion by joining Roseanne's narrative to those for which the institution stands. As Harney-Mahajan claims, "Barry positions Roseanne to tell a story that has been lost . . . , [and thus] the novel . . . enters into an ongoing debate in Ireland about social justice" (56). This may be true, but the form of telling and the resultant convergence of the characters' histories are critical to that action.

28. In a related but distinct observation, Garratt suggests that the novel's structure, with its "inclusion of flashbacks, . . . disregard for chronology, . . . fragmentation in expression, [and] interruption of the story line," "attempts to mimic traumatic experience while offering objective description of trauma as a subject" (*Trauma and History in the Irish Novel*, 142).

29. On the view in trauma novels that "the national story is so entwined with the personal that one implies the other," see Garratt, *Trauma and History in the Irish Novel*, 145. For one example of the interrelation of the personal and the political in Irish fiction, see Costello-Sullivan, *Mother/Country*.

30. For a different reading of the novel's conclusion in terms of forgiveness and happiness, see Harney-Mahajan, "Provoking Forgiveness" 69–71.

31. Banville, "A Century of Looking the Other Way."

32. Laub, "Truth and Testimony," 70.

4. "Stories Are a Different Kind of True"

1. Barry, *The Secret Scripture*, 3–4.

2. Anne Speckhard, Nadejda Tarabrina, Valery Krasnov, and Natalia Mufel, "Stockholm Effects and Psychological Responses to Captivity in Hostages Held by Suicide Terrorists," *Traumatology* 11, no. 2 (June 2005): 123, citing R. R. Corrado and E. Tompkins, doi:10.1177/153476560501100206.

3. Emma Donoghue, *Room* (New York: Little, Brown, 2010), 11; all references are to this edition and are subsequently given parenthetically by page number.

4. Herman, *Trauma and Recovery*, 75.

5. "As is almost always the case, when passivity is the demanded outcome the hostage must choose strategies to restrain the self from protest behaviors, hysteria, and emotional outbursts that, if indulged, can become the basis for his or her victimization: even death" (Speckhard et al., "Stockholm Effects," 123).

6. Speckhard et al., "Stockholm Effects," 122, paraphrasing M. Lassagne.

7. Herman, *Trauma and Recovery*, 75.

8. Herman, *Trauma and Recovery*, 79.

9. Speckhard et al., "Stockholm Effects," 127.

10. George Orwell, quoted in Herman, *Trauma and Recovery*, 87, emphasis in original. Herman notes that "psychological language does not have a name for this complex array of mental maneuvers, at once conscious and unconscious" (87).

11. Herman, *Trauma and Recovery*, 89–90.

12. Herman, *Trauma and Recovery*, 89.

13. Kinga Földváry, "In Search of a Lost Future: The Posthuman Child," *European Journal of English Studies* 18, no. 2 (2014): 216.

14. Although Földváry claims that "the little boy's lineage is never explicitly traced back to Old Nick" ("Posthuman Child," 217), the narrative makes quite clear that Nick is his father through rape when Nick tells Ma, "Don't forget where you got him" (74).

15. The very structure of the phrase "mine-not-Ma's" illustrates the boy's difficulty in seeing a separation between them; the hyphens ironically unite them even as they syntactically divide them.

16. On Jack's sense of himself as betraying the "blurring between the human and the nonhuman" and his difficulty in trying to "distinguish between himself as a human and things as being other," see Dominique Hétu, "Of Wonder and Encounter: Textures of Human and Nonhuman Relationality," *Mosaic* 48, no. 3 (Sept. 2015): 159–74, esp. 162–64, quote here on 163.

17. On the mirror stage, see Jacques Lacan, *The Seminar of Jacques Lacan*, book II: *The Ego in Freud's Theory and in the Technique of Psychoanalysis 1954–1955*, ed. Jacques-Alain Miller, trans. Sylvana Tomaselli (Cambridge: Cambridge Univ. Press, 1988), 49–52.

18. Mary Grace Elliott, "'Remembering How to Be Me': The Inherent Schism of Motherhood in Twentieth-Century American Literature," *The Quint* 4, no. 4 (Sept. 2012): 76.

19. Elliott, "'Remembering How to Be Me,'" 75.

20. LaCapra, *Writing History, Writing Trauma*, 90.

21. Földváry, "In Search of a Lost Future," 217. I would suggest that Földváry's observation highlights how Jack inhabits the fictive narrative of Room constructed by his mother and his struggle to negotiate her revision of that narrative after the trauma, which I discuss later in the chapter.

22. For insight into how the portrait of Ma's outbursts is consistent with the "outbursts of rage" common to former captives, see Herman, *Trauma and Recovery*, 94–95.

23. Laura Moss, "'A Science of Uncertainty': Bioethics, Narrative Competence, and Turning to the 'What If' of Fiction," *Studies in Canadian Literature* 40, no. 2 (2015): 14–15.

24. For a reading that productively complicates the easy juxtaposition of Room and the outside world as unreal and real, respectively, see Sandra Dinter, "Plato's Cave Revisited: Epistemology, Perception, and Romantic Childhood in Emma Donoghue's *Room*," *C21 Literature* 2, no. 1 (2013): 53–69, esp. 65–68.

25. Hétu, "Of Wonder and Encounter," 160.

26. On the role of the "posthuman," see Földváry, "In Search of a Lost Future." On "nonhuman relationality" and the role of objects in "negotiations between life and death," see Hétu, "Of Wonder and Encounter," 160. For a reading of *Room* as "point[ing] to [the romantic model of childhood's] factitious and obsolete quality as a cultural construct," see Dinter, "Plato's Cave Revisited," passim, quote here on 57.

27. Földváry, "In Search of a Lost Future," 207; Dinter, "Plato's Cave Revisited," 65.

28. It is impossible—at least for me—not to notice the echoes of such criticism in the mocking portrait Donoghue provides of intellectual TV commentators: "But surely, at a symbolic level, Jack's the child sacrifice," she says, "cemented into the foundations to placate the spirits" (*Room*, 293).

29. McGlynn, "'No Difference between the Different Kinds of Yesterday,'" 34. Room is tellingly closed off from the kinds of domestic commodification that novels such as *The Gathering* work against.

30. Földváry, "In Search of a Lost Future," 217.

31. Michel de Certeau, *The Practice of Everyday Life* (Berkeley: Univ. of California Press, 1984), 117, emphasis in original. De Certeau ruminates on the difference between "space" and "place" as filled with meaning and devoid of meaning, respectively.

32. Földváry, "In Search of a Lost Future," 217.

33. Sybil Steinberg, "*PW* Talks with Emma Donoghue," *Publishers Weekly*, July 12, 2010.

5. "Nothing Is Entirely by Itself"

1. Joseph Lennon, "'A Country of Elsewheres': An Interview with Colum McCann," *New Hibernia Review* 16, no. 2 (Summer 2012): 104. See also Joel Lovell, "Colum McCann's Radical Empathy," *New York Times Magazine*, May 30, 2013, at http://www.mytimes.com/2013/06/02/magazine/xolum-mccanns-radical-empathy.html?_r=1.

2. Alison Garden, "'Making It Up to Tell the Truth': An Interview with Colum McCann," *Symbiosis* 2014 (2014): 1. The result of this embrace of empathy is sometimes critical aggravation; readers at times find the endings of McCann's novels too neat or too sentimental, an interpretation that McCann rejects. See Kathleen Costello-Sullivan, "An Interview with Colum McCann," *TriQuarterly*, Apr. 25, 2017, at https://www.triquarterly.org/interviews/interview-colum-mccann.

3. Flannery, *Colum McCann*, 205.

4. Flannery, *Colum McCann*, 203.

5. McCann, *Let the Great World Spin*, 306; all references are to the 2009 Random House edition and are subsequently given parenthetically by page number.

6. Promotional blurb from *Esquire magazine*, in McCann, *Let the Great World Spin*.

7. Eóin Flannery, "Internationalizing 9/11: Hope and Redemption in Nadeem Aslam's *The Wasted Vigil* (2008) and Colum McCann's *Let the Great World Spin* (2009)," *English* 62, no. 238 (2013): 294.

8. Sinéad Moynihan, "'Upground and Belowground Topographies': The Chronotopes of Skyscraper and Subway in Colum McCann's New York Novels before and after 9/11," *Studies in American Fiction* 39, no. 2 (Fall 2012): 270.

9. In contrast, Caroline Chamberlin Hellman reads *Let the Great World Spin* as "an elegy to the victims of 9/11, relayed through the stories of characters representing a spectrum of New York experience" ("New York Unearthed: 9/11, *Let the Great World Spin*, and the Archaeology of Grief," in *The City since 9/11: Literature, Film, Television*, ed. Keith Wilhite [Madison, NJ: Farleigh Dickinson Univ. Press, 2016], 58). Similarly, Regina Schober reads the novel as specifically a "contemporary reflection on post 9/11 America" ("'It's about Being Connected': Reframing the Network in Colum McCann's Post 9/11 Novel *Let the Great World Spin*," *Zeitschrift fur Anglistik und Amerikanistik* 60, no. 4 [Oct. 2012]: 393).

10. Flannery, *Colum McCann*, 7.

11. *TransAtlantic* in many ways continues McCann's evolution toward increasingly interconnected, international texts. It not only surveys a breadth of discrete places and histories but also challenges received notions of identity by blurring the very temporal, historical, and national divides that differentiate those places and histories, shrinking the boundaries that separate individual lives. McCann thus engages at once both the boundedness and the fluidity of identity constructions, as they are complicated through and by international contexts, and suggests that geographical and national distances are more easily crossed than one might be led to believe. This novel, too, thus offers a comforting sense of community and commonality in a life, and a world, sometimes marked by great pain. See Colum McCann, *TransAtlantic: A Novel* (New York: Random House, 2013).

12. Brett Anthony Johnson, "Interview with Colum McCann," 2009 National Book Award Winner Fiction, National Book Foundation, n.d., at http://www.nationalbook.org/nba2009_f_mccann_interv.html#.V1V24_krKM8.

13. Flannery, "Internationalizing 9/11," 309, 294. Laura P. Z. Izarra similarly notes that "the watchers, despite their indifference and reservation, experience a brief moment of communion with the other" ("Let the Great Narrative Spin: A Poetics of Relations," *Brazilian Journal of Irish Studies*, Nov. 2012, 83).

14. For a careful analysis of the paralleling of these two dates, see Bertrand Cardin, *Colum McCann's Intertexts: "Books Talk to One Another"* (Cork: Cork Univ. Press, 2016), 132–43, esp. 134–36.

15. Moynihan, "'Upground and Belowground Topographies,'" 282.

16. In her reading of *This Side of Brightness* and *Let the Great World Spin*, Moynihan notes McCann's tendency to "[insist] on the proximity in time and space of the subway and skyscraper to such an extent that the two become almost inextricable from one another," thus enabling McCann to "interrogate the relationship between trauma and time" as well as "the ethics of representation" ("'Upground and Belowground Topographies,'" 280–81). For a reading of the skyscraper as "spotlighting equilibrium" and balancing the "ordinary, earth-bound" with "acrobatic balance" in *Let the Great World Spin* and *This Side of Brightness*, see Flannery, "Internationalizing 9/11," 313.

17. Garden, "'Making It Up,'" 3.

18. Schober, "'It's about Being Connected,'" 392.

19. Elizabeth Cullingford, "American Dreams: Emigration of Exile in Contemporary Irish Fiction?" *Éire–Ireland* 49, nos. 3–4 (Fall–Winter 2014): 86. Cullingford notes that Corrigan is modeled on liberal-theology-inspired Jesuit Daniel Berrigan, SJ, a notorious protestor against the Vietnam War and a vocal advocate for peace. As McCann has stated about the time he wrote the novel, "I was contemplating the Daniel Berrigans of the world, the good people, the decent and moral ones, who needed to be celebrated, too. And I thought: That has got to be part of my narrative" (Kathleen Costello-Sullivan, "An Interview with Colum McCann," *TriQuarterly*, Apr. 25, 2017, at https://www.triquarterly.org/interviews/interview-colum-mccann). Flannery also identifies Corrigan as "arguably the central personality" in the novel (*Colum McCann*, 216).

20. Interestingly, Izarra reads Corrigan's marginal lifestyle as a metaphorical parallel to Petit's, claiming in passing that "the man in the sky . . . equals Corrigan's state of mind" ("Let the Great Narrative Spin," 85).

21. Moynihan, "'Upground and Belowground Topographies,'" 286. In reading the skyscraper and subway as "challeng[ing] the notion of an easy opposition between creation and destruction," Moynihan in fact suggests that the foil to Petit is Fernando, the subway artist (282–83).

22. Schober, "'It's about Being Connected,'" 396–97.

23. Moynihan reads the parallel between "skyscraper and subway" as a means "to consider . . . the ethics of representation and the limits of what is acceptable . . . to confront artistically" ("'Upground and Belowground Topographies,'" 281).

24. Flannery, *Colum McCann*, 214, 216.

25. Schober, "'It's about Being Connected,'" 395. For a thorough analysis of Corrigan's materiality (as opposed to the tightrope walker's ethereality), see Flannery, *Colum McCann*, 216–19.

26. Flannery, *Colum McCann*, 209.

27. Flannery, "Internationalizing 9/11," 309.

28. Flannery, *Colum McCann*, 215.

29. Flannery, "Internationalizing 9/11," 313.

30. Flannery, *Colum McCann*, 218.

31. Flannery notes there is "a remoteness to Corrigan at the same time, which again is suggestive of his presence as an angelic or Christ-like figure" (*Colum McCann*, 219).

32. Flannery, *Colum McCann*, 219.

33. For an interesting reading of the novel through intertextual connectedness rather than through connectedness as a narrative device per se, see Cardin, *Colum McCann's Intertexts*, 118–31.

34. For a reading of the novel in terms of emigration as suggesting that "globalised Ireland is beginning to resemble everywhere else," see Cullingford, "American Dreams," 84–89, quote here on 89. For a reading of the novel in terms of "exile and mobility," see Flannery, *Colum McCann*, 209.

35. Garden, "'Making It Up to Tell the Truth,'" 9, emphasis in original.

36. Quoted in Flannery, *Colum McCann*, 15.

37. Costello-Sullivan, "Interview with Colum McCann."

38. Quoted in Flannery, "Internationalizing 9/11," 295.

39. Flannery, "Internationalizing 9/11," 309, 294.

40. Cardin, *Colum McCann's Intertexts*, 137.

41. Costello-Sullivan, "Interview with Colum McCann."

42. Colum McCann, "Walking an Inch off the Ground," expanded version of "Author, Author: Stories Are There to Be Told," *Guardian*, Sept. 5, 2009, reprinted in *Let the Great World Spin*, 359

43. Phil Klay, "Colum McCann Talks New Novel 'TransAtlantic' and Narrative4," *Daily Beast*, June 14, 2013, at https://www.thedailybeast.com/colum-mccann-talks-new-novel-transatlantic-and-narrative4.

6. Trauma, Recovery, and Intertextual Redemption in Colm Tóibín's *Nora Webster*

1. For a reading of *The Blackwater Lightship* in these terms, see Costello-Sullivan, *Mother/Country*, 123–54.

2. Joseph Wiesenfarth, "An Interview with Colm Tóibín," *Contemporary Literature* 50, no. 1 (Spring 2009): 11. As I argue elsewhere, however, it would be a mistake to read Tóibín's work as strictly or primarily autobiographical. On the impact of his family history on his work, see Costello-Sullivan, *Mother/Country*, 6–13. Tóibín himself reminds us of this caveat in an interview: "I've been mining material that's very personal and I've also been adding material that's invented" (quoted in Brenda

Cronin, "Colm Tóibín Explores His Irish Hometown in *Nora Webster*," *Wall Street Journal*, Sept. 29, 2014, at https://www.wsj.com/articles/colm-toibin-explores-his-irish-hometown-in-nora-webster-1412007935).

3. Nonetheless, few reviews have contextualized *Nora Webster* within Tóibín's larger oeuvre. For example, although Tessa Hadley recognizes the novel's resonances with *Brooklyn*, she reads the later novel essentially as exploring the concept that "a man is dead before his time, [and] his family is stricken" ("*Nora Webster* by Colm Tóibín—a Rare and Tremendous Achievement," *Guardian*, Oct. 11, 2015, at https://www.theguardian.com/books/2014/oct/11/nora-webster-colm-toibin-review-rare-achievement). Similarly, Janet Maslin's reading of *Nora Webster* as about Nora's "gradual, subtle reawakening" and her assertion that "grief has made [Nora] a terrible, selfish parent" ("A Change in the Climate for an Icy Irish Matron," *New York Times*, Oct. 13, 2014, at https://www.nytimes.com/2014/10/14/books/nora-webster-by-colm-toibin.html?_r=0) do not sufficiently consider either the novel's echoes of other Tóibín works or the complex ways in which Nora remains limited throughout. A notable exception to this tendency to read *Nora Webster* in isolation is Roy Foster's review "Keeping the Pressure On: *Nora Webster*" (*Irish Times*, Oct. 11, 2014, at https://www.irishtimes.com/culture/books/keeping-the-pressure-on-nora-webster-1.1955005), which shows his mastery of and thorough familiarity with Tóibín's oeuvre.

4. Colm Tóibín, *Nora Webster* (New York: Scribner, 2014), 4; all references are to this edition and are subsequently made parenthetically by page number.

5. Colm Tóibín, "A Priest in the Family," in *Mothers and Sons*, 137.

6. As Katherine Powers asserts, "Tóibín conveys the indecency of small-town one-upmanship and schadenfreude beautifully and understatedly" ("Review: *Nora Webster* by Colm Tóibín," *Chicago Tribune*, Sept. 26, 2014, at http://www.chicagotribune.com/lifestyles/books/ct-prj-nora-webster-colm-toibin-20140926-story.html).

7. Tóibín, "A Priest in the Family," 143.

8. Tóibín, *The Blackwater Lightship*, 137.

9. Colm Tóibín, "The Name of the Game," in *Mothers and Sons*, 83.

10. Tóibín, "A Priest in the Family," 149.

11. Colm Tóibín, *Brooklyn* (New York: Scribner, 2009), 214.

12. Costello-Sullivan, *Mother/Country*, 20 n. 67.

13. This inability to say something when the need arises is consistent, too, with the mechanisms of Eilis's family in *Brooklyn*: "Eilis would have given anything to be able to say plainly that she did not want to go. . . . [Her family] could do everything except say out loud what it was they were thinking" (Tóibín, *Brooklyn*, 32).

14. Colm Tóibín, *The Heather Blazing* (New York: Penguin, 1992), 28.

15. This is a different use of silence than Roy Foster identifies in observing that a "dominant theme here concerns things unsaid, and silence" because "Nora knows the power of keeping her mouth shut" ("Keeping the Pressure On").

16. Maslin, "A Change in the Climate."

17. Colm Tóibín, *The South* (New York: Penguin, 1990), 14.

18. Wiesenfarth, "An Interview with Colm Tóibín," 9.

19. See Colm Tóibín, "A Song," in *Mothers and Sons*, 41–49. On the representation of the lost or absent mother in Tóibín's fiction, see Costello-Sullivan, *Mother/Country*, esp. 6–7; see also John McCourt, "A Battle for Space: Mothers and Sons," in *Reading Colm Tóibín*, ed. Paul Delaney (Dublin: Liffey Press, 2008), 148–66, and Anne Fogarty, "After Oedipus? Mothers and Sons in the Fiction of Colm Tóibín," in *Reading Colm Tóibín*, ed. Delaney, 167–81.

20. Foster, "Keeping the Pressure On."

21. The possible exception, at least to me, is May Lacey in *Brooklyn*, whose cold rejection of her daughter and selfish focus on her own grief are never truly recuperated in that novel. Interestingly, however, we finally see some of May's perspective in *Nora Webster* when she explains why she was so cold, stating, "I just didn't want to lose Eily" (5).

22. Tóibín, "The Name of the Game," 97–98; see also 56–58 and 88–89. Of course, both Nancy and Nora also use their widowhood to their advantage at times: Nancy wonders if she should have "become the stricken widow" to manipulate a bank manager (58), and Nora "left silence and did not move" to guilt a man into hanging her curtains for her (333).

23. One might consider Katherine's sense of vulnerability in *The South* when she observes, "There are men everywhere watching you" (6). This focus may be a reflection not only of the challenges Tóibín's own mother faced but also of the influence on Tóibín of author Mary Lavin, who so effectively presenced Irish widows in her short stories. For a review that focuses on the pressures on Nora as a woman among others, claiming that "Nora lives in a world of female surveillance," see Buzzy Jackson, "*Nora Webster* by Colm Tóibín," *Boston Globe*, Oct. 9, 2014, at https://www.bostonglobe.com/arts/books/2014/10/09/book-review-nora-webster-colm-toibin/7dqXOGW8GOqUtpLYgDfqaK/story.html.

24. For more on Katherine's doubleness and the representation of motherhood in *The South*, see Costello-Sullivan, *Mother/Country*, 35–64, quote on 36.

25. Tóibín, *The South*, 90.

26. Tóibín, *The South*, 205.

27. For a detailed reading of troubled mother-child relationships in *The South*, see Costello-Sullivan, *Mother/Country*, 44–45, 60–64.

28. Tóibín, *The Blackwater Lightship*, 210.

29. Tóibín, *The Blackwater Lightship*, 211.

30. Tóibín, *The Blackwater Lightship*, 192.

31. This scene is resonant with the short story "One Minus One," in which the speaker recognizes that although his mother is gone and so is any opportunity

for their relationship, he feels "almost . . . relief" (in *Empty Family*, 84). Similarly, Nora muses that she "did not feel remorse" and recognizes the lost opportunity to connect (343).

32. Texts that resonate with this dynamic include "A Song" and "One Minus One": in "A Song," although Noel has the opportunity to confront his mother, he ultimately cannot bring himself to do so, and the narrator in "One Minus One" has a similar sense of lost opportunity, as we have seen. In contrast to Nora, the narrator in the former story muses at length about the impact of his mother's emotional abandonment of him.

33. Foster, "Keeping the Pressure On."

34. Even Eamon Redmond in *The Heather Blazing*, who also cannot meet his mother, recognizes the damage he has suffered; "I learned never to need anything from anybody. . . . I don't believe that anyone has ever wanted me" (228). Of course, although he is not a great father and is one of the grown children in Tóibín's canon, he is differentiated from the abandoning mother figure and from Nora by gender.

35. Foster, "Keeping the Pressure On."

36. Herman, *Trauma and Recovery*, 35.

37. Eibhear Walshe, *A Different Story: The Writings of Colm Tóibín* (Dublin: Irish Academic Press, 2013), 160, 166.

38. Nora's brandishing of the scissors at Ms. Kavanagh, when she does not even know why she is holding them, bespeaks a similar kind of aggrieved rage. It is also resonant with Mary's brandishing of the kitchen knife against the offending apostles when they invoke her dead husband in *The Testament of Mary* ([New York: Scriber and Simon and Schuster, 2012], 14–16), as does Ms. Kavanagh to Nora.

39. Herman, *Trauma and Recovery*, 55.

40. In many respects, *The Blackwater Lightship* is the closest to *Nora Webster* in its approach to sympathy for the mother figure, as when Dora notes that Lily "couldn't get over losing" (88) her husband and in its brief windows into Lily's perspective, noted earlier in this chapter. Nonetheless, I am arguing that *Nora Webster*'s sustained engagement with Nora's perspective shifts our sympathy and the narrative perspective meaningfully toward the mother's point of view. Self-reflection and existential meditation by the sea are a common pattern in Tóibín.

41. Nora's envisioning of Maurice is consistent with the reappearance of lost loved ones throughout Tóibín's canon: for example, in *Brooklyn* Eilis imagines she sees her father (90), and in the story "The Street" (in *The Empty Family: Stories* [New York: Scribner, 2011]), Malik imagines he sees his dead aunt (232).

42. Again, Lily in *The Blackwater Lightship* is an apt example: our ability to sympathize with her is often compromised by her selfish foregrounding of her needs: "I did what I could for you . . . and you never gave me an inch" (211). In contrast, Nora's pain is treated in its own right, and she is represented as a person in need of care.

43. Ron Charles, "Colm Tóibín's *Nora Webster*: A Masterful Portrait of a Grieving Woman Finding Herself," *Washington Post*, Oct. 7, 2014, at https://www.washington post.com/entertainment/books/colm-toibins-nora-webster-a-masterful-portrait-of -a-grieving-woman-finding-herself/2014/10/07/524108f6-4b0a-11e4-b72e-d60a92 29cc10_story.html.

44. Charles, "Colm Tóibín's *Nora Webster*."

45. Wiesenfarth, "An Interview with Colm Tóibín," 11. On the personal resonances of this work, see Susan Page, guest host, "Colm Tóibín: *Nora Webster*, a Novel," *Diane Rehm Show*, National Public Radio, Oct. 16, 2014, at https://thediane rehmshow.org/shows/2014-10-16/colm-Tóibín-nora-webster-novel.

Works Cited

Associated Press. "Correction: Ireland—Children's Mass Graves Story." June 20, 2014. At http://news.yahoo.com/correction-ireland-childrens-mass-graves-story-184828902.html.

Banville, John. *Birchwood.* 1973. Reprint. London: Minerva, 1992.

———. "A Century of Looking the Other Way." *New York Times*, May 22, 2009. At http://www.nytimes.com/2009/05/23/opinion/23banville.html.

———. *The Infinities.* New York: Knopf, 2010.

———. *The Sea.* New York: Vintage, 2005.

———. *Shroud.* 2002. Reprint. New York: Vintage International, 2004.

———. *The Untouchable.* 1997. Reprint. New York: Vintage, 1998.

Barry, Sebastian. *The Secret Scripture.* London: Viking, 2008.

Beckett, Samuel. "Texts for Nothing." In *The Complete Short Prose 1929–1989*, 100–154. New York: Grove Press, 1995.

Beiner, Guy. *Remembering the Year of the French: Irish Folk History and Social Memory.* Madison: Univ. of Wisconsin Press, 2007.

Bennett, Ronan. "*The Country Girls*' Home Truths." *Guardian*, May 3, 2002. At https://www.theguardian.com/books/2002/may/04/fiction.reviews1.

Boland, Rosita. "Tuam Mother and Baby Home: The Trouble with the Septic Tank Story." *Irish Times*, June 7, 2014. At http://www.irishtimes.com/news/social-affairs/tuam-mother-and-baby-home-the-trouble-with-the-septic-tank-story-1.1823393?page=3.

Bracken, Claire, and Susan Cahill, eds. *Anne Enright.* Dublin: Irish Academic Press, 2011.

———. "An Interview with Anne Enright, August 2009," In *Anne Enright*, edited by Claire Bracken and Susan Cahill, 13–32. Dublin: Irish Academic Press, 2011.

———. Introduction to *Anne Enright*, edited by Claire Bracken and Susan Cahill, 1–12. Dublin: Irish Academic Press, 2011.

Brousseau, Danielle C., Marvin J. McDonald, and Joanne E. Stephen. "The Moderating Effect of Relationship Quality on Partner Secondary Traumatic Stress among Couples Coping with Cancer." *Families, Systems, and Health* 29, no. 2 (2011): 114–26.

Cahill, Susan. "'Dreaming of Upholstered Breasts,' or, How to Find Your Way Back Home: Dislocation in *What Are You Like?*" In *Anne Enright*, edited by Claire Bracken and Susan Cahill, 87–106. Dublin: Irish Academic Press, 2011.

———. "A Girl Is a Half-Formed Thing? Girlhood, Trauma, and Resistance in Post-Tiger Irish Literature." *LIT: Literature, Interpretation, Theory* 28, no. 2 (2017): 153–71.

———. *Irish Literature in the Celtic Tiger Years 1990–2008: Gender, Bodies, Memory.* New York: Continuum International, 2011.

Cardin, Bertrand. *Colum McCann's Intertexts: "Books Talk to One Another."* Cork: Cork Univ. Press, 2016.

Caruth, Cathy. Preface to *Trauma: Explorations in Memory*, edited by Cathy Caruth, vii–ix. Baltimore: Johns Hopkins Univ. Press, 1995.

———. "Trauma and Experience: Introduction." In *Trauma: Explorations in Memory*, edited by Cathy Caruth, 3–12. Baltimore: Johns Hopkins Univ. Press, 1995.

———, ed. *Trauma: Explorations in Memory.* Baltimore: Johns Hopkins Univ. Press, 1995.

Carville, Conor. "'Keeping That Wound Green: Irish Studies and Traumaculture." In *What Rough Beasts? Irish and Scottish Studies in the New Millennium*, edited by Shane Alcobia-Murphy, 45–71. Newcastle, UK: Cambridge Scholars, 2008.

Charles, Ron. "Colm Tóibín's *Nora Webster*: A Masterful Portrait of a Grieving Woman Finding Herself." *Washington Post*, Oct. 7, 2014. At https://www.washingtonpost.com/entertainment/books/colm-toibins-nora-webster-a-masterful-portrait-of-a-grieving-woman-finding-herself/2014/10/07/524108f6-4b0a-11e4-b72e-d60a9229cc10_story.html.

Cleary, Joe. "'Misplaced Ideas'? Colonialism, Location, and Dislocation in Irish Studies." In *Ireland and Postcolonial Theory*, edited by Clare Carroll and Patricia King, 16–45. Notre Dame, IN: Univ. of Notre Dame Press, 2003.

Conrad, Kathryn A. *Locked in the Family Cell: Gender, Sexuality, and Political Agency in Irish National Discourse.* Madison: Univ. of Wisconsin Press, 2004.

Cook, Bruce. "Irish Censorship: The Case of John McGahern." *Catholic World* 206 (1967): 176–79.

Costello-Sullivan, Kathleen. "An Interview with Colum McCann." *Tri-Quarterly*, Apr. 25, 2017. At http://www.triquarterly.org/interviews/interview-colum-mccann.

———. *Mother/Country: Politics of the Personal in the Fiction of Colm Tóibín.* Oxford: Peter Lang, 2012.

———. "Silence and Power in Anglo-Irish Women's Fiction." In *Back to the Present, Forward to the Past: Irish Writing and History since 1798*, vol. 1, edited by Patricia A. Lynch, Joachim Fischer, and Brian Coates, 279–88. Amsterdam: Rodopi, 2006.

Coughlan, Patricia. "Banville, the Feminine, and the Scenes of Eros." In "John Banville," special issue of *Irish University Review* 36, no. 1 (Spring–Summer 2006): 81–101.

Cronin, Brenda. "Colm Tóibín Explores His Irish Hometown in *Nora Webster.*" *Wall Street Journal*, Sept. 29, 2014. At https://www.wsj.com/articles/colm-toibin-explores-his-irish-hometown-in-nora-webster-1412007935.

Cullingford, Elizabeth. "American Dreams: Emigration of Exile in Contemporary Irish Fiction?" *Éire–Ireland* 49, nos. 3–4 (Fall–Winter 2014): 60–94.

Dawson, Graham. *Making Peace with the Past? Memory, Trauma, and the Irish Troubles.* Manchester: Manchester Univ. Press, 2007.

———. "The Meaning of 'Moving On': From Trauma to the History and Memories of Emotions in 'Post-conflict' Northern Ireland." In "Moving Memory: The Dynamics of the Past in Irish Culture," edited by Emilie Pine, special issue of *Irish University Review* 47, no. 1 (Spring–Summer 2017): 82–102.

De Certeau, Michel. *The Practice of Everyday Life.* Berkeley: Univ. of California Press, 1984.

Delaney, Paul, ed. *Reading Colm Tóibín.* Dublin: Liffey Press, 2008.

Dell'Amico, Carole. "Anne Enright's *The Gathering*: Trauma, Testimony, Memory." *New Hibernia Review* 14, no. 3 (Fómhar/Autumn 2010): 59–74.

"Digde: Aithbe Damsa Bés Mara (Digde's Lament) (c. 900)." In *Irish Women's Writing and Traditions*, vol. 4 of In *The Field Day Anthology of Irish Writing*, edited by Angela Bourke, Siobhán Kilfeather, Maria Luddy, Margaret Mac Curtain, Gerardine Meaney, Máirín Ní Dhonnchadha, Mary O'Dowd, and Clair Wills, 111–14. New York: New York Univ. Press, 2002.

Dinter, Sandra. "Plato's Cave Revisited: Epistemology, Perception, and Romantic Childhood in Emma Donoghue's *Room*." *C21 Literature* 2, no. 1 (2013): 53–69.

Dobrogoszcz, Tomas. "The Eerie Re-visioning of Airy Past in John Banville's *The Sea*." In *The Playful Air/Light(ness) in Irish Literature and Culture*, edited by Marta Goszczyńska and Katarzyna Poloczek, 57–66. Newcastle upon Tyne, UK: Cambridge Scholars, 2011.

Donoghue, Emma. *Room*. New York: Little, Brown, 2010.

Edgeworth, Maria. *Maria Edgeworth's Letters from Ireland*. Edited by Valerie Pakenham. Dublin: Lilliput Press, 2018.

Eliot, T. S. "The Lovesong of J. Alfred Prufrock." In *The Norton Anthology of Poetry*, shorter 5th ed., edited by Margaret Ferguson, Mary Jo Salter, and Jon Saltworthy, 862–66. New York: Norton, 2005.

Elliott, Mary Grace. "'Remembering How to Be Me': The Inherent Schism of Motherhood in Twentieth-Century American Literature." *The Quint* 4, no. 4 (Sept. 2012): 67–80.

English, Bridget. "Laying Out the Bones: Death, Trauma, and the Irish Family in Colm Tóibín's *The Blackwater Lightship* and Anne Enright's *The Gathering*." In *New Voices, Inherited Lines: Literary and Cultural Representations of the Irish Family*, edited by Yvonne O'Keeffe and Claudia Reese, 203–23. Oxford: Peter Lang, 2013.

Enright, Anne. *The Gathering*. London: Jonathan Cape, 2007.

———. Review of *A Girl Is a Half-Formed Thing* by Eimear McBride. *Guardian*, Sept. 20, 2013. At https://www.theguardian.com/books/2013/sep/20/girl-half-formed-thing-review.

Facchinello, Monica. "'The Old Illusion of Belonging': Distinctive Style, Bad Faith, and John Banville's *The Sea*." *Estudios Irlandeses* 5, no. 10 (2010): 33–44.

Fasching, Hannelore. "'The New Drama of Being a Mother about Which so Little Has Been Written': Maternal Subjectivity and the Mother Icon in Anne Enright's Writing." In *New Voices, Inherited Lines: Literary *and Cultural Representations of the Irish Family*, edited by Yvonne O'Keeffe and Claudia Reese, 183–201. Oxford: Peter Lang, 2013.

Felman, Shoshana, and Dori Laub. *Testimony: Crisis of Witnessing in Literature, Psychoanalysis, and History*. New York: Routledge, 1992.

Finnane, Mark. *Insanity and the Insane in Post-Famine Ireland*. London: Croom Helm; Totowa, NJ: Barnes & Noble Books, 1981.

Flannery, Eóin. *Colum McCann and the Aesthetics of Redemption*. Dublin: Irish Academic Press, 2011.

———. "Internationalizing 9/11: Hope and Redemption in Nadeem Aslam's *The Wasted Vigil* (2008) and Colum McCann's *Let the Great World Spin* (2009)." *English* 62, no. 238 (2013): 294–315.

Fogarty, Anne. "After Oedipus? Mothers and Sons in the Fiction of Colm Tóibín." In *Reading Colm Tóibín*, edited by Paul Delaney, 167–81. Dublin: Liffey Press, 2008.

Földváry, Kinga. "In Search of a Lost Future: The Posthuman Child." *European Journal of English Studies* 18, no. 2 (2014): 207–20.

Foster, Roy. "Keeping the Pressure On: *Nora Webster*." *Irish Times*, Oct. 11, 2014. At https://www.irishtimes.com/culture/books/keeping-the-pressure-on-nora-webster-1.1955005.

Frawley, Oona. Introduction to *History and Modernity*, vol. 1 of *Memory Ireland*, edited by Oona Frawley, xiii–xxiv. Syracuse, NY: Syracuse Univ. Press, 2011.

Friberg, Hedda. "'In the Murky Sea of Memory': Memory's Miscues in John Banville's *The Sea*." *An Sionnach* 1, no. 2 (Fall 2005): 111–23.

Friberg-Harnesk, Hedda. "Waters and Memories Always Divide: Sites of Memory in John Banville's *The Sea*." In *Recovering Memory: Irish Representations of Past and Present*, edited by Hedda Friberg-Hanesk, Irense Gilsenan Nordin, and Lene Yding Pedersen, 244–62. Newcastle, UK: Cambridge Scholars, 2007.

Gardam, Sarah C. "'Default[ing] to the Oldest Scar': A Psychoanalytic Investigation of Subjectivity in Anne Enright's *The Gathering*." *Études Irlandaises* 34, no. 1 (Spring 2009): 99–112.

Garden, Alison. "'Making It Up to Tell the Truth': An Interview with Colum McCann." *Symbiosis* 2014 (2014): 1–19.

Garratt, Robert F. *Trauma and History in the Irish Novel: The Return of the Dead*. London: Palgrave Macmillan, 2011.

Goarzin, Anne. "Articulating Trauma." In "Trauma et mémoire en Irlande: Perspectives on Trauma in Irish History, Literature, and Culture," edited by Anne Goarzin, special issue of *Études Irlandaises* 36, no. 1 (Spring–Summer 2011): 1–22.

Hadley, Tessa. "*Nora Webster* by Colm Tóibín—a Rare and Tremendous Achievement." *Guardian*, Oct. 11, 2015. At https://www.theguardian.com/books/2014/oct/11/nora-webster-colm-toibin-review-rare-achievement.

Hand, Derek. *John Banville: Exploring Fictions.* Dublin: Liffey Press, 2002.

Harney-Mahajan, Tara. "Provoking Forgiveness in Sebastian Barry's *The Secret Scripture*." *New Hibernia Review/Iris Éireannach Nua* 16, no. 2 (Summer 2012): 54–71.

Harte, Liam. "Mourning Remains Unresolved: Trauma and Survival in Anne Enright's *The Gathering*." *LIT: Literature, Interpretation, Theory* 21 (2010): 187–204.

Hatipoğlu, Gülden. "Palimpsests of History in Sebastian Barry's *The Secret Scripture*." In *The Adaptation of History: Essays on Ways of Telling the Past*, edited by Lawrence Raw and Defne Ersin Tutan, 153–60. Jefferson, NC: McFarland, 2013.

Hellman, Caroline Chamberlin. "New York Unearthed: 9/11, *Let the Great World Spin*, and the Archaeology of Grief." In *The City since 9/11: Literature, Film, Television*, edited by Keith Wilhite, 57–70. Madison, NJ: Farleigh Dickinson Univ. Press, 2016.

Herbe, Sarah. "Memory, Reliability, and Old Age in Sebastian Barry's *The Secret Scripture*: A Reading of the Novel as Fictional Life Writing." *EnterText* 11 (2014): 24–41.

Herman, Judith Lewis. *Trauma and Recovery: The Aftermath of Violence—from Domestic Abuse to Political Terror.* New York: Basic Books, 1992.

Hétu, Dominique. "Of Wonder and Encounter: Textures of Human and Nonhuman Relationality." *Mosaic* 48, no. 3 (Sept. 2015): 159–74.

Hogan, Linda. "Clerical and Religious Child Abuse: Ireland and Beyond." *Theological Studies* 72 (2011): 170–86.

Imhof, Rüdiger. "*The Sea*: 'Was't Well Done?'" In "John Banville," special issue of *Irish University Review* 36, no. 1 (Spring–Summer 2006): 165–81.

Izarra, Laura P. Z. "Let the Great Narrative Spin: A Poetics of Relations." *Brazilian Journal of Irish Studies*, Nov. 2012, 79–87.

Jackson, Buzzy. "*Nora Webster* by Colm Tóibín." *Boston Globe*, Oct. 9, 2014. At https://www.bostonglobe.com/arts/books/2014/10/09/book-review-nora-webster-colm-toibin/7dqXOGW8GOqUtpLYgDfqaK/story.html.

Johnson, Brett Anthony. "Interview with Colum McCann." 2009 National Book Award Winner Fiction, National Book Foundation, n.d. At http://www.nationalbook.org/nba2009_f_mccann_interv.html#.V1V24_krKM8.

Joyce, James. "Araby." In *Dubliners*, rev. ed., 29–48. New York: Penguin Books, 1996.

Kelleher, Margaret. *The Feminization of the Famine: Expressions of the Inexpressible?* Cork: Cork Univ. Press, 1997.

Kenny, John. *John Banville*. Dublin: Irish Academic Press, 2009.

Kiberd, Declan. "Irish Literature and History." Appendix in R. F. Foster, *Illustrated History of Ireland*, 306–7. Oxford: Oxford Univ. Press, 1989.

Klay, Phil. "Colum McCann Talks New Novel 'TransAtlantic' and Narrative4." *Daily Beast*, June 14, 2013. At https://www.thedailybeast.com/colum-mccann-talks-new-novel-transatlantic-and-narrative4.

Lacan, Jacques. *The Seminar of Jacques Lacan*. Book II: *The Ego in Freud's Theory and in the Technique of Psychoanalysis 1954–1955*. Edited by Jacques-Alain Miller. Translated by Sylvana Tomaselli. Cambridge: Cambridge Univ. Press, 1988.

LaCapra, Dominick. *Writing History, Writing Trauma: Parallax Re-visions of Culture and Society*. Baltimore: Johns Hopkins Univ. Press, 2001.

Laub, Dori. "Bearing Witness, or the Vicissitudes of Listening." In *Testimony: Crises of Witnessing in Literature, Psychoanalysis, and History*, edited by Shoshana Felman and Dori Laub, 57–87. New York: Routledge, 1992.

———. "Truth and Testimony: The Process and the Struggle." In *Trauma: Explorations in Memory*, edited by Cathy Caruth, 61–75. Baltimore: Johns Hopkins Univ. Press, 1995.

Lennon, Joseph. "'A Country of Elsewheres': An Interview with Colum McCann." *New Hibernia Review* 16, no. 2 (Summer 2012): 98–111.

Llena, Carmen Zamorano. "'The Figures of the Far Past Come Back at the End': Unmasking the Desired Self through Reminiscence in Late Adulthood in John Banville's *The Sea*." In *Flaming Embers: Literary Testimonies on Ageing and Desire*, edited by Nela Bureu Ramos, 87–112. Bern: Peter Lang, 2010.

Lovell, Joel. "Colum McCann's Radical Empathy." *New York Times Magazine*, May 30, 2013. At http://www.mytimes.com/2013/06/02/magazine/xolum-mccanns-radical-empathy.html?_r=1.

Luddy, Maria. *Women and Philanthropy in Nineteenth-Century Ireland.* Cambridge: Cambridge Univ. Press, 1995.

Maher, Eamon. *"The Church and Its Spire": John McGahern and the Catholic Question.* Dublin: Columba Press, 2011.

Maslin, Janet. "A Change in the Climate for an Icy Irish Matron." *New York Times*, Oct. 13, 2014. At https://www.nytimes.com/2014/10/14/books/nora-webster-by-colm-toibin.html?_r=0.

McBride, Eimear. *A Girl Is a Half-Formed Thing.* Norwich, UK: Faber and Faber, 2013.

McCann, Colum. *Let the Great World Spin.* New York: Random House, 2009.

———. *TransAtlantic: A Novel.* New York: Random House, 2013.

———. "Walking an Inch off the Ground." Expanded version of "Author, Author: Stories Are There to Be Told," *Guardian*, Sept. 5, 2009. In *Let the Great World Spin*, 357–60. New York: Random House, 2009.

McCourt, John. "A Battle for Space: Mothers and Sons." In *Reading Colm Tóibín*, edited by Paul Delaney, 148–66. Dublin: Liffey Press, 2008.

McGahern, John. *The Dark.* New York: Penguin Books, 1965.

McGlynn, Mary. "'No Difference between the Different Kinds of Yesterday': The Neoliberal Present in *The Green Road*, *The Devil I Know*, and *The Lives of Women*." *LIT: Literature, Interpretation, Theory* 28, no. 1 (2017): 34–54.

McGreevey, Ronan. "Tuam Case 'Reminder of a Darker Past in Ireland.'" *Irish Times*, June 4, 2014. At http://www.irishtimes.com/news/social-affairs/tuam-case-reminder-of-a-darker-past-in-ireland-1.1820349.

McKeon, Belinda. "John Banville, the Art of Fiction No. 200." *Paris Review* 188 (Spring 2009). At https://www.theparisreview.org/interviews/5907/john-banville-the-art-of-fiction-no-200-john-banville.

McKeon, Michael. *The Origins of the English Novel 1600–1740.* Baltimore: Johns Hopkins Univ. Press, 1987.

McMinn, Joseph. *John Banville: A Critical Study.* Dublin: Gill and Macmillan, 1991.

McNamara, Denise. "Campaign to Recognise 800 Dead Tuam Babies." *Connaght Tribune*, Feb. 12, 2014. At http://connachttribune.ie/campaign-recognise-800-dead-tuam-babies/.

Moss, Laura. "'A Science of Uncertainty': Bioethics, Narrative Competence, and Turning to the 'What If' of Fiction." *Studies in Canadian Literature* 40, no. 2 (2015): 5–24.

Moynihan, Sinéad. "'Upground and Belowground Topographies': The Chronotopes of Skyscraper and Subway in Colum McCann's New York Novels before and after 9/11." *Studies in American Fiction* 39, no. 2 (Fall 2012): 269–90.

Mulhall, Anne. "'Now the Blood Is in the Room': The Spectral Feminine in the Work of Anne Enright." In *Anne Enright*, edited by Claire Bracken and Susan Cahill, 67–86. Dublin: Irish Academic Press, 2011.

O'Brien, Carl. "Call to Extend Mother and Baby Homes Inquiry to Mental Homes." *Irish Times*, June 16, 2014. At http://www.irishtimes.com/news/social-affairs/call-to-extend-mother-and-baby-homes-inquiry-to-mental-homes-1.1833367.

O'Brien, Edna. *Down by the River.* New York: Plume, 1997.

———. *The Little Red Chairs: A Novel.* New York: Little, Brown, 2016.

O'Keeffe, Yvonne, and Claudia Reese, eds. *New Voices, Inherited Lines: Literary and Cultural Representations of the Irish Family*. Oxford: Peter Lang, 2013.

O'Neill, Joseph. "A Heartening Way with the Big Things" (interview). *Guardian*, May 6, 1990.

O'Neill, Margaret. "The *Caoineadh*, Psychoanalytic Theory, and Contemporary Irish Writing: Anne Enright's *The Gathering*." In *Folklore and Modern Irish Writing*, edited by Anne Markey and Anne O'Connor, 191–203. Dublin: Irish Academic Press, 2014.

O'Toole, Fintan. "If Shame Has Gone, Why Do We Use Secret Abortions in England to Preserve the Myth of Holy Ireland?" *Irish Times*, June 10, 2014. At http://www.irishtimes.com/news/social-affairs/if-shame-has-gone-why-do-we-use-secret-abortions-in-england-to-preserve-the-myth-of-holy-ireland-1.1826199?page=2.

———. Introductory remarks. Launch of *Digital Dubliners*, a multimedia guide created by students at Boston College, Ireland House, Dublin, June 11, 2014.

Page, Susan, guest host. "Colm Tóibín: *Nora Webster*, a Novel." *Diane Rehm Show*, National Public Radio, Oct. 16, 2014. At https://thedianerehmshow.org/shows/2014-10-16/colm-Tóibín-nora-webster-novel.

Pizzetta, Candis P. "Division of Maternal Effort in Anne Enright's *The Gathering*." In *Constructing the Literary Self: Race and Gender in*

Twentieth-Century Literature, edited by Patsy J. Daniels, 199–212. Newcastle upon Tyne, UK: Cambridge Scholars, 2013.

Powell, Kersti Tarien. *Irish Fiction: An Introduction*. Annotated ed. London: Bloomsbury Academic, 2004.

Powers, Katherine. "Review: *Nora Webster* by Colm Tóibín." *Chicago Tribune*, Sept. 26, 2014. At http://www.chicagotribune.com/lifestyles/books/ct-prj-nora-webster-colm-toibin-20140926-story.html.

Ricoeur, Paul. "Memory and Forgetting." In *Questioning Ethics: Debates in Contemporary Philosophy*, edited by Richard Kearney and Mark Dooley, 5–11. London: Routledge, 1999.

Ryan, James. *Seeds of Doubt*. London: Weidenfeld & Nicholson, 2001.

Schneider, Ana-Karina. "Skin as a Trope of Liminality in Anne Enright's *The Gathering*." *Contemporary Women's Writing* 8, no. 2 (July 2014): 206–22.

Schober, Regina. "'It's about Being Connected': Reframing the Network in Colum McCann's Post 9/11 Novel *Let the Great World Spin*." *Zeitschrift fur Anglistik und Amerikanistik* 60, no. 4 (Oct. 2012): 391–402.

Siegel, Elisabeth. "'Another Fleeting Image': Pictorial Memory in John Banville's *The Sea*." In *Intermedialities*, edited by Warner Huber, Evelyne Keitel, and Gunter Süß, 107–17. Trier, Germany: Wissenshaftlicher Verlag Trier, 2007.

Smith, James M. *Ireland's Magdalen Laundries and the Nation's Architecture of Containment*. Notre Dame, IN: Univ. of Notre Dame Press, 2007.

Speckhard, Anne, Nadejda Tarabrina, Valery Krasnov, and Natalia Mufel. "Stockholm Effects and Psychological Responses to Captivity in Hostages Held by Suicide Terrorists." *Traumatology* 11, no. 2 (June 2005): 121–40. doi:10.1177/153476560501100206.

Steinberg, Sybil. "*PW* Talks with Emma Donoghue." *Publishers Weekly*, July 12, 2010.

Sydora, Laura. "'Everyone Wants a Bit of Me': Historicizing Motherhood in Anne Enright's *The Gathering*." *Women's Studies* 44 (Mar. 2015): 239–63.

Tancke, Ulrike. "Trauma and Violence in Contemporary Fiction: Theorising Narrative Deception and Narrative Complicity." In *Deceptive Fictions: Narrating Trauma and Violence in Contemporary Writing*, 1–17. Newcastle upon Tyne, UK: Cambridge Scholars, 2015.

Tóibín, Colm. *Beauty in a Broken Place*. Dublin: Lilliput Press, 2004.

———. *The Blackwater Lightship: A Novel*. New York: Scribner, 1999.

———. *Brooklyn*. New York: Scribner, 2009.

———. *The Empty Family: Stories*. New York: Scribner, 2011.

———. *The Heather Blazing*. New York: Penguin, 1992.

———. *Mothers and Sons*. New York: Scribner, 2007.

———. "The Name of the Game." In *Mothers and Sons*, 51–108. New York: Scribner, 2007.

———. *Nora Webster*. New York: Scribner, 2014.

———. "One Minus One." In *The Empty Family: Stories*, 69–84. New York: Scribner, 2011.

———. "A Priest in the Family." In *Mothers and Sons*, 133–52. New York: Scribner, 2007.

———. "A Song." In *Mothers and Sons*, 41–49. New York: Scribner, 2007.

———. *The South*. New York: Penguin, 1990.

———. "The Street." In *The Empty Family: Stories*, 207–75. New York: Scribner, 2011.

———. *The Testament of Mary*. New York: Scribner and Simon and Schuster, 2012.

Vandelanotte, Lieven. "'Where Am I, Lurking in What Place of Vantage?': The Discourse of Distance in John Banville's Fiction." *English Text Construction* 3, no. 2 (2010): 203–25.

Van der Kolk, Bessel A., and Onno van der Hart. "The Intrusive Past: The Flexibility of Memory and the Engraving of Trauma." In *Trauma: Explorations in Memory*, edited by Cathy Caruth, 158–82. Baltimore: Johns Hopkins Univ. Press, 1995.

Walshe, Eibhear. *A Different Story: The Writings of Colm Tóibín*. Dublin: Irish Academic Press, 2013.

Watkiss, Joanne. "Ghosts in the Head: Mourning, Memory, and Derridean 'Trace' in John Banville's *The Sea*." *Irish Journal of Gothic and Horror Studies* 2 (Mar. 2007). At http://irishgothichorrorjournal.homestead.com/theseabanville.html.

Watt, Ian. *The Rise of the Novel: Studies in Dafoe, Richardson, and Fielding*. Berkeley: Univ. of California Press, 2000.

Wiesenfarth, Joseph. "An Interview with Colm Tóibín." *Contemporary Literature* 50, no. 1 (Spring 2009): 1–27.

Zwierlein, Anne-Julia. "Lost at Sea: Melancholia and Maritime Mindscapes in Early 21st-Century British and Irish Fiction." In *Narrating Loss: Representations of Mourning, Nostalgia, and Melancholia in Contemporary Anglophone Fictions*, edited by Brigitte Johanna Glaser and Barbara Puschmann-Nalenz, 161–77. Trier, Germany: Wissenschaftlicher Verlag Trier, 2014.

Index

Kathleen Costello-Sullivan is professor of modern Irish literature and dean of the College of Arts and Sciences at Le Moyne College in Syracuse, New York, where she founded and directs an Irish literature program. She is the author of *Mother/Country: Politics of the Personal in the Fiction of Colm Tóibín* (2012) and editor of critical editions of *Carmilla* by Sheridan Le Fanu (Syracuse University Press, 2013) and *Poor Women!* by Norah Hoult (2016).